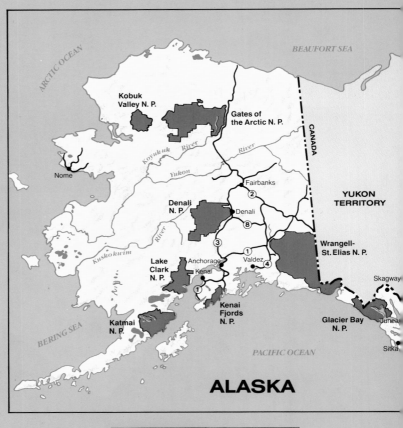

ALASKA

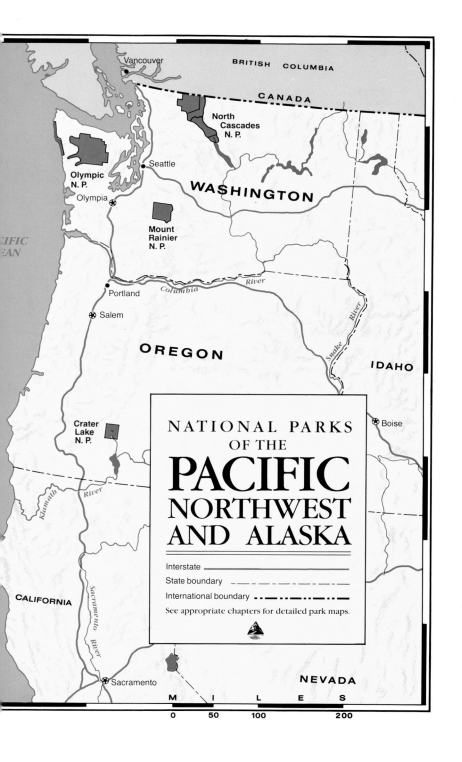

Vancouver

BRITISH COLUMBIA

CANADA

North
Cascades
N. P.

WASHINGTON

Seattle

Olympic
N. P.

Olympia

Mount
Rainier
N. P.

CIFIC
EAN

Portland

Columbia River

Snake River

IDAHO

Salem

OREGON

Boise

Crater
Lake
N. P.

NATIONAL PARKS

OF THE

PACIFIC
NORTHWEST
AND ALASKA

Klamath River

Interstate ————————

State boundary — — — — — —

International boundary ▪—▪—▪—▪—▪

See appropriate chapters for detailed park maps.

CALIFORNIA

Sacramento River

Sacramento

NEVADA

M   I   L   E   S

0   50   100   200

THE SIERRA CLUB GUIDES TO THE
NATIONAL PARKS
OF THE
PACIFIC
NORTHWEST
AND ALASKA

Published by
Stewart, Tabori & Chang

Distributed by
R A N D O M   H O U S E

Library of Congress Cataloging-in-Publication Data

The Sierra Club guides to the national parks of the Pacific Northwest and Alaska /
(text by Robert Belous . . . et al.). — Rev. and updated.
p. cm. — (The sierra Club guides to the national parks)
Includes Index.
Cover title: Pacific Northwest and Alaska.
ISBN 0-679-76495-X (alk. paper)
1. National parks and reserves—Northwest, Pacific—Guidebooks. 2. National
parks and reserves—Alaska—Guidebooks. 3. Northwest, Pacific—Guidebooks. 4.
Alaska—Guidebooks. I. Belous, Robert. II. Sierra Club. III. Title: Pacific
Northwest and Alaska IV. Series.
F852.3.S54 1996
917.95'0443—dc20   96-11449
                                                                          CIP

TEXT BY:
Robert Belous: Glacier Bay, Kenai Fjords, Kobuk Valley, and Wrangell-St. Elias
Barbara B. Decker and Robert W. Decker: Crater Lake and Mount Rainier
Kim Heacox: Denali, North Cascades, and Olympic
John Kauffmann: Gates of the Arctic
Susan Tollefson: Katmai and Lake Clark

Text revisions throughout this edition by the Project Editor.

Photo credits are on pp. 392–393

PROJECT EDITOR: Donald Young
CONSULTING EDITOR: James V. Murfin (First Edition)
DESIGNER: J. C. Suarès
PHOTO EDITOR: Amla Sanghvi
COPY EDITOR: Randy Blunk (Revised Edition)
ART AND PRODUCTION: Alice Wong, Lisa Vaughn, Melanie Random,
Evangeline Yao, Christopher Young (Revised Edition)

Created by Stewart, Tabori & Chang, Inc., 575 Broadway, New York, NY 10012

Printed in Singapore

4689753

Revised Edition

Cover Photographs: Mount Rainier (© Manuel Rodriguez); Dall Sheep (© Tom
Bean); Starfish (© Bill West); Illustration and map (© Bill Russell). Frontispiece:
Caribou at Wonder Lake, Denali National Park and Preserve (© Mike Tollefson).
Back cover: Wizard Island, Crater Lake National Park (© Pat O'Hara)

The fifty-four national parks of the United States contain many glorious natural splendors. Each year, tens of millions of Americans and growing numbers of visitors from around the world contemplate the beauty of snow-capped mountains, cascading waterfalls, groves of soaring trees, glistening surf-kissed beaches, and deep and mysterious red-rock canyons. Herds of large mammals enhance the setting in some parks, and uncounted numbers of other animals, birds, crawly things, and plants occupy their own niches as participants in nature's grand design.

The National Park System contains about 375 units, but the five volumes of *The Sierra Club Guides to the National Parks* feature only those units designated as a "national park" or as a "national park and preserve." An act of Congress is required for the establishment of a park. The world's first national park—Yellowstone—was created in 1872. The list has grown steadily, as the American people, through their elected representatives, demonstrated many times their commitment to preserving parks for the enjoyment of themselves and of generations yet to come. In 1994 alone, three more parks were added to the list.

The Sierra Club was founded in California in 1892 by the naturalist John Muir and some of his friends. One of the oldest and largest conservation organizations, the Club, which now has more than 550,000 members, has been in the forefront of many efforts to create new parks.

This series has been produced with the cooperation of the Sierra Club and with the participation of the National Park Service and Random House. Leading nature writers and photographers have contributed to the guides. This revised edition contains new chapters on the six parks established since the mid-1980s. As well, the chapters on the forty-eight other parks have been thoroughly reviewed and completely updated.

We hope you will enjoy exploring the parks, and we know these guides will enhance your experience.

—*Donald Young, Editor*

The Alaska National Interest Lands Conservation Act of 1980

CONGRESS IN 1980 PASSED THE ALASKA NATIONAL Interest Lands Conservation Act (ANILCA), creating a gift for all the American people—100 million acres of new parks, monuments, wildlife refuges, and national forests, almost all in pristine condition. Overnight, the national-park and wildlife systems more than doubled in size.

Until Alaska became a state, 99 percent of it was owned by the federal government. The 1959 statehood bill provided that 104.6 million acres (of a total of 375 million) would be transferred to the state. Alaska's Inuits (Eskimos), Aleuts, and Indians pressed their own claims. Congress in 1971 approved the Alaska Native Claims Settlement Act (ANCSA), which gave the Natives 44 million acres and $962.5 million. In 1967, Sierra Club president Edgar Wayburn had persuaded the Club to make the preservation of Alaska's wild lands a top priority. His lobbying paid off with the inclusion in ANCSA of a clause that authorized the Secretary of the Interior to study up to 80 million acres suitable for addition to, or creation as, units of the four national systems. Congress had to implement the clause by 1978.

A nine-year struggle ensued. The Sierra Club and other conservation organizations formed the Alaska Coalition, which utilized professional lobbying and grass-roots efforts. Alaskan politicians and mining and forest-industry companies sought to block or weaken a parks bill. Conservationists and employees of the Interior Department trudged through primeval Alaska, evaluating areas for preservation. A strong bill that went beyond recommendations by Interior passed twice in the House of Representatives, but senators favoring a weaker bill delayed action in the Senate. In December 1978, with the statutory limit of the 1971 act about to expire, Jimmy Carter used emergency authority to create national monuments by presidential proclamation. With Ronald Reagan's election in 1980, conservationists concluded that the prospect of getting any bill passed after his inauguration was dim. During a "lame duck" session of Congress, they accepted a compromise Senate bill. Carter signed ANILCA on December 2, 1980.

—Donald Young

An Alaskan Perspective

ALASKA'S NATIONAL PARKS CONTAIN 39 MILLION acres. These vast realms challenge visitors to adjust their expectations and perspective and are a distinct departure from their counterparts elsewhere. Generally, park areas can be classified into three settings. (1) In the remote bush country, visitors are on their own. Support facilities are absent, and the weather and terrain pose difficult challenges. Trails and a refined catalog of resources are nonexistent. (2) Intermediate areas—equivalent to wilderness parklands in other states—offer some visitor aids and a degree of resource interpretation. Basic visitor facilities are available, usually at or near a headquarters site. (3) Long-established units, such as Denali, provide services and accommodations that are comparable to those found at other national parks. Resource interpretation can enrich short visits. But such parks also contain wild terrain beyond the core area of visitor facilities.

Thousands of acres of private or state lands lie within Alaska's parks. Mining claims exist in remote settings. Visitors should ask about land status, or "inner boundaries," before selecting routes, campsites, and destinations. Native allotments—often situated along rivers or lakes or near caribou migration routes—constitute a special class of private land. Allotment lands represent special ties between Natives and their homelands. The Alaska National Interest Lands Conservation Act (1980) allows local Native and non-Native people to hunt, fish, trap, and gather subsistence resources in park areas that they used in the past. Tent frames and fish racks may be unattended, but they will be used during the next seasonal round of harvest activity. Disturbing equipment or interfering with hunting or fishing are serious forms of trespass.

Information in the "Sites, Trails, and Trips" sections of this book is necessarily spare. In these young and vast parklands, biotic systems are only vaguely understood. Natural features have not been reduced to the trail-guide format common to many parks. Indeed, the National Park Service seeks to preserve the challenge and character of these last wild places. The conservationist Aldo Leopold asked: "Of what avail are forty freedoms without a blank spot on the map?" The absence of complete data is not intended to dissuade visitors, but to preserve an opportunity for discovery, self-reliance, and deep adventure.

—Robert Belous

M A P S

CONTENTS

CRATER
LAKE
NATIONAL PARK

The view of Wizard Island from Watchman Peak, which is on the rim of Crater Lake

CRATER LAKE NATIONAL PARK
P.O. BOX 7, CRATER LAKE, OREGON 97604
TEL.: (503) 594-2211

HIGHLIGHTS: Rim Drive • Crater Lake • Pumice Desert • Wizard Island • Discovery Point • The Watchman • Devil's Backbone • Llao Rock • Vidae Falls • The Pinnacles • Mount Scott

ACCESS: From west and south, take Oregon 62. Crater Lake access road open all winter, weather permitting. Oregon 138 to North Entrance, open mid-June to mid-October.

HOURS: Roads are open 24 hours.

FEES: At entrance, for vehicles and bus passengers. Golden Eagle, Golden Age, and Golden Access passes accepted. Camping fee.

PARKING: Available at Rim Village.

GAS: Mazama Village; open Memorial Day to mid-October.

FOOD: Crater Lake Lodge dining room (summer only) and cafeteria.

LODGING: In park at Crater Lake Lodge, from mid-May to October.

VISITOR CENTER: Rim Village Visitor Center. Weather updates, naturalist talks; books and maps for sale; trip planning assistance and backcountry permits.

MUSEUMS: Exhibits at park headquarters, Visitor Center, and Sinnott Memorial.

GIFT SHOP: At cafeteria in Rim Village.

PETS: Permitted on short leashes, except on trails or indoors.

PICNICKING: At designated sites.

HIKING: Winter, ranger-guided snowshoe hike near lake rim; group hikes arranged through park headquarters. Summer, 140 miles of trails.

BACKPACKING: Throughout park; permit required.

CAMPGROUNDS: Mazama Campground, 198 sites for tents or campers; Lost Creek Campground, 16 sites for tents only, open in late July. First-come availability. Firewood for sale. Fires only in fireplaces.

TOURS: Boat tours daily, July to mid-September, when weather permits.

OTHER ACTIVITIES: Geology talks hourly, from June to early September, at Sinnott Memorial Overlook. Horses permitted on some backcountry trails.

FACILITIES FOR DISABLED: Scripts of talks available for hearing impaired. Most facilities, viewpoints, and some restrooms accessible to wheelchairs.

For additional information, see also Sites, Trails, and Trips on pages 35–43 and the map on pages 16–17.

Sunrise over the caldera; Mount Scott stands on the horizon.

A MORE DRAMATIC SETTING WOULD BE HARD to imagine: a magnificent blue lake, 6 miles across, cradled in the shattered top of what was once a 12,000-foot volcano. Steep, jagged cliffs surround the lake, rising as high as 2,000 feet above placid waters that are more intensely blue than the Oregon sky on a clear day.

The result of an enormous volcanic eruption that occurred about 7,700 years ago, this lovely lake in the crown of Mount Mazama is the central feature of Crater Lake National Park, situated along the crest of the Cascade Range in southern Oregon. Crater Lake is famous for its depth as well as for its surpassing beauty: at 1,932 feet, it is the deepest lake in the United States and the seventh deepest in the world.

Elevations in the park vary from 4,400 feet at the south entrance to 8,926 feet at Mount Scott, a volcanic cone east of the lake. Most of the landscape is clothed in deep conifer forests, but in the summertime wildflowers bloom lavishly in a headlong rush to outrace the early fall snows. Almost 600 plant species have been identified in Crater Lake National Park, and all have colonized there since the area was devastated by the volcanic eruption.

A 33-mile rim road circling the lake provides splendid panoramic views from numerous overlooks, and 145 miles of trail make

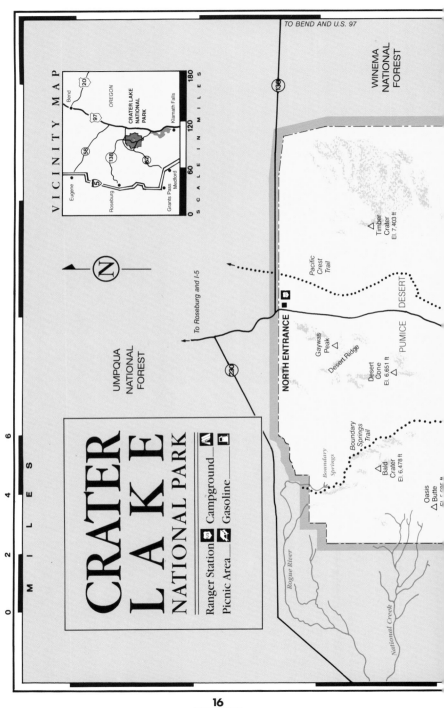

CRATER LAKE NATIONAL PARK

Ranger Station
Campground
Picnic Area
Gasoline

UMPQUA NATIONAL FOREST

WINEMA NATIONAL FOREST

TO BEND AND U.S. 97

To Roseburg and I-5

NORTH ENTRANCE

Pacific Crest Trail

Timber Crater
El 7,403 ft

Gaywas Peak

Desert Ridge

Desert Cone
El 6,651 ft

PUMICE DESERT

Boundary Springs Trail

Boundary Springs

Bald Crater
El 6,478 ft

Oasis Butte

Rogue River

National Creek

VICINITY MAP

OREGON

Bend

Eugene

Roseburg

Grants Pass

Medford

Klamath Falls

CRATER LAKE NATIONAL PARK

SCALE IN MILES
0   60   120   180

M I L E S
0   2   4   6

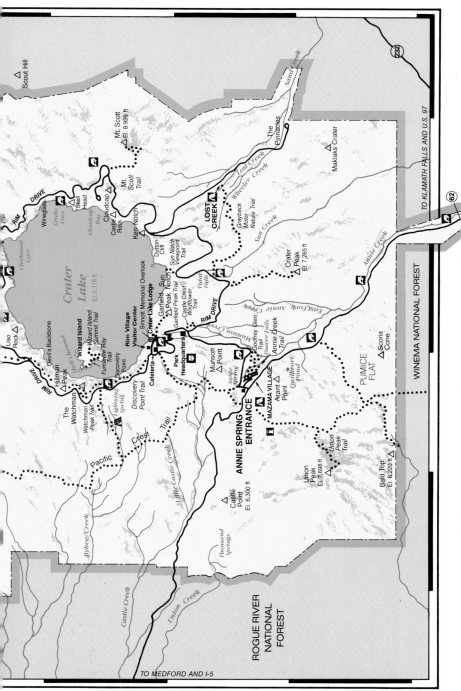

more viewing points available to those who have time to hike. But the summer season is short at Crater Lake, and from October to July the park is buried in snow. Nonetheless, the road to the rim from the south is kept open all year to allow an unforgettable view of the deep blue lake shining in brilliant contrast to the icy crater rim with its stands of snow-draped conifers. With good reason, Crater Lake is often called the Jewel of the Cascades.

History

The First Americans and the Angry Gods

Human beings witnessed the huge volcanic eruption that created Crater Lake 7,700 years ago. In fact, archeological evidence shows that Native Americans were living in the Pacific Northwest 6,000 years before the eruption. At the end of the last ice age, about 12,000 years ago, living conditions were relatively good in south-central Oregon; large and small animals were abundant, and the wetlands provided not only fish but huge flocks of migrating waterfowl. Edible plants were also plentiful.

In cliff shelters above the wet lowlands, scientists have found evidence of a way of life that continued for thousands of years. Arrowheads, stone knives, and scrapers used to prepare skins are common in the earliest layers; grinding stones seem to have come into use a bit later, as food preparation became more complex and more use was made of roots and seeds.

When the climate warmed and the glaciers retreated, some lakes and marshes gradually dried up and were replaced by spreading grasslands and forests. As water grew scarce, groups of Indians settled in the Fort Rock area, about 55 miles east of Mount Mazama, and in similar places near cool springs and sheltering caves. Others moved to the south, where the Modoc Indians lived along the shores of Klamath Lake.

Many of these Indians had observed volcanic disturbances. The whole Pacific Northwest is an active area, dotted with the fifteen major volcanoes of the Cascade Range; Mount Mazama itself had erupted many times in the thousands of years preceding its final explosion and collapse.

But the cataclysmic eruption of about 5700 B.C. was of far greater dimensions than the others. Some people died in avalanches of hot ash, and the survivors' environment was disrupted for many years thereafter. Choking blankets of ash covered the ground for miles around, burying plants and smothering small animals and birds. In a cave near Fort Rock, archeologists found a collection of sagebrush sandals charred and buried by a rain of hot volcanic ash from Mount Mazama. Heavy ash from the eruption clogged the water in streams, lakes, and marshes, killing the fish and water plants. Over many years, volcanic ash weathers into fertile soil, but the immediate effects of a heavy ashfall are ruinous.

The deep blue lake that formed in the caldera of the collapsed volcano was a mysterious, sacred place to the Natives. Their legends tell of a time when god-chiefs fought so fiercely that mountaintops were smashed and the pieces hurled through the sky, raining hot rocks on the villages, and of rivers of fire that swept down the mountains, sending the people fleeing to Klamath Lake for safety.

The Klamath Indians tell of Llao, the Chief of the Below World, whose throne was on the rim of what is now Crater Lake. He ruled over a race of giant crayfish who lived in the cold waters below. His archenemy was Skell, the Chief of the Upper World. Through treachery, Skell captured Llao and dismembered him, throwing the pieces into the lake, where the crayfish ate them, not knowing they were feasting on their king. When the crayfish realized what had happened they wept copiously, and their tears raised the lake to its present level. Llao's head became an island, which is now called Wizard Island.

Western American grandeur—the first photograph taken of Crater Lake, 1874.

The lake was so sacred that most Indians were forbidden to gaze upon its blue waters or even to speak of it. Indeed, the first parties of whites who explored the Oregon territory had not been told of its existence.

Accidental Discoveries

The American exploration of the Northwest, which included the Lewis and Clark Expedition (1804-1806), opened vast tracts of land to fur traders and settlers. In 1853, rumors of gold were sweeping the West, fueled by rich strikes in California and Oregon. On June 12, 1853, a small number of prospectors made their way up what is now called Mount Mazama, looking for a "lost" gold mine. Instead, they stumbled upon a beautiful lake in a hollowed-out mountaintop, where no one would expect a lake to be. They reported their discovery, naming it Deep Blue Lake, but gold fever was much stronger than curiosity, and no one else saw the lake for nearly ten years.

In 1862, another group of miners happened upon the lake, and in 1865 two soldiers from Fort Klamath came upon it while hunting deer. They brought several parties of adventurous civilians to see their discovery, its fame spread, and the lake's "tourist era" began. Its name was changed to Blue Lake and then to Lake Majesty, but the name Crater Lake ultimately came into use.

Establishment of the Park

William Gladstone Steel deserves most of the credit for preserving Crater Lake. In an accident of history, the Kansas schoolboy read a description of the beauties of Crater Lake one day in 1870 in a newspaper wrapped around his school lunch. He kept the story to read and reread, obsessed with the idea of seeing the lake in person. It took 15 years, but in 1885 Steel, with a group from Portland, Oregon, stood speechless with wonder on the rim of Crater Lake.

The idea of making this scenic treasure a national park was born that day and became Steel's lifework. For the next 17 years he lobbied, lectured, wrote articles, and circulated petitions in support of the idea, devoting most of his personal fortune to the cause.

In 1886, meanwhile, a U.S. Geological Survey party led by Captain Clarence Dutton managed to haul a 26-foot boat, the *Cleetwood*, to the top of the mountain and lower it over the steep cliffs into the water. From this boat they made detailed maps of the lake and took the first soundings that established the depth of Crater Lake at more than 1,900 feet. Measurements taken since have identified the lake's deepest point at 1,932 feet, about a mile

Top: William Gladstone Steel, far right, with local and Oregon State officials.
Bottom: Members of the U.S. Geological Survey sound the lake in 1886.

from the rim shore.

In 1896 the Mazamas, a Portland mountaineering club organized by Steel, met at Crater Lake and heard reports from scientists who had conducted studies there. When club members learned that the lake had a name but the mountain did not, they proposed that it be called Mount Mazama, and the name was adopted—surely one of the few instances in which a mountain has been named for a climbing club instead of the other way around.

Steel continued to lobby for park status for Crater Lake. Finally, in 1902, after Steel made a personal appeal to President Theodore Roosevelt, Congress passed the legislation, Roosevelt signed the bill, and Crater Lake became America's sixth national park.

The tranquil beauty of Crater Lake gives no hint that it was born in catastrophic violence, but studies of the cliffs, of charred trees buried in the now-cool pumice, and of the rest of the geological record lead inescapably to this conclusion.

The Destruction of a Mountaintop

Careful field studies by three generations of geologists—J. S. Diller in 1902, Howel Williams in 1942, and Charles Bacon in 1983—all confirm that Crater Lake fills a huge pit formed by the explosion and collapse of the summit of Mount Mazama, a great volcanic peak. The cone of Mount Mazama had grown slowly for 500,000 years, but the explosion and collapse occurred in recent geologic time. ("Recent" to geologists means since the last ice age, which ended about 12,000 years ago.)

Many unknowns persist, but a great deal of geological history has been pieced together from the wreckage left by the volcanic eruption. Charcoal from the burned and buried trees can be dated by measuring the amount of a radioactive isotope known as carbon 14 they contain. Carbon 14 dating of trees buried on Mount Mazama during the eruption places the time of their destruction at about 7,700 years ago.

Observations of the 1980 eruption of Mount St. Helens and eyewitness accounts of the Krakatau eruption in Indonesia in 1883 provide insights into the Crater Lake eruption. From descriptions of these smaller eruptions and from clues in the wreckage of Mount Mazama, Williams and Bacon have worked out this sequence of events:

Small but incessant earthquakes shook the mountain for months as molten rock (magma) pushed upward to the surface. Gases trapped in the magma began to expand violently. The initial explosion formed a vent, and gas-charged molten rock sprayed out in fragments of hot volcanic ash. Within a few hours, a rapidly growing volcanic ash cloud probably reached an altitude of 20 to 30 miles.

The fallout of pumice (chunks of frothy volcanic glass) and volcanic ash (fine fragments of volcanic glass and silicate crystals) from this eruption cloud was enormous. Ash beds more than 60 feet thick are found near the present caldera rim. With the wind blowing to the northeast, the fallout was more than 2 feet thick at Newberry Volcano, 65 miles from Crater Lake. Half-inch accumu-

Opposite: Morning light on Watchman Peak, with Mount McLaughlin in the distance.

lations of fine ash sifted down over Canada, more than 700 miles downwind. The total mass of hot fragments from this initial eruption phase amounted to about 6 cubic miles of magma. By contrast, the 1980 eruption of Mount St. Helens involved only about one-tenth of a cubic mile of magma. The beginning of the Crater Lake eruption was 50 times as large as the Mount St. Helens eruption, and much more was about to happen.

The jetting ash column continued to enlarge the eruption vent, allowing an ever-increasing volume of magma to boil out. As the exploding mixture of gas and hot rock fragments became denser, it was unable to rise in a high cloud; instead it poured out in a pyroclastic flow—one of the most dangerous and destructive aspects of a volcanic eruption. This ashflow that swept down the canyons on the flanks of Mount Mazama was so hot that when it finally stopped it became welded into hard, solid rock.

At this stage so much magma had been expelled from below that the summit of the volcano began to collapse along the great circular fracture that now forms the cliffs encircling Crater Lake. The collapse permitted a still greater volume of ash to pour out and sweep down the canyons in fiery avalanches that were concealed from sight by their own enormous clouds of dark gray ash. Ashflows are not thick and viscous like liquid lava flows; instead, these turbulent mixtures of hot gas and fine ash move downslope at the speed of hurricane winds.

Hot gas fused volcanic ash into these erosion-resistant spires, the Pinnacles.

In minutes these ashflows traveled 35 miles southwest down the Rogue River Valley and south down the Sun Creek Valley. A great blanket spewed eastward over the plateau that crosses the present location of U.S. 97, carrying blocks of pumice measuring up to 10 feet across. These ashflow deposits are 200 to 300 feet thick where they filled deep canyons.

The evidence suggests that the entire eruption was continuous and lasted only a few days. During that great spasm more than 13 cubic miles of magma jetted out and boiled over from the restless underground reservoir, and the top mile of Mount Mazama, 6 miles across, fell into the hellish void below. An area four times the size of the present national park was devastated by the hot ashflows, and an even greater area to the northeast was covered by 5 feet or more of pumice and ash.

If human survivors had the courage to walk into this area after the ash in the air had cleared, they must scarcely have believed their eyes. Where before a majestic snow-capped mountain had stood encircled by great conifer forests, there was now a truncated cone within which lay a vast, steaming pit 4,000 feet deep, containing pools of vile-smelling sulfurous water. In all directions buff-gray ash and pumice covered the land. Each filled canyon was now a valley of ten thousand smokes.

The Formation of Crater Lake

How could the present beauty of Crater Lake have evolved from such destruction? At first only the jagged, empty caldera remained, but the pit had no outlet; rain and snowmelt, and perhaps springs on the deep crater walls, poured water into the basin faster than it could seep out. Slowly a small, fetid lake began to form.

Year by year the lake rose and cleansed itself with waters from rain and melting snow. After about 500 to 1,000 years, the rate of seepage from the lake's holding basin came into balance with the annual input. Snowbanks cloaked the volcanic scars in winter, and rain, sun, and seeds slowly covered the volcanic soil with summer plants, then brush, and finally forest again.

Smaller eruptions occurred after the great collapse, forming Wizard Island and two other volcanic features that lie hidden beneath the lake's surface, but none has occurred for at least 5,000 years.

Will Wizard Island or some other vent in or near Crater Lake erupt again? Probably. Measurements from some areas of the lake bottom indicate that the volcanic fires beneath the surface are not dead. It will probably not occur in our lifetime, but we cannot be sure; the earth has guarded the secrets of its molten interior well.

Overleaf: Cracks develop in volcanic rock when water freezes and expands.

Climate

Crater Lake's year is divided into two seasons: a long, snowy winter and a short but beautiful summer. July, August, and September are usually clear and sunny, with almost no rain except for an occasional thundershower. Summer days are warm—around 80° F—with nighttime temperatures dropping to the low 40s.

But when storms start down the Pacific Northwest storm track in the fall, Crater Lake's heavy winter begins. The air carried by the storm systems is warmed by the Japan Current and laden with moisture. It cools as it ascends the mountains, condensing to fall to earth as snow crystals. The yearly snowfall at Crater Lake is prodigious, averaging 44 feet, but because fallen snow compacts and some melts on warmer days, not that much is on the ground at one time. A record snowpack of 21 feet was measured in April 1983. Most snow is gone by June, but it is not unusual to find snowbanks at the park's higher elevations even during the month of July.

The Lake

Because Crater Lake's winter is so long and its snowfall so heavy, the lake might be expected to freeze over, but it almost never does. Its great depth allows the heat stored from the summer sun to escape slowly and keeps the surface just above freezing.

The vivid blue of Crater Lake seems to leave even the most voluble person at a loss for words. A writer who stationed himself at the rim some years ago, to capture on tape the exclamations of people seeing Crater Lake for the first time, left after only one day, grumbling that he never again wanted to hear the word "Wow!"

The color results from the lake's purity; the water has almost no organic matter and few dissolved minerals. In such pure water, sunlight's longer wavelengths of red, yellow, and green are absorbed at a certain depth, but wavelengths at the blue end of the visible light spectrum penetrate deeper and instead of being absorbed are reflected and scattered by water molecules to produce the intense blueness.

No streams flow into or out of Crater Lake; the lake's water comes only from snow, rain, and a few springs, and it is lost only by evaporation and seepage. The lake level remains stable, seldom varying as much as 3 feet even in the wettest years.

Opposite: Climax mountain hemlock forests are generally found at lower mountain elevations.

Wildlife

No fish swam in Crater Lake until 1888, when William Steel hand-carried buckets of fingerling trout up the Mountainside and down the rim. Stocking continued until 1941, and there is now a self-perpetuating population of rainbow trout and kokanee salmon that feed on various water insects and plankton. Dolly Varden trout, which thrive throughout Sun Creek, south of the lake, are the only fish that occur naturally in the park.

About sixty kinds of mammals are found in the park, but most are seldom seen. The park's largest animals are the black bear and the elk. In 1917, fifteen Rocky Mountain elk were brought to the park from Yellowstone National Park. They joined a small population of another subspecies, the Roosevelt elk. This subspecies, once widespread but now scarce, can also be seen in Redwood National Park in California. Black-tailed and mule deer can sometimes be seen in the wet meadow sections, while fat, yellow-bellied marmots and rabbit-like pikas scurry among the rocks found at higher elevations.

By far the most conspicuous mammals are the golden-mantled ground squirrels and the Townsend's chipmunks, foraging in campgrounds and at every road turnout.

In winter, Crater Lake's animals deal with the deep snowpack in several ways. Deer and elk migrate to milder, lower elevations. Some, like the chipmunks and marmots, hibernate, while others, like black bears, go into a lighter sleep that is called a brumal. Pine martens and snowshoe hares travel over the snow in search of food; voles and shrews live in tunnels under the snow, sometimes tunneling upward to the surface for a look around.

Crater Lake's long winter is difficult for the bird population, too; only the hardiest, including the bold Clark's nutcracker, Steller's and gray jays, blue and ruffed grouse, and mountain chickadee, are year-round residents.

As the season warms, summer breeding birds such as horned larks, pine siskins, and robins arrive, and large flocks of migrating birds stop by briefly. Ravens soar above the crater rim, and hawks ride the thermals over the higher peaks. The ultimate treat for a birdwatcher is to catch sight of a magnificent golden or bald eagle. These great birds with a wingspread of 7 feet are occasionally seen along the caldera rim, although sightings are now becoming less frequent.

Opposite: The magnificent bald eagle has a 7-foot wingspread.
Overleaf: Sitka columbine, one of the many wildflowers that flourish in the park.
Inset: Shooting star.

Trees and Flowers

Except for the Pumice Desert in the northern part of the park, Crater Lake National Park is almost entirely forested and contains an impressive variety of tree species for an area its size. All these plants have recolonized since the big eruption.

Four life zones—characteristic groupings of plants and animals determined largely by climate—are represented. The park's lowest elevations are in the Transition zone, dominated by ponderosa pines, the largest trees in the park. With them grow sugar pines, white firs, and a few patches of Douglas-fir. Above the Transition zone is the Canadian zone, characterized by Shasta red firs, lodgepole pine (usually the first tree to appear in an area devastated by fire or volcanic eruption), and the first mountain hemlocks, with their droopy tops.

The crater rim is in the Hudsonian life zone; here are fine stands of sturdy mountain hemlock and Shasta red fir. Higher still, on the northern rim and on the windswept summit of Mount Scott, are gnarled whitebark pines, contorted by their battle with wind and weather. The hard seeds produced by these craggy trees are the favorite food of the Clark's nutcracker. The bird tears the cones apart to get at the tasty seeds, scattering some seeds in the process and caching others—many of which germinate the next season.

Most of the trees in the park are evergreens, but scattered deciduous trees such as bigleaf maples dot the mountainsides in fall with splashes of orange and red, while stands of quaking aspen provide swaths of brilliant yellow.

Though forest dominates Crater Lake's landscape, summer brings a grand display of wildflowers as well. Some, like the long leaf arnica, Crater Lake currant, and smooth woodrush, thrive on the shady forest floor, but the most colorful show takes place in the park's moist, open meadows. The flowering season is short, so there is a rapid succession of blooms in June, July, and August.

Fields of pink spreading phlox follow receding snowfields, quickly trailed by columbine, shooting star, paintbrush, lupine, and dozens of other flowers in a rainbow of colors. Five kinds of monkeyflower are found in Crater Lake National Park, including a dwarf variety that prefers the Pumice Desert.

On the high, drier slopes grow bright red shoots of Newberry knotweed; western pasque flower, whose white blooms turn to frowsy tassels, by midsummer; and a wooly white *Eriogonum* that bears the inelegant common name "dirty socks." Several members of the phlox family turn the highest elevations into rock gardens for the few short weeks of a Cascade summer.

The famous Phantom Ship is a remnant from one of the many eruptions that exploded from the summit of Mount Mazama.

SITES, TRAILS, AND TRIPS

The Rim Drive

The best way to enjoy the Rim Drive is to start at Sinnott Memorial Overlook in Rim Village and drive clockwise around Crater Lake. (Visitors in trailers should check about parking.) Try to allow at least half a day to make the Rim Drive circle. Mileages given are cumulative from the Rim Village Visitor Center parking lot.

The Sinnott Overlook provides an excellent survey of the entire lake and of many of the landmarks on the rim. The lake surface is at an elevation of 6,176 feet, and the rim's elevation averages about 7,000 feet. The view from left to right shows The Watchman on the west rim, Wizard Island, Llao Rock, Cleetwood Cove, the Wineglass, Skell Head, and Redcloud Cliff. These features are shown on park maps and also on the relief model in the memorial; locating and identifying them at the start of the drive around the lake helps put the caldera—the great collapse basin that holds the lake—into better perspective.

John Wesley Hillman and his group of prospectors came upon the lake at or near Discovery Point, 1.9 miles from Rim Village, on June 12, 1853. At the rim, where the pumice from the great eruption has eroded away, the older gray lavas of Mount Mazama show signs of the scratching and polishing of glaciers that once crept down from the now-vanished slopes of the mountain.

The Wizard Island Overlook is at 4.1 miles. William Steel named Wizard Island for its fancied resemblance to a pointed sorcerer's cap. The island formed after the caldera collapse. The cone is made of cinders that were ejected red-hot from the island's small summit crater and piled up into a loose cone like a giant anthill. The crumpled hills near the base of the cinder cone are lava flows. The ages of its oldest trees indicate that the island was formed more than 5,000 years ago. Wizard Island rises 760 feet above lake level; its summit crater is 300 feet wide and 90 feet deep. These numbers, not small, give some idea of how the vast scale of Crater Lake makes all of the area's features appear smaller than they really are.

The high peak just skirted by the Rim Drive and now to the south is *The Watchman*, a thick lava flow about 50,000 years old. The dark ridge that extends beneath The Watchman is the remains of a dike—molten rock intruded through a crack in the rocks. Cliffs such as these expose the insides of ancient volcanoes to geologists for close study.

To the north on the rim is the sharp crest of *Hillman Peak*, a 70,000-year-old volcano that was cut in half by the caldera collapse. Ancient beds of pale yellow to reddish brown ash and cinders contrast with the darker lava flows.

At *Diamond Lake Viewpoint* (4.9 miles), the views are directed away from Crater Lake itself. About 15 miles to the north is the spire of Mount Thielsen, 9,182 feet. Its summit is the plug of a volcano that has been stripped of less-durable rocks by glacial erosion. The treeless region below Mount Thielsen is called the Pumice Desert. This area is covered by ashflow deposits from the glowing avalanches of the Crater Lake eruption. On a clear day the snowy Middle and South peaks of the Three Sisters volcanoes, 85 miles to the north, can be seen to the left of Mount Thielsen. Farther to the left of Mount Thielsen, but only 3 miles from the viewpoint, is Red Cone, a volcanic vent about 40,000 years old, and beyond it is part of Diamond Lake.

At 5.8 miles, a short trail leads to *Devil's Backbone*, a 50-foot-thick dike of resistant rock that forms a wall from rim to lake surface. Only a small portion of the dike is exposed in this outcrop. Because the dike had formed and cooled before the caldera collapse, it must be older than 7,700 years. The dike in turn cuts through rocks of Hillman Peak volcano, so it must be younger than 70,000 years. These interrelationships of volcanic rock bodies help geologists to work out the sequence of activity at Crater Lake and at other volcanic centers. Just beyond Devil's Backbone, the road

Opposite: Crater Lake is the seventh deepest lake in the world.

leading toward the north entrance to the park branches to the left and then crosses the Pumice Desert.

At 6.3 miles, the massive cliff on the rim ahead is *Llao Rock*, a 1,200-foot-thick lava flow that extends halfway down to the lake surface. This is one of four massive flows of thick, viscous lava that preceded the caldera-forming eruption by less than two hundred years. The other related flows are Redcloud on the east rim, Grouse Hill northeast of Llao Rock, and Cleetwood, a flow that was still so hot and plastic at the time of the Crater Lake eruption that it flowed back toward its source down the newly formed caldera rim. A layer of pumice appears as a light band beneath the bowl-shaped remnant of Llao Rock. Much of Llao Rock fell into the caldera, just as Indian legend says; however, Wizard Island, at least geologically, is not Llao's severed head. The Rim Drive skirts Llao Rock and then returns to the rim for another view of its east face and of Wizard Island at 9.9 miles.

Cleetwood Trail (at 11.2 miles) descends 1.1 miles from the rim at this point to the boat landing, the starting point for the launch trip around Crater Lake.

Cleetwood Cove Overlook is at 11.5 miles. The cove takes its name from the boat *Cleetwood* used to sound the lake in 1886. The top of Merriam Cone, a submerged volcanic peak of roughly the same age as Wizard Island, is 486 feet beneath the lake surface to the southwest of Cleetwood Cove. From the 1,900-foot-deep lake bottom, Merriam Cone rises 1,400 feet, but it is still easily hidden in the vast depths of Crater Lake.

TRAILS OF CRATER LAKE NATIONAL PARK

Crater Lake has more than 140 miles of trails that vary from 1 mile to 33 miles in length. Most of them are still buried in snow in June and early July.

PACIFIC CREST TRAIL: This trail follows a mountainous course from Mexico to Canada. The Crater Lake portion is divided into three sections. The first extends from the southern park boundary to Oregon 62; 6.3 miles one way; 3-3.5 hours; from south, moderately steep first 1.2 miles, gentle grades after. Second section begins at a pullout on Oregon 62, .8 mile west of south park entrance station, and ends at the North Entrance Road; 17.9 miles one way; 7.5 hours; level and maintained; the trail was rerouted in 1994 to provide hikers with a view of the lake, but stock animals are not allowed on the new route and must stay on the former route; small mammals and some signs of elk may be seen; elevation 5,450-6,500 feet. Third section begins at the North Entrance Road and continues on to the park's north boundary; 8.9 miles one way; 3.5 hours; level; elevation 6,000-6,500 feet. Total Pacific Crest Trail within park: 33.1 miles one way; 14-15 hours.

WESTERN TRAILS

WATCHMAN PEAK TRAIL: Starts at Watchman Overlook northwest of Rim Village; ends at Watchman Peak; .8 mile one way; 1 hour; follows an old roadbed for short distance at base, then switchbacks to lookout station at top for spectacular view of lake; moderately steep; lookout used in summer to watch for fires; elevation 7,600-8,056 feet.

CRATER SPRINGS TRAIL: Starts at junction with Pacific Crest Trail 13 miles north from Oregon 62; ends at Forest Service road .5 mile beyond park boundary, 2.2 miles past Crater Springs; 6.1 miles one way; 3 hours; fairly level path passing through lodgepole pine forest; subalpine firs near springs; Sphagnum Bog, a very wet meadow area, lies a short distance from springs; fragile plant life; deer common along trail.

BOUNDARY SPRINGS TRAIL: Starts at junction with Pacific Crest Trail, 3.2 miles from North Entrance Road pullout; ends at Rogue River Crossing, 1.2 miles past Boundary Springs; 7.1 miles one way; 2.5 hours; drops gently from trail head through lodgepole pine forests to springs, which produce large volumes of water even in dry weather; deer, elk, and coyote have been sighted along trial. A spur trail runs generally southwest from the Boundary Springs Trail, passes west of Bald Crater and Oasis Butte, and connects with the Crater Springs Trail to create the Boundary Springs-Sphagnum Bog Loop Trail.

CRATER LAKE TRAILS

CLEETWOOD COVE TRAIL: Starts at parking area on Rim Drive 4.5 miles east of junction with the North Entrance Road; ends at tour-boat concession, Cleetwood Cove dock on lake; 1.1 miles one way; .5-1 hour; only trail leading to Crater Lake; descends from one of lowest points on rim and is one of steepest trails in park (the elevation gain on the climb back up is 700 feet); views of lake through forest of hemlock and Shasta red fir; limited wildlife.

WIZARD ISLAND SUMMIT TRAIL: Starts at boat dock on Wizard Island; ends at island summit (cinder cone rim); .9 mile one way; .5 hour; moderately steep trail through mountain hemlock and Shasta red fir forest to the crater; watch for black garter snakes, squirrels, and an abundance of birds.

FUMAROLE BAY TRAIL: Starts .2 mile from boat dock along Summit Trail; ends at Fumarole Bay on western shore of Wizard Island; .7 mile one way; .5 hour; level but with large rocks to traverse; leads through forest to exceptionally clear water bay; fishing permitted but swimming is quite cold in water seldom warming above 55° F.

EASTERN AND SOUTHERN TRAILS

MOUNT SCOTT TRAIL: Starts at Rim Drive pullout 17.9 miles clockwise from Rim Village; ends at summit of Mount Scott; 2.5 miles one way; 2.5-3 hours; fairly steep switchbacks to summit; small mammals abundant; one of the most spectacular views in park.

SUN NOTCH VIEWPOINT TRAIL: Starts at Rim Drive parking area; ends at rim above Phantom Ship; .25 mile one way; .25 hour; short path to rim for excellent view of 300-foot-long lava island.

Palisade Point (13.1 miles) is one of the low sections on the rim, just over 500 feet above the lake.

At *Skell Head* (15.5 miles), a large turnout provides an excellent panoramic view of the lake from the east rim, making it a fine complement to the opposite view from Wizard Island Overlook. Skell Head consists of thick lavas much older than Llao Rock. The remnants, cast in stone, of the Klamath gods Skell and Llao thus face each other still across the cauldron of their battleground.

Sun Notch, visible on the south crater rim (left), is the valley of a glacier that once descended from the 12,000-foot snowfields of ancient Mount Mazama, whose summit was just south of (though high above) the present lake center. Four Empire State Buildings, one on top of another, would reach from the present lake surface up to that missing summit; another one could be hidden upright beneath the lake with 400 feet to spare.

Mount Scott (17.9 miles) is the highest peak in the park at 8,926 feet. The trail to the summit leaves from this turnout.

At 18.2 miles, a spur road to the right goes to the highest rim overlook at Cloudcap. It is perched on the edge of *Redcloud Cliff*, a 600-foot-thick viscous lava flow similar to Llao Rock. The thick layer of pumice on top of Redcloud Cliff is sparsely covered by small plants and wildflowers that can exist under severe conditions—little soil, high winds, and a short growing season. Twisted whitebark pines are stunted by these alpine conditions into almost bonsai forms.

Just below Redcloud Cliff is a turreted cluster of pink to yellowish brown rocks called Pumice Castle. These are the remnants of layered pumice and ash from an earlier generation of explosive volcanism occurring about 50,000 years ago.

Kerr Notch (24.1 miles), a low point on the rim, is the remains of a glacial valley similar to Sun Notch. Phantom Ship, a small island that is the resistant ridge of a volcanic dike, is beautifully framed by the hemlocks, firs, and pines growing in Kerr Notch. Phantom Ship is dwarfed by the precipitous rim cliffs, but its "sails" are as high as a 16-story building.

The rim road now turns away from the lake to avoid the high summit of Dutton Cliff.

At *Vidae Falls* (29.6 miles) is a picnic area set beside a mountain stream that is fringed with wildflowers. The falls are a series of cascades about 100 feet high. The narrow, dark canyon makes a striking contrast to the open, bright views across Crater Lake.

The *Castle Crest Wildflower Trail* (32.5 miles), a half-mile loop, provides a fine ending to the Rim Drive. Park headquarters (32.9 miles) and Rim Village (35.9 miles) complete the circuit of Crater Lake.

Pinnacles Road

The Pinnacles Road is 12 miles round trip from the southeast rim of Crater Lake near Kerr Notch. The Pinnacles are eroded spires and needles of rock, some more than 100 feet high, formed out of glowing avalanche deposits from the Crater Lake eruption. The rock columns formed when hot gases, escaping through vertical cracks in the ashflow that filled Wheeler Canyon, cemented fragments of loose pumice into vertical pipes. Wheeler Creek then eroded away the uncemented deposits, leaving the more durable pinnacles standing in stark relief.

The erosion in Wheeler Canyon also reveals that the lower portion of the ashflow deposit is a much lighter color than the gray upper layer. This color change indicates a reduced silica content in the magma being emitted in the later stages of the eruption.

Trails

The hiking season is short at Crater Lake, roughly from the Fourth of July until Labor Day, though a few trails may be free of snow by mid-June. Winter use becomes more popular every year; cross-country skiing and snowshoeing from Rim Village are encouraged. A tour of the rim may be completed on skis in two or three days. Information on 25 more miles of marked ski routes is available at park headquarters. Forecasts on the likelihood of avalanches are also issued.

Except for a 33-mile section of the Pacific Crest Trail—the 2,250-mile trail that passes through the park on its way from Mexico to Canada—most of Crater Lake's trails are short and well suited to day hiking. (The Pacific Crest Trail stays to the west of the lake).

The Lake Trails and Launch Trip. The only trail that leads down to Crater Lake from the rim is the Cleetwood Cove Trail, the most popular trail in the park. It leaves from one of the lowest points on the rim, but it still makes use of 1.1 miles of steep switchbacks in its descent to the water. The trail passes through the characteristic mountain hemlock-Shasta red fir forest to lake level.

From the boat dock at the foot of the trail, tour boats operate during the summer months, weather permitting. The launch trip, guided by a ranger-naturalist, takes about two hours. It circles the lake counterclockwise near the 25-mile shoreline, stopping now and then for a closer look at immense rock formations looming up from the clear water.

The launch passes Llao Rock and Devil's Backbone and glides

through Skell Channel before docking at Wizard Island for a short stop. Passengers are offered the opportunity to hike to the summit of Wizard Island and catch a later boat for the rest of the tour.

The *Wizard Island Summit Trail,* just over a mile long, rises in a fairly steep spiral loop to the summit crater. The lower part of the trail is in hemlock-red fir forest, but the upper part of this pumice cone supports only whitebark pine, pinemat manzanita, and some patches of alpine flowers—saxifrage, Newberry knotweed, and pasque flower.

Wizard Island is the home of one of Crater Lake's most unusual animals, an all-black variety of the valley garter snake, which has evolved to match the island's black lava almost perfectly. On the mainland, valley garter snakes have yellow stripes. The ubiquitous chipmunks and ground squirrels live on Wizard Island too.

After leaving Wizard Island, the launch continues its trip around the lake, circling Phantom Ship, a jagged rock formation that rises 160 feet above the water, and docks at Cleetwood Cove.

The Nature Trails. The half-mile *Castle Crest Wildflower Trail* leads through dense mountain hemlock and red fir, where few flowers can grow, and then enters a lush, damp meadow bright with a multitude of flowers. Violets, shooting stars, monkeyflowers, and dozens of other moisture-loving plants bloom here in succession throughout the summer. As the trail leads from the meadow to a sunny, dry slope, the vegetation again changes; here are pussypaws, phlox, gilia, and other plants that prefer dry habitats. Birds are attracted to Castle Crest too, especially hummingbirds, juncos, and chickadees.

At *Godfrey Glen,* 2 miles below park headquarters, a 1.5-mile nature trail leads through a forest of hemlock and fir that overlooks a canyon wall sculptured with bizarre fluting and spires. This valley was once filled to a depth of 250 feet by an avalanche of hot ash and rock fragments from the great eruption. As hot gases boiled out of these deposits in fumaroles (steam vents), the vent walls were cemented by the hot vapors. When Munson Creek later cut through the loose material to form a new canyon, the old fumaroles were more resistant to erosion, and now stand as spires and pinnacles.

Forest plants along the trail include the strange white coral root, pipsissewa, and Crater Lake currant. Godfrey Glen itself is a meadow, verdant and lush with flowers during the short summer season.

The 1.7-mile *Annie Creek Trail* leaves from the Mazama Campground and winds to the bottom of Annie Creek Canyon, a V-shaped canyon carved in the pumice that filled the old canyon. The creek was named for Annie Gaines, the first woman to descend Crater Lake's walls.

The trail follows the stream through gardens of creekside wild-flowers—lupine, monkeyflowers, and paintbrush, to name just a few. As the trail leaves the canyon, it passes several pinnacles on the canyon wall, remnants of ancient fumaroles similar to those at Godfrey Glen.

Other Trails. A park ranger should be consulted before one begins the long *Boundary Springs-Sphagnum Bog Loop Trail* through the remote northwestern corner of the park. Both Boundary Springs and Sphagnum Bog, which is fed by Crater Spring, support a delicate flora of mosses and herbs. Four species of insectivorous plants are found at Sphagnum Bog.

Among the many short trails, three provide especially fine panoramic views of the Crater Lake area.

The *Watchman Peak Trail* is a fairly steep .8-mile hike, but the views of the lake, Wizard Island, and surrounding countryside at trail's end make the climb worthwhile. The peak got its name from a U.S. Geological Survey party that used it as a signal point when mapping the lake in 1886. Clark's nutcrackers are often seen (and heard) along the trail, feeding on the seeds of the whitebark pines. The trail, which sometimes is not clear of snow until early August, branches off from the Rim Road 3.7 miles from Rim Village.

The *Garfield Peak Trail* starts from Crater Lake Lodge on the rim, and winds for a moderately steep 1.7 miles to the top of the peak 2,000 feet above the lake. The views from the summit are incomparable. All of Crater Lake's major landmarks are visible, as are mountain peaks as far away as California's Mount Shasta.

Wildflowers are abundant, with pentstemon, paintbrush, and phlox on the drier slopes, and valerian following the retreating snowbanks. This is a good place to see wildlife, too—pikas and marmots scurry among the rocks, while hawks and falcons soar over the slopes.

The summit of *Mount Scott*, at 8,926 feet the highest point in the park, is reached by a 2.5-mile trail from Rim Drive. This fairly steep switchback trail, which gains more than 1,200 feet in elevation, crosses pumice deposits with scattered stands of whitebark pine and a lovely array of wildflowers, including pasque flower, Newberry knotweed, woolly sunflower, phacelia, and dozens of others as the season progresses.

The summit provides a panoramic view of Crater Lake and its surrounding cliffs, as well as of peaks more than 100 miles in the distance. A fire lookout station at the summit guards the neighboring countryside. Mount Scott is a prime spot for birdwatching; in spring and fall several kinds of hawks and occasionally falcons and eagles follow migratory routes, soaring over the summit.

DENALI
NATIONAL PARK
AND PRESERVE

Mount McKinley, "the roof of North America," rises to 20,320 feet above sea level.

DENALI NATIONAL PARK AND PRESERVE
BOX 9, DENALI PARK, ALASKA 99755
TEL.: (907) 683-2294

HIGHLIGHTS: Mount McKinley • Wonder Lake • Wild Animals • Savage River Canyon • Outer Range • Sanctuary River • Muldrow Glacier • Kantishna Hills • Triple Lakes • Mount Healy

ACCESS: From Fairbanks or Anchorage, either Alaska 3 or daily summer service provided by Alaska Railroad and Alaska Yukon Motorcoaches.

SEASON: Year-round, but road into park not plowed in winter; best time from late May to early September.

FEES: For entrance, shuttle-bus tour, and camping.

PARKING: At Visitor Center and Riley Creek.

GAS: Near Denali National Park Hotel. Fuel, oil, propane, and air available. Open late May to late September.

FOOD: Denali Dining Room and Whistle Stop Snack Shop in hotel. Grocery store.

LODGING: Denali National Park Hotel; reservations advised, open late May to mid-September.

VISITOR CENTER: Denali Visitor Center, 0.7 mile west of Alaska 3. Eielson Visitor Center is a 4-hour shuttle bus ride from Denali Visitor Center. Naturalist talks, dog sled demonstration, walks, wilderness instruction.

GIFT SHOP: McKinley Gift Shop in Denali Park Hotel. Sells Alaskan crafts.

PETS: Not encouraged, but permitted on leash, except in backcountry, on trails, or in public buildings.

HIKING: Permitted. Sections of park may be closed to entry. Proper gear and weather conditions required; treat water.

BACKPACKING: Permit required, available at Visitor Center.

CAMPGROUNDS: 225 sites available, some by reservation (800-622-7275); may be full by 11 A.M. in summer; 14-day limit in summer. Group campground available. Some sites for trailers; hookups available only outside park. Fires only in grills. Information and required registration at Visitor Center.

TOURS: Guided bus tour for tundra wildlife viewing; reservations suggested (800-622-7275). Denali Wilderness Air Tour.

OTHER ACTIVITIES: Cross-country skiing, from November to March; advanced mountain climbing.

FACILITIES FOR DISABLED: Most buses, buildings, and marked campsites.

For additional information, see also Sites, Trails, and Trips on pages 64–75 and the maps on pages 48–49 and 75.

WHEN DENALI PARK SHALL BE MADE easy of access with accommodations and facilities for travel . . . it is not difficult to anticipate the enjoyment and inspiration visitors will receive."

Charles Sheldon, a naturalist and hunter, prophetically penned these words in his journal while camped on the moraine of Peters Glacier. Above him loomed Denali, "the high one"—the name he preferred for the mountain he loved. Before him spread the open tundra, blanketed in snow, noiseless and pure. He recognized the tracks of fox, moose, and ptarmigan. In the distance, ravens called and wolves howled. It was January 1908.

A Dall Sheep; this species ranges from British Columbia to Alaska.

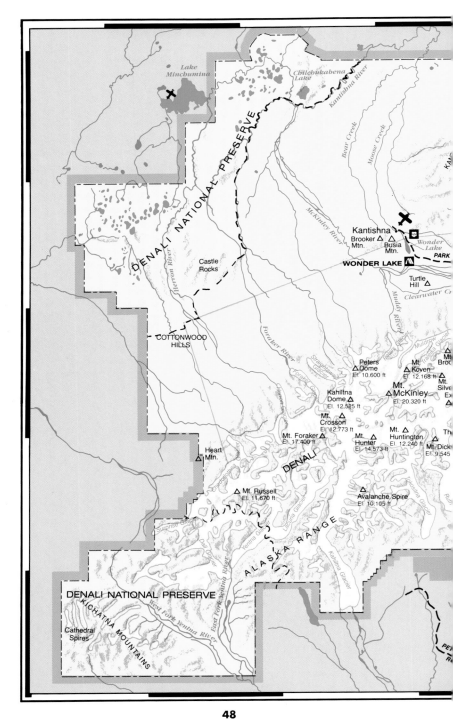

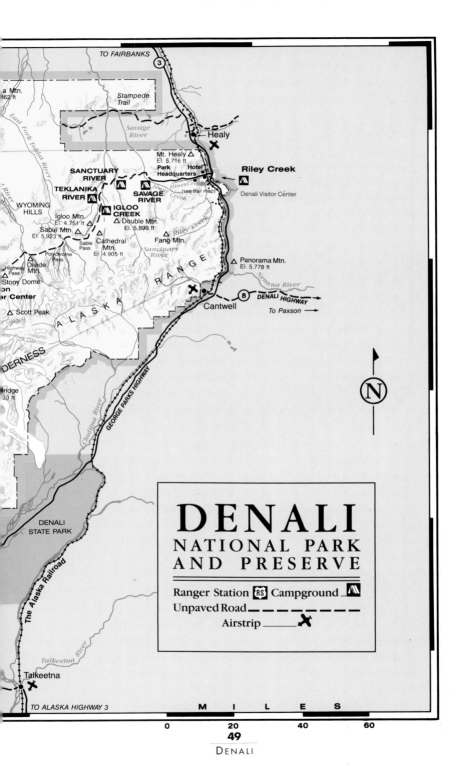

TO FAIRBANKS

3

Stampede
Trail

a Mtn.
862 ft

Savage
River

Healy

Mt. Healy △
El. 5,716 ft

Park
Headquarters

Hotel

Riley Creek

Denali Visitor Center

SANCTUARY
RIVER

TEKLANIKA
RIVER

SAVAGE
RIVER

(see trail map)

WYOMING
HILLS

Igloo Mtn.
El. 4,751 ft

IGLOO
CREEK

△ Double Mtn.
El. 5,899 ft

Sable Mtn.
El. 5,923 ft

Sable
Pass

Cathedral
Mtn.
El. 4,905 ft

Fang Mtn.

Polychrome
Pass

Sanctuary
River

Divide
△ Mtn.

Highway
△ Pass

Stony Dome

n

r Center

△ Scott Peak

△ Panorama Mtn.
El. 5,778 ft

Nenana River

8 DENALI HIGHWAY

Cantwell

To Paxson →

A L A S K A   R A N G E

DERNESS

ridge
33 ft

GEORGE PARKS HIGHWAY

N

DENALI
STATE PARK

DENALI

NATIONAL PARK
AND PRESERVE

Ranger Station **RS** Campground 🏕

Unpaved Road — — — — — —

Airstrip ✈

The Alaska Railroad

Talkeetna

Talkeetna

TO ALASKA HIGHWAY 3

M   I   L   E   S

0   20   40   60

Establishment of the Park

Charles Sheldon spent that entire winter in Denali. He and his partner, Harry Karstens, made forays by dog team into the wild land from a cabin they had built on the Toklat River. They mushed their teams up ridges and down rivers, and they made careful notes on the natural history. When Sheldon left Denali, he was devoted to its beauty and determined to preserve it. After years of political battle in Washington, D.C., he hand-delivered a bill for signature to the White House. His dream came true on February 16, 1917, when President Woodrow Wilson created Mount McKinley National Park, Alaska's first national park. Sheldon's former partner, Harry Karstens, became the first superintendent in 1921.

With passage of the Alaska National Interest Lands Conservation Act (ANILCA) in 1980, the 1.9-million-acre Mount McKinley National Park became the 6-million-acre Denali National Park and Preserve. Reigning over this old land and new park is Mount McKinley, now protected on all sides, uplifting the human spirit, making its own weather, and birthing the seventeen glaciers that spill down-slope to carve and shape the land. At 20,320 feet above sea level and 17,000 feet above its base, Mount McKinley is the tallest mountain in North America. Mountaineers from all over the world come to climb it; visitors want to see it, photograph it. The sudden appearance of the lofty white summit above gray clouds, especially after days of waiting, can be an exhilirating experience, for the mountain is always higher and bigger than expected.

Although Mount McKinley is the geographical focal point of the park, preservation of the wildlife was Sheldon's foremost concern. He realized the irreplaceable natural treasure the mammal populations here represented, as well as the fragility of their habitats. Yet he did not measure this importance in dollars and cents but as a resource essential to the spiritual health of the human race.

The enlargement of the park in 1980 was intended to provide protection for entire ecosystems, based on improved understanding of wildlife population dynamics and of the steps necessary to save species. Although legislative compromise frustrated the achievement of this goal, at least temporarily, Denali National Park and Preserve is a magnificent home for wildlife in the heart of Alaska, crowned by the incomparable granite massif called McKinley.

The Athapaskans

Athapaskans, the aboriginal peoples of Alaska's interior, probably had no permanent villages in present-day Denali National Park, preferring the relative hospitableness of the open lowlands to the north. Small bands, however, made summer migrations into the park, building blinds and waiting for caribou or moose. Perhaps, too, they collected blueberries in August near Wonder Lake, as visitors do today. Although archeological evidence indicates that in this land the Athapaskans were seasonal visitors, all their stories refer to the huge mountain they could see throughout the year. They called it Denali, the name Alaskans prefer today.

Early Explorers

In 1794, Captain George Vancouver sailed into upper Cook Inlet to survey Knik Arm. On the far northwest horizon he noted "distant stupendous mountains covered with snow and apparently detached from one another." Were these Mount McKinley and Mount Foraker, about 140 miles away? Probably.

A second reference to these peaks appeared on a map published in 1839 by the Imperial Russian Academy of Sciences, though a

The McKinley Depot, circa 1920, was a stop on the Seward–Fairbanks Alaska Railroad.

Russian map published 22 years later omitted reference to them. When the United States purchased Alaska from Russia in 1867, the 1861 map served as a major reference. The first American explorers into Alaska's heartland, therefore, had no idea what lay before them.

In 1878, Arthur Harper journeyed up the Tanana River, and from the present site of Fairbanks he described a "great ice mountain to the south." Thirty-five years later, his son, Walter Harper, would become the first man to stand atop that mountain.

Near the turn of the century, several topographers—George Eldridge, Robert Muldrow, and Alfred Brooks among them—accurately described and measured Mount McKinley. Muldrow calculated its great height (missing by only 144 feet) and the world (especially mountaineers) took notice. A prospector, William A. Dickey, named the mountain after learning that William McKinley had been nominated for president in 1896.

To the Roof of North America

The first man to attempt the summit was James Wickersham, Alaska's federal judge in the young town of Fairbanks.

The Sourdough Expedition of 1910 mistakenly climbed the lower of McKinley's peaks.

Unfortunately, he approached the mountain by way of Peters Glacier and was abruptly turned back at 10,000 feet by a steep north-facing precipice. Later named in his honor, the Wickersham Wall has seldom been scaled.

Seven years later, in 1910, four Kantishna miners announced in a Fairbanks saloon their intention to climb Mount McKinley. Known as the Sourdough Party, Thomas Lloyd, Charles McGonagall, William Taylor, and Peter Anderson mushed sled dogs up the Muldrow Glacier to about 12,000 feet on the mountain's northeast flank. Over the following days, with doughnuts and hot chocolate in their packs and a 14-foot spruce pole in hand, Taylor and Anderson climbed to the top, only to discover that the North Peak (19,470 feet) on which they stood was lower than the South Peak two miles away. They had been deceived because from Fairbanks to Kantishna, the North Peak appears higher than the South Peak and actually obstructs views of it. Nonetheless, they planted the spruce pole for proof and headed down. Anderson then tried to reach the South Peak, but inclement weather forced him back. On returning to Fairbanks, the Sourdoughs met with some skepticism in addition to praise. Not everyone believed their story,

The owner of Cann Studio in Fairbanks gets ready for some aerial photography, 1927.

for not even the most powerful telescopes in Fairbanks could spot the spruce pole.

The Parker-Brown Expedition of 1912 made a serious attempt to reach the South Peak, but it failed after being hit hard by a blizzard only 600 feet below the summit.

In 1913, Archdeacon Hudson Stuck and veteran explorer Harry Karstens organized an assault on Mount McKinley. Walter Harper and Robert Tatum, employed by Stuck at the Nenana Episcopal Mission, joined the team. Their expedition would take 53 days. From 11,000 to 15,000 feet, they were obliged to carve a 3-mile-long staircase into the ice. The weather remained calm, however, and on June 7 the four men reached McKinley's true summit, the roof of North America. Across from them was the North Peak, 800 feet lower, crowned by a spruce pole still standing after three years. Mount McKinley had been climbed and the Sourdoughs vindicated.

In 1932, the Lindley-Liek Expedition climbed both the North and South peaks. Concurrently, the Carpe-Koven Expedition arrived on the mountain to measure cosmic rays from the earth's magnetic field. Upon returning from their success, the first expedition discovered that Allen Carpe and Theodore Koven had fallen into crevasses and died. They were the first climbers known to have lost their lives on Mount McKinley.

Altogether, through 1994, seventy-nine climbers have died on Mount McKinley, and at least 200 have suffered serious injuries. Yet several thousand have stood on the top. About half of the climbers who attempt the ascent each year succeed. Most begin at about 7,500 feet where a skiplane from Talkeetna lands them on the south-facing Kahiltna Glacier. The fly-in landing takes place on land added to the park in 1980; the fly-in tradition was retained even though the area is now in the park. Following the popular West Buttress Route, the climb is essentially a long hard walk, with success or failure depending largely upon the vagaries of the weather.

GEOLOGY

The geologic history of Denali National Park and Preserve records a half billion years of successive processes that shaped and reshaped the land. Denali's geology includes some of Alaska's oldest rocks as well as the largest crustal break on the North American continent.

The Denali Fault

The Denali Fault arcs 600 miles across the heart of Alaska from the Canadian border to Bristol Bay. About 60 million years ago, when the fault first ripped open, lava flowed across the flat land and

Glacial erratics are carried off by glaciers and later deposited when the glacier melts.

hardened into rhyolite and basalt. Volcanic ash interbedded with the igneous rocks, and together they began to build into a range of new mountains. The land buckled, fractured, and folded along the fault; great blocks of the earth's crust lifted higher and higher.

Deep in the fault was a chamber of magma that did not flow forth and harden rapidly but instead remained buried. It cooled very gradually into granite, a crystalline and weather-resistant rock. Then the granite lifted as a great massif until it breached the surface, dwarfed the mountains, and crowned the continent over 20,000 feet above the sea. This is Mount McKinley, surrounded by the Alaska Range.

Younger Mountains, Older Rocks

The Outer Range rises just north of the central Alaska Range. It includes Mount Healy, Healy Ridge, Primrose Ridge, and Mount Wright. Curiously, these mountains are younger than those in the Alaska Range, yet they contain rocks eight times older.

Long before the birth of the Alaska Range, shallow seas flooded Alaska's interior and deposited large amounts of sediment. Layer upon layer of sediment cemented and eventually metamorphosed into a hard rock consisting of compacted flakes of mica and quartz. This is Birch Creek Schist, about 550 million years old and very resistant to erosion.

Overleaf: Debris precipitated by Muldrow Glacier forms its lateral moraine.

But if the schist is resistant, how could the Sanctuary, Savage, and Nenana rivers have cut through it? It is a matter of what came first. The rivers flowed strongly off the Alaska Range before the Outer Range existed. At whatever rate the new mountains lifted, the pre-established rivers cut into the Schist faster, splitting the Outer Range and maintaining their paths. Running water thus carved canyons and exposed some of the oldest rocks in Alaska.

Savage River Canyon offers the park's best exposures of Birch Creek Schist. As for the basalts, rhyolites, and ash created 40 to 60 million years ago along the Denali Fault, they are most visible in the cliffs near Polychrome Pass. Chemical weathering (oxidation) has colored iron in the basalt dark brown, while the ash has turned white, yellow, pink, purple, red, and green.

Ice and Water

Ice has been the chief architect of many of the landforms visible today in Denali National Park and Preserve. And where ice left off, water picked up.

Sometime between one and two million years ago, worldwide temperatures fell by a few degrees. In consequence, sea level dropped several hundred feet and the polar ice caps expanded. A land bridge joining Siberia and Alaska was left behind by the receding ocean, and the first people to enter North America walked across it.

This was the ice age, or Pleistocene epoch, when continental glaciers advanced and retreated at least four times over northern North America. Glaciers filled the Alaska Range. Then as now, the south side of the range received more precipitation from storms off the Gulf of Alaska than the north side did, and for this reason it produced larger glaciers. On the mountains' north slopes, the great ice rivers flowed down valleys and abutted against the Outer Range. This accounts for the marked contrast between the broad U-shaped valleys in the Alaska Range, which were carved by glaciers, and narrow V-shaped canyons in the Outer Range, which were cut by water. Savage River Canyon is a good example of the latter.

Many other signatures of the Pleistocene epoch are also in evidence. As the glaciers retreated, they stranded huge transported boulders—called erratics—on the valleys and ridges. Large blocks of ice were also abandoned; the ice then melted, leaving potholes that later filled with water, features known as kettle ponds. More subtle evidence can be found in bedded sediments that record the speed and volume of water discharge off the ice from thousands of years ago; the slower the water velocity, the finer the sediment.

Probably the most curious and surprising features are the braided rivers. During the last great melting, about 12,000 years ago, a tremendous volume of water flowed across the valleys. The rivers may have carried fifty or one hundred times more water then than now, cutting and filling the rock channels that dwarf them today. Huge dams of ice and rock probably formed in the narrow canyons of the Outer Range, causing lakes to pool in the valleys, where they deposited sediments and then suddenly drained when the dams broke. These periods of alternating quiet and turbulent waters built alluvial terraces visible today on the banks above the rivers. The top of each terrace records a former water level.

Today, the rivers form braids for several reasons. Permafrost lies beneath many rivers and inhibits the deepening of channels. Also, ice jams that occur in the fall and spring force the water into new channels. Finally, the erratic weather—be it heavy rain or a long period of sunshine—can swell the rivers, which spill into many new braids.

NATURAL HISTORY

Weather and Climate

Denali National Park and Preserve, which is about 200 miles south of the Arctic Circle, lies entirely within the earth's subarctic climate zone. Residents say there are only three seasons: June, July, and winter. In some years, that seems like an exaggeration in favor of June and July.

Winter descends cold and clear, with temperatures (measured at park headquarters) dropping to severe levels. The record low is — 52° F. The mountain temperatures are even more severe. In 1913, the Stuck-Karstens climbing party left an alcohol thermometer at 15,000 feet on Mount McKinley. Nineteen years later, the Lindley-Liek Expedition discovered it. The reading was below the very bottom of the scale: - 95° F, which, if accurate, represents one of the coldest temperatures recorded in North America.

Accumulations of snow in the winter lowlands seldom amount to more than 3 feet. The snow whitens the Denali landscape and insulates tundra plants and animals from cold, desiccating winds. Darkness, too, prevails in winter. December and January are brooding months with only 5 to 6 hours of pale light per day. For many, however, the colorful displays of the northern lights (aurora borealis) are ample compensation.

In summertime, plants race to reproduce, mammals climb from their burrows and dens, and wildflowers and insects explode on the scene. Migrating birds arrive from the south, while the fur and feathers of some resident animals turn from white to brown. The sun arcs high over the mountains, swinging around the sky for 20 hours in a day. Temperatures can climb to 50° F (the record high is actually 90° F) or drop to 20° F. Rain is common during the summer. It falls lightly for days or weeks at a time, and accounts for most of the park's 15 inches of average annual precipitation. Visitors should carry light clothing, plus wool clothing and raingear.

Upon arriving, visitors to Denali National Park and Preserve usually have one interest in the weather that preempts all others: "Is Mount McKinley clear or clouded?" It tends to be clouded more often than not because the huge mountain readily builds its own weather from surrounding unstable air masses. On any given day, from June through August, the chances of seeing the summit are about 35 to 40 percent.

Taiga and Tundra

More than 450 species of trees, shrubs, and herbs grow in Denali National Park and Preserve. Each is a study in natural strategy and resilience. Essentially dormant for nine months of the year, they come to life at winter's end with branches, blossoms, and berries. Their adaptations are beyond imagination, yet within discovery; every detail has a purpose, and every form has a function.

Taiga and tundra describe the two dominant vegetation types in the Alaska interior. The terms are used loosely because many variations exist within and between them.

Taiga (pronounced TIE-ga) is a Russian word meaning "land of little sticks" and refers to the forests of the Far North. The major species in Denali are white spruce and black spruce, with a sprinkling of aspen, paper birch, balsam poplar, and tamarack. There is far less difference between the two species of spruce than their names imply, and, in fact, most visitors would have difficulty distinguishing them. White spruce prefer dry soils and develop comparatively full profiles. Black spruce favor wet soils, grow in a thin and tapering outline, and often look sickly. Beneath the spruce live shade-tolerant plants such as Labrador tea, dwarf dogwood, wild rose, bluebells, blueberry, crowberry, and lowbush cranberry.

The treeline in the park ranges from about 2,000 feet on exposed ridges to about 2,800 feet in protected valleys—and where the taiga ends, the tundra begins. There are two types of tundra: wet and dry. Wet tundra is characterized by waist-high willow and dwarf birch, often interspersed along ponds with horsetails, sedges, and grasses. Dry (or alpine) tundra carpets the upper ridges and rocky slopes of Denali from about 3,500 to 7,500 feet. Wildflowers hug the earth in rosette, button, and mat shapes, creating their own hospitable microclimates beneath the wind and

Opposite: The rock ptarmigan is a year-round resident of Denali.

cold. White mountain avens, moss campion, alpine azalea, arctic bell heather, saxifrages, louseworts, geraniums, harebells, and many, many more grow on the leeward sides of rocks and in the bottoms of depressions. Examining any of the dozens of different tundra blossoms close up is like discovering worlds within a world. Simple designs frame elegant details, and colors fuse into rich alpine bouquets. It is a grand occasion for becoming pleasantly lost.

A Wildlife Park

Denali is a wildlife park. The sweeping vistas lend themselves to open viewing. Migrating caribou can be seen half a mile away, or a nesting sandpiper can be spotted as it moves about in the immediate foreground. The animals fit into the landscape as integral parts of the greater whole, manifesting subarctic laws of adversity and beauty. And the element of surprise sharpens every sight into an acute memory. The sudden appearance of an eagle, a bear, or a moose always makes the heart race faster.

About 155 species of birds occur in Denali, most of them as summer residents. They come from Siberia, Japan, Hawaii, California, Costa Rica, Antarctica, and many points in between. Some species, such as the red-throated loon, sandhill crane, and oldsquaw, pause briefly on their way to and from nesting grounds farther north. Others live here year-round, including the great horned owl, the raven, and the white-tailed, rock, and willow ptarmigan. The majority, however, arrive to court, mate, nest, feed, and fledge at locations throughout the Denali taiga and tundra. Sandpipers and plovers settle inconspicuously into the tundra; mew gulls perch atop spruce; buffleheads and goldeneyes use woodpecker holes in tree snags. And as suddenly as they arrive, they leave—on the wing, southbound, joined by the new generation.

Ranging in size from the tiny yellow-cheeked vole to the 1,600-pound Alaska bull moose, thirty-seven species of mammals live in the park. All are year-round residents. Sure-footed Dall sheep inhabit the high country, falling prey to avalanches, rock slides, and eagles far more often than to wolves and bears. Omnivorous red foxes roam widely, at home in both the tundra and the taiga.

Grizzly bears are equally omnivorous and opportunistic. They feast on berries, dig for arctic ground squirrels, and partake of whatever carrion they can find. During the grizzly's courting season, mid-May to mid-July, pairs may travel together for a week to ten days. The female (sow) mates once every three years. The male (boar) leaves the sow after mating. The one-pound cubs (there are usually two), blind and deaf at birth, are born in the winter den. They remain with their mother for up to three years. When the sow

The call of the sandhill crane is long, harsh, and shrill.

is ready to mate again, the cubs leave or are chased away by the sow or her new suitor.

Wolves work the open tundra, but these wary animals are seldom seen. Adolph Murie, a mammalogist from Minnesota, spent more than twenty consecutive summers in the park, beginning in the early 1920s. In his classic study, *The Wolves of Mount McKinley* (1944), Murie concluded that wolf predation had a "salutary effect" on the Dall-sheep population and that the two species appeared to be in equilibrium.

In the taiga, snowshoe-hare populations boom and crash roughly every ten years. In delayed response, the numbers of lynx and goshawks—chief predators of the hares—follow a similar cycle.

A more disconcerting population change among Denali wildlife is that of the caribou. In the 1940s the herd numbered about 25,000. By the mid-1980s, fewer than 3,000 survived. Why? No one is certain. The caribou numbers have no doubt risen and fallen before. Indeed, nature tends toward cycles. But was this crash "natural"? Or was the element of human encroachment involved? From 1960 to 1980, visitation to Denali jumped almost 30-fold. More people:

fewer caribou. With this situation specifically in mind, Congress enlarged the park in 1980 to afford the caribou protection in both their calving and wintering grounds. A severe winter, 1990-91, further reduced the herd size; in 1994 there were 1,800 caribou.

SITES, TRAILS, AND TRIPS

In 1923, Congress appropriated $5,000 for construction of a road through the park. Fifteen years later, the road from the railroad station to Wonder Lake was completed. Visitors arrived by train back then; not until 1972 was the George Parks Highway (Alaska 3) constructed between Anchorage and Fairbanks. Visits to the park quintupled in 1972, and today over 300,000 visitors arrive each summer from around the world. More than half are Alaska residents.

Camping and "Carrying Capacity"

No hiker or camper, no matter how conscientious, can visit Denali National Park and Preserve without putting a strain on the delicate biota. The pre-1980 portion of the park has been designated by Congress as the Denali Wilderness and the National Park Service has divided it into backcountry management units of various shapes and sizes. Each unit has a "carrying capacity"—a designated maximum number of people in the unit at any given time above which, careful research has suggested, the environmental impact would be irreparable. Some units are more sensitive or smaller than others and thus have lower carrying capacities. The same is true for campgrounds. The result: Denali's backcountry can accommodate only a limited number of visitors at a time. At this time, no reservations are required for backcountry camping, but campground sites may be reserved. For those without reservations, the best pre-arrival plan is to allow ample time and to stress flexibility—the more days allowed for waiting, the better.

This is a management system designed to maintain Denali's pristine environment. Mistakes in the states farther south have become lessons learned by the National Park Service in Alaska. In effect, the idea of carrying capacity has been developed to keep history from repeating itself.

The Park Road

Shuttle buses travel the park road between the Park Visitor Center and Wonder Lake Campground at intervals of 30 or 60 min-

Opposite: Tundra moss colonizes rocky areas at high elevations.

utes. They run from early morning to late evening. This system is critical to the management of resources in the park. The buses reduce traffic and thereby increase wildlife-viewing opportunities along the road. When one passenger sees an animal, the bus stops and forty people see it. Invariably, travelers on the shuttle buses see more than those in private vehicles. The buses stop almost anywhere to let passengers on or off.

In its 90 miles, the park road crosses rivers, climbs mountains, and enters some of the richest wildlife habitat in Alaska. It begins off the George Parks Highway, 235 miles north of Anchorage and 120 miles south of Fairbanks.

The *Denali Park Visitor Center* (.7 mile from the Parks Highway turnoff) is the summertime home base of the park. The information center has campground and backcountry permits, shuttle-bus schedules, current brochures, park literature, weather information, and schedules of various interpretive activities such as guided nature walks, sled-dog demonstrations, campfire talks, and movie and slide presentations.

The *Denali Park Railroad Station* (1.2 miles; 1,732 feet) was built in 1921 when the Alaska Railroad was completed from Seward to Fairbanks. That station was replaced in 1989. The train stops here daily in the summer but only on passenger request in winter. The original hotel burned to the ground on Labor Day 1972 and has been replaced by a temporary structure on the site.

Nearby is *Morino Campground*, named after pioneer Maurice Morino, who built a roadhouse near the present railroad station. This is a backpackers' campground, designed for walk-in tent campers only.

The road climbs along the steep north bank of Hines Creek to *park headquarters*, 3.1 miles from the park entrance. This complex of buildings is open all year and includes ranger-naturalist offices and administrative and maintenance facilities. The Denali sled dogs live here in their kennels beyond the large maintenance garage. In the winter, the dogs take rangers on patrol, and in the summer, they are used in demonstrations for visitors.

For the next 6 miles, the road climbs steadily through the taiga. As the spruce open into tundra, space becomes an extraordinary element of the Denali landscape. Open vistas spread between the Alaska Range to the south and the Outer Range, along which the road winds, to the north. Here also is the first opportunity to see Mount McKinley—weather permitting—about 70 air miles to the southwest.

Near the *Savage River Campground* (12.5 miles; 2,780 feet) is the site of the old Savage Road Camp. Stagecoaches once shuttled visitors from Riley Creek to here, where a good night's lodging consisted of a cot in a canvas tent. The camp operated from 1926 to 1941.

Savage River Check Station (14.8 miles) is the farthest private vehicles are allowed to travel into the park without a permit. Vehicles registered for Teklanika campground may proceed to mile 28.7.

Primrose Ridge roughly parallels the road to the north between the Savage and Sanctuary rivers. Its slopes support a rich array of wildflowers and provide an outstanding view of the Alaska Range.

The alpine poppy.

The *Sanctuary River* (22.5 miles; 2,470 feet) slices through the Outer Range between Mount Wright and Primrose Ridge. Near its headwaters, high in the Alaska Range, are spring calving grounds of the caribou.

The road breaches a low pass and then enters a dwarf birch and spruce forest along the Teklanika River. *Teklanika* is an Athapaskan word meaning "much gravel, little water." It could be appropriately applied to any of Denali's major rivers.

At 28.7 miles, the road passes *Teklanika River Campground* and at 30 miles, crosses the river (2,663 feet). Wildlife viewing is often good here, as bear, wolf, moose, and fox work the shoreline. Early and late in the summer, waterfowl gather in the ponds near the entrance to the campground. *Igloo Creek* separates Igloo and Cathedral mountains, both favorite haunts of Dall sheep.

Sable Pass has become synonymous with grizzly bears. They can sometimes be observed for hours here, roaming the tundra. The Sable Pass Wildlife Restricted Area extends roughly from *Tattler Creek* (37 miles) to the *East Fork River Bridge* (42 miles). All the acreage here within 1 mile of the road (excluding the road itself) has been permanently closed to the public since 1952.

The *East Fork of the Toklat River* (3,057 feet) shows better than any other the braided characteristics of Denali's rivers. It was here, too, that Adolph Murie lived with his family in the late 1930s and conducted his classic wolf study.

Polychrome Pass (45.3 miles; 3,704 feet) offers a breath-taking view south to the Plains of Murie and the Alaska Range. Clearly visible on the plains below are numerous glacial features such as erratics, kettle ponds, and outwash alluvial terraces.

Beyond Polychrome Pass, the road drops down and skirts the ghostly looking *Porcupine Forest*. Many decades ago, a population of porcupines was trapped here by heavy snow. The starving animals quickly exhausted their primary food, tree bark, and continued to girdle the spruce, gnawing at the green wood. By spring, most of the trees and porcupines were dead.

The *Toklat River* (52.4 miles; 3,400 feet) is one of the largest rivers on the north side of the Alaska Range. It flows 50 miles north to the Tanana, which later joins the mighty Yukon. *Divide Mountain* (5,195 feet) separates the upper two forks of the Toklat just south of the road.

Migrating caribou and winter sled-dog patrols cross *Highway Pass* (57.5 miles) each year. The sled-dog trail parallels the road and is barely visible in the valley to the south. Ground-nesting birds such as plovers and jaegers can also be observed here.

Bergh Lake was created on July 18, 1952, when a massive landslide dammed *Stony Creek* (59.8 miles; 3,610 feet) just downstream and north of the road. By the mid-1980s the lake had been reduced to one-half its former size, and it was subsequently washed out altogether.

At 61 miles (3,720 feet), the road crests between *Stony Hill* to the north and *Stony Dome* to the south. On a clear day—which is rare—Mount McKinley rises in the distance between them, about 40 air miles away. Also visible from here are the peaks of Mounts Mather (12,123 feet), Silverthrone (13,220 feet), and Brooks (11,880 feet). In the foreground, caribou have worn paths during their annual migratory movements. The topography concentrates them here as they move between the less constricted Highway Pass and Thorofare Pass areas. The trails often braid, recalling the rivers the caribou must cross.

Eielson Visitor Center honors Carl Ben Eielson, who, in 1924, first landed a plane in Mount McKinley National Park. Five years later he died while flying over Siberia. The Visitor Center (65.2 miles; 3,730 feet) sits on a terrace overlooking the Thorofare River where Eielson touched down his World War I Jenny. Across the river rises the Alaska Range, crowned by Mount McKinley, 33 miles to the southwest.

Arctic ground squirrels abound near the Visitor Center. They are likable animals that easily win the hearts and handouts of visitors. This causes a serious problem, however. Overfeeding by people has created a population boom among the squirrels here which, in turn, has attracted increasing numbers of grizzly bears looking for a squirrel meal. Bears and people do not mix. The best solution, therefore, is to refrain from feeding the squirrels.

Beyond Eielson Visitor Center, the road cuts along steeply eroded cliffs of ancient volcanic rock. Golden eagles soar here, hunting for squirrels. Gyrfalcons dive past the cliffs almost too fast to be identified.

The road jogs to the right, and the mountain slopes smooth out into rolling hills at about 68 miles.

Muldrow Glacier first appears to the south at 61 miles and remains visible until about 83 miles. Blanketed in rock and sediment, it at first looks nothing like a river of ice. Yet the Muldrow is the largest glacier on the north side of the Alaska Range, spilling down for 32 miles and 16,000 feet from just beneath McKinley's summit. It was named by Alfred Brooks in remembrance of Robert Muldrow, a young topographer who, in 1898, made the first instrument-aided determination of the altitude and position of Mount McKinley

For the next 15 miles the road winds over old glacial moraines—hummocky landforms deposited thousands of years ago when the Muldrow Glacier filled the McKinley River Valley below.

Between 74 and 77 miles are numerous small lakes called the beaver ponds. Beaver, muskrat, and waterfowl live here. Moose often wade belly deep and dunk their heads for aquatic vegetation. The wood frog—the only species of amphibian in Alaska's interior—lives here, too.

At 82.5 miles, *Wonder Lake* appears, 3 miles long, 280 feet deep, and glittering amid the coniferous slopes like a jewel pinned on a cloth of green. According to local legend, two turn-of-the-century miners from Kantishna stumbled through the forest and happened upon the beautiful body of water. One turned to the other and exclaimed, "I wonder how we missed this before!" In true pioneer tradition, the name I Wonder stuck. It has since been shortened to its present form.

The road divides at 83.5 miles. A mile and a half down and to the left is *Wonder Lake Campground*. To the right, the road parallels Wonder Lake and approaches the *Kantishna Hills*.

Photographers often gravitate to *Reflection Pond* (84.7 miles; 2,350 feet) at dawn or dusk when clear days offer mirror-calm images of Mount McKinley and Mount Foraker. White cotton grass, which is actually a sedge, rings the ponds below and frames reflections of the mountains.

The *Wonder Lake Ranger Station* (85.5 miles; 2,095 feet) is a time-honored old structure, now cracked and leaning on its foundation. In winter, it serves as the final destination of the sled-dog teams. Wonder Lake bears a thick covering of ice and snow then, a white void criss-crossed with the tracks of hares, wolves, ptarmigan, moose, lynx, and other winter residents. During summer, loons and grebes nest along the shore of the lake, while many other species stop to rest here on their way to and from breeding grounds far to the north.

From the Wonder Lake cabin, the North Peak of Mount McKinley is 27.5 miles distant. Hidden behind it is the true summit, the South Peak. This deceptive view fooled many early mountain climbers on McKinley, most notably the Sourdoughs, who probably would have reached the mountain's true summit had they realized where it was.

Continuing north, the road passes *Bald Knob* at 86.7 miles. A short walk up the hill provides a splendid view of Mount McKinley reflected in Wonder Lake. As with those seen in Reflection Pond, the images are usually best during calm hours early or late in the day.

The road ends at the mining town of *Kantishna*, at 89.8 miles. In 1905, Kantishna boomed with gold fever, swelled to several thousand people, and collapsed shortly thereafter. Mining continues in the hills nearby, but the quaintness is gone. Picks and shovels have been replaced with earth movers and hydraulics that rip open the land and silt the streams. Present and future mining is limited to ground already disturbed. Because of the regulatory difficulties associated with mining in a national park, many of the owners of mineral rights are offering their assets for sale to the Park Service. By 1994, more than 60 percent of the potential mining claims had already been purchased.

Frontcountry Trails

Hiking opportunities are endless in Denali National Park and Preserve. The country seems to stretch forever, inviting hikers down rivers and up ridges. And it is quite natural, on reaching a destination, to wonder whether anyone has ever been there before.

Options include hiking a trail in the frontcountry, walking along the park road, joining a naturalist for a hike, or setting off across the tundra almost anywhere. Two important preliminary steps are to check which backcountry units are closed or full and to register at the Visitor Center for any overnight trips.

The Denali frontcountry—the area around the buildings near the entrance to the park—has several trails that originate near the train station/hotel complex.

Triple Lakes Trail. The Triple Lakes Trail is a 4-mile round-trip route from the trail head on the George Parks Highway, about 5 miles south of the park entrance and just north of McKinley Village. These lakes are deep enough to support a population of small grayling, and waterfowl often pause there en route to or from summer nesting grounds. The middle lake is the largest, about .5 mile long.

Horseshoe Lake Trail. The 1.5-mile-long Horseshoe Lake Trail attracts visitors of all ages and hiking abilities. Beginning at the railroad tracks on the Park Road, it winds through stands of aspen and spruce, crosses a service road and a stream, climbs a short hill, and divides. The left fork leads up Mount Healy. The right fork continues to Horseshoe Lake, leading to an overlook above the lake.

Thousands of years ago, the Nenana River flowed in a sweeping oxbow bend. As huge glaciers retreated, the river swelled, shifted its course, and eventually pinched off the oxbow bend, isolating a quiet, horseshoe-shaped lake whose waters no longer flowed. Sediment fills the lake now, and the shores encroach little by little each year. In a few centuries—or maybe a few decades—the lake will become a meadow, and the beaver (who also played a role in building the lake), muskrat, and moose that visit today will go elsewhere.

The trail descends steeply from the overlook to the lake and meanders about the shore. It is a short walk to the Nenana River.

Mount Healy Overlook Trail. This trail climbs from the taiga to the tundra, 1,700 feet in 3 miles. It begins with the Taiga Loop Trail (behind the hotel) and branches off to the left just beyond the stream crossing.

The trail passes through several transition zones of plant and animal life. The spruce give way to thickets of alder growing on an old road and on a World War 11 military ski run. Alder flourish in such disturbed areas and add nitrogen, an essential element for plant growth, to the soil.

Above the alder and into the open light, the trail enters a realm of wildflowers. Lavender spires of monkshood, larkspur, and tall Jacob's ladder reach for the sky. Monkshood and larkspur are related to the buttercup and mix attractively with the yellow dusting of black-tipped groundsel and goldenrod, relatives of the sunflower. Bluebells, wintergreens, and anemones bow toward the earth, while wild rhubarb and fireweed nod high in the wind.

Continuing its ascent, the trail reaches the timberline above paper birch and groves of aspen. It switches back over talus slopes and finally arrives at the overlook. Although the trail continues onward, the top of Mount Healy is still 1,000 feet up and many false summits rise between it and the overlook.

Overleaf: The "moss mat" thrives over chalky soils that are saturated with seepage water.

Like bouquets of miniature blossoms, alpine wildflowers carpet the overlook. Here, too, live the arctic ground squirrel and the pika, a small nonhibernating relative of rabbits and hares. If the sky is clear, Mount McKinley can be seen about 80 miles away on the western horizon.

Backcountry Trips

There are no maintained trails in the Denali backcountry. In the lower states, the National Park Service urges hikers to stay on designated trails. But hikers in the Denali backcountry should not walk single file; the objective is to avoid making trails. Repeated impact from footfalls and scuffing creates serious damage to fragile plantlife. Loose slopes and areas that permafrost underlies are especially susceptible. This land scars easily and heals slowly. Hikers should spread out and emulate the braided rivers, the wide valleys, the entire topography.

The Denali backcountry has countless exciting places to explore, but many of the backcountry management units may be temporarily closed or full. Travel options should be left open. The best procedure is to talk to a ranger and plan accordingly. With a little patience and a lot of built-in adjustment time, hiking opportunities increase immensely. Backcountry trips in Denali might include hiking in one or several of the following types of terrain.

Ridgetops and Hills. Mount Wright, Primrose Ridge, Healy Ridge, Eielson Ridge, Stony Hill, and Stony Dome all can be climbed round trip from the road in a day. The lower slopes often support waist-high willow and dwarf birch, but with each step upward the walking becomes easier as woody plants disperse and delicate ground-hugging vegetation carpets the rock and thin soil. The ridgetops offer displays of wildflowers and views of the Alaska Range. Pikas, marmots, and arctic ground squirrels are common, and Dall sheep sometimes graze atop Mount Wright and Primrose Ridge.

Mountaintops. Cathedral Mountain, Igloo Mountain, Sable Mountain (via Tattler Creek), Mount Eielson, and many others are strenuous climbs up unconsolidated rock. Climbing them requires care.

Braided Rivers. This area forms a rich wildlife habitat. Wolves, red fox, grizzlies, moose, and caribou follow the shorelines. Many species of willow thrive, some maturing at only a few inches in height and others towering tens of feet tall. Fireweed and oxytrope blossom on small terraces near the water's edge; they are annuals and therefore set new seed each year. Sandpipers, surfbirds, and wandering tattlers occasionally feed along rivulets of the river, now and then sounding a plaintive call that is muffled by the river's murmuring.

Remote Areas. In Denali's vast realm, other sites beckon the truly resourceful explorer. Of course, climbing Mount McKinley is an important attraction of the park. Those climbers who are sincerely interested in making the ascent should contact the park directly.

There are countless other routes to hike. The open land and far vistas can almost mesmerize a lover of wilderness. Special treats for the wilderness walker are rainbows, bear tracks, and the midnight moon over Mount McKinley. Sights such as these are the essence of Denali National Park and Preserve.

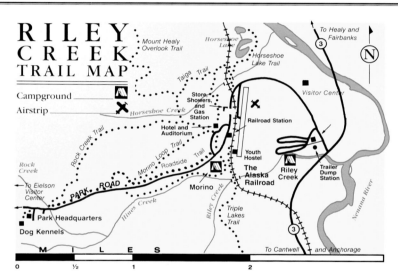

TRAILS OF DENALI NATIONAL PARK AND PRESERVE

Several trails begin near the Denali Visitor Center. They are shown above. At the Visitor Center, ask for the flier "Entrance Area Trails." In addition to the trails described in previous pages, the Entrance Area Trails include the following:

TAIGA LOOP TRAIL: Starts and ends at the Denali Park Hotel parking lot; 1.3 miles; 1 hour; elevation change 150 feet; easy.

MORINO LOOP TRAIL: Starts and ends at the Denali Park Hotel parking lot; 1.3 miles; 1 hour; elevation change 100 feet; easy.

ROCK CREEK TRAIL: Starts at Denali Park Hotel; ends at Park Headquarters; 2.3 miles, one way; 2 hours, one way; elevation change 400 feet; moderate.

Overleaf: At elevations ranging from 2,000 to 2,800 feet, the taiga gives way to the tundra.

GATES

OF THE ARCTIC
NATIONAL PARK
AND PRESERVE

The Arrigetch Peaks are listed on the National Register of Natural Landmarks.

Gates of the Arctic
National Park and Preserve
P.O. Box 74680, Fairbanks, Alaska 99707
Tel.: (907) 456-0281

Highlights: North Fork, Koyukuk River • Boreal Mountain and Frigid Crags • Kobuk River • Chandler Lake • Noatak River • Brooks Range • Arctic Tundra • Arrigetch Peaks • Mount Igikpak

Access: By air from Fairbanks to Bettles and Anaktuvuk Pass. Cross-country hiking from Dalton Highway, which parallels the park at a distance of 5 to 15 miles.

Season: Best time from June to September. Winter trips possible from February to April.

Fees: None.

Gas, Food, Lodging: Available in Anaktuvuk Pass, Bettles, and Coldfoot. Gas in Coldfoot.

Visitor Center: Park headquarters in Fairbanks serves as a Visitor Center. Bettles and Anaktuvuk stations can also provide trip-planning assistance. Coldfoot has a joint-agency Visitor Center with displays, interpretive programs, and trip planning.

Pets: Pack dogs only are allowed in park.

Hiking: Unrestricted hiking. Prepare for wilderness experience requiring complete self-sufficiency. Treat all water.

Backpacking: No facilities, trails, or campgrounds available. Food and stoves must be carried. Minimum-impact camping must be practiced. Bearproof storage containers strongly recommended.

Campgrounds: No designated campgrounds.

Tours: Concessionaire-guided hiking and rafting trips; no National Park Service tours. Information available at park headquarters.

Other Activities: Cross-country skiing in late winter and early spring; kayaking, fishing with Alaska State license.

Facilities for Disabled: All visitor contact offices in Fairbanks, Bettles, Anaktuvuk Pass, and Coldfoot are handicap accessible.

For additional information, see also Sites, Trails, and Trips on pages 94–97 and the map on pages 82–83.

GAUNT, AUSTERE, CHALLENGING, YET exquisite in its subtle beauties, Gates of the Arctic is America's ultimate national park. Lying entirely north of the Arctic Circle, it embraces the heart of the nation's last great mountain wilderness, the Brooks Range. Just as Alaska is termed the "Last Frontier" for enterprise and adventure, so Gates of the Arctic is a final mountain frontier for those who wish to perpetuate true wilderness.

Compared with most national parks, Gates of the Arctic is immense. The park section alone is more than 200 miles wide and 140 miles deep. It is bordered on the south, in part, by a unit of the preserve (where hunting is permitted) and on the west by the huge Noatak National Preserve. Kobuk Valley National Park is also nearby to the west, and to the east, beyond the trans-Alaska oil pipeline, the Arctic National Wildlife Refuge stretches to the Canadian border. Thus, a great deal of the Brooks Range region—but far from all of it, unfortunately—enjoys protection, and much of it is in the National Wilderness Preservation System.

In the far north, environmental protection requires broad scope. Animals like the caribou, grizzly bear, and wolf must roam across hundreds of miles to survive in this spare and hungry land. With plant and animal productivity low, replenishment is slow. A disruption in the chain of interdependent organisms can have serious consequences. Wounds to the land are slow to heal. The human presence must be slight and gentle, lest it have a severe, even permanent, adverse impact.

Gates of the Arctic's stern landscape is no place for the ill-prepared.

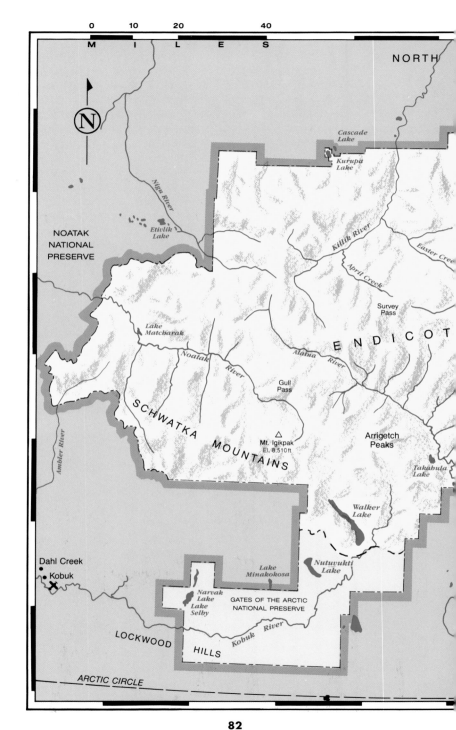

MILES

0   10   20   40

NORTH

N

Nigu River

Cascade Lake

Kurupa Lake

Etivlik Lake

Killik River

Easter Creek

April Creek

NOATAK NATIONAL PRESERVE

Survey Pass

Lake Matcharak

E N D I C O T

Noatak River

Alatna River

Gull Pass

S C H W A T K A

Mt. Igikpak
El. 8,510 ft

Arrigetch Peaks

M O U N T A I N S

Takahula Lake

Ambler River

Walker Lake

Dahl Creek

Nutuvukti Lake

Kobuk

Narvak Lake
Lake Selby

Lake Minakokosa

GATES OF THE ARCTIC NATIONAL PRESERVE

LOCKWOOD

HILLS

Kobuk River

ARCTIC CIRCLE

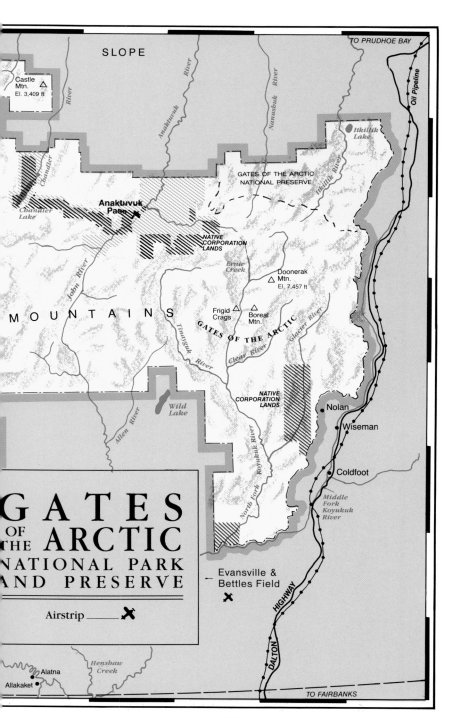

SLOPE

Castle
Mtn.
El. 3,409 ft

River

Anaktuvuk River

Nanushuk River

TO PRUDHOE BAY

Oil Pipeline

Itkillik Lake

GATES OF THE ARCTIC
NATIONAL PRESERVE

Chandler River

Chandler Lake

Anaktuvuk Pass

NATIVE
CORPORATION
LANDS

Itkillik River

John River

Ernie Creek

Doonerak Mtn.
El. 7,457 ft

M O U N T A I N S

Frigid
Crags

Boreal
Mtn.

GATES OF THE ARCTIC

Glacier River

Tinayguk River

Clear River

Allen River

Wild
Lake

NATIVE
CORPORATION
LANDS

Koyukuk River

Nolan

Wiseman

North Fork Koyukuk River

Coldfoot

Middle
Fork
Koyukuk
River

G A T E S
OF
THE ARCTIC
NATIONAL PARK
AND PRESERVE

Airstrip ✈

Evansville &
Bettles Field
✖

HIGHWAY

DALTON

Henshaw
Creek

Alatna

Allakaket

TO FAIRBANKS

Inupiat and Athapaskans

Standing on some nameless summit in Gates of the Arctic National Park and Preserve, one might imagine that no other human had ever set foot there. Such elation and sense of discovery is what this park is all about. Forbidding as it seems, however, this lonely landscape has been hunting ground and, often, home for Native Americans for thousands of years. Although they had to cope with its wild moods, the land was not wilderness to them. Coupled with the sea, it served as their meager larder. They roamed it at need and knew it intimately.

The earliest evidence of human occupation of the park dates to as early as 10,000 years ago, when glaciers had only recently receded. Through succeeding millenniums, bands of Inupiat (as "Eskimos" prefer to be called) and Athapaskan Indians lived here from time to time in small, scattered, nomadic units. Inupiats of the Kobuk and Noatak valleys hunted, fished, and trapped in what are now the southwestern and western portions of the park. Others subsisted on the North Slope. Koyukon Athapaskans journeyed into the park area from their settlements on the Koyukuk River to the south. Earlier Athapaskan groups had occupied territory in the heart of the range but eventually withdrew eastward into the Yukon Basin.

At the turn of the twentieth century, a drastic decline in the caribou population, in addition to other economic factors, drained the central Brooks Range of Native inhabitants. In the 1930s, the Nunamiut, an Inupiat group that lived primarily by hunting caribou, began to return from the Arctic coast, where they had been attracted by work for the whaling fleets and fur markets. In the 1950s and early 1960s, the construction of a church, school, and post office, and the concentration of supply services at Anaktuvuk Pass drew their scattered settlements into a village. Their large enclave of Native-owned land is now bordered on three sides by the park and preserve, some of which they also use for subsistence hunting, fishing, and trapping.

Filling In the Blanks

Before the 1880s, white explorers had only glimpsed the Brooks Range from the sea. In that decade, however, Lieutenant Henry Allen of the U.S. Army explored the Koyukuk River to its confluence with the John River, and at the least viewed the park area from the south. The Revenue Service's Lieutenant J. C. Cantwell

"Mosquito protection," as practiced in this region early in the twentieth century.

commanded expeditions up the Kobuk River to Walker Lake and well up the Noatak River. At the same time, Navy Lieutenant George Stoney, having established a winter camp on the Kobuk, sledded to Chandler Lake, through the heart of what is now park territory. The region was much more thoroughly explored between 1899 and 1926 by men of the U.S. Geological Survey. In expeditions of amazing audacity and rigor, they sledded, canoed, portaged, and hiked countless miles of river and terrain to map it and examine its geological formations.

The tide of gold seekers in the late nineteenth and early twentieth centuries surged up to the southern edges of the central Brooks Range. Bettles, Wiseman, and other miners' settlements served as departure points for trapping, prospecting, and small-scale mining activities in the region. The Koyukuk's North Fork and adjacent valleys, however, remained unmapped and little-known until a forester on leave, Robert Marshall, arrived in 1929 with a keen urge to explore "blank spaces" in arctic Alaska. With sourdough companions, he sledded, tramped, and mapped the region, climbing at least twenty-eight peaks during four visits, the last in 1939. Marshall, who became a founder of the Wilderness Society, wrote excitedly of the wild freshness, solitude, and exhilaration that he had experienced.

Establishment of the Park

Marshall's eloquence is revealed in the names he gave to the mountain bastions that flank the yawning U-shaped valley of the North Fork of the Koyukuk. The huge fist of rock to the east he christened Boreal Mountain. The bristling precipice to the west he called Frigid Crags. Seeing them as portals to his land of adventure, Marshall named the pair Gates of the Arctic. "Fortunately this gorge was not in the continental United States, where its wild sublimity would almost certainly have been commercially exploited," Marshall wrote at the time.

So evocative is the phrase "Gates of the Arctic" that it has consistently been favored as the name for a park in a region of many splendid gateways to the far north. Marshall himself was first to recommend protection for the northland. "In the name of a balanced use of American resources, let's keep northern Alaska largely a wilderness," he wrote.

As Alaska's resources of national-park caliber gained increasing attention in the decades after World War II, and because the eastern Brooks Range had already been designated a national wildlife range, studies of potential parks focused on the country that Marshall had extolled. In 1968 a two-unit national monument was proposed that would embrace the North Fork country and Walker Lake, the Arrigetch Peaks, and the Noatak headwaters region farther west. The glacial lake and the granite spires of the Arrigetch were placed on the National Register of Natural Landmarks.

The Alaska Native Claims Settlement Act of 1971 authorized comprehensive park studies in "The Great Land," and among the recommendations was a Gates of the Arctic National Park. Congress authorized its establishment in the Alaska National Interest Lands Conservation Act of 1980. Land selections of the state and of the Native people and mineral interests took precedence in many areas, so the park did not encompass subarctic and arctic ecosystems to the extent that had been proposed by the Park Service and the Department of the Interior. Nonetheless, the act did ensure survival of the natural environment on a greater scale than the proposed national monument of 1968 would have been able to do.

GEOLOGY

Above the Arctic Circle, the Rocky Mountain spine of North America bends sharply westward to become the Brooks Range. Named for a distinguished director of U.S. geological work in Alaska, Alfred H. Brooks, it runs east to west, crossing the entire state. It forms the Arctic Divide—separating north-flowing waters from the Yukon drainage—and the Continental Divide as well.

Mixed-up Rocks

The Brooks Range is geologically distinct from the continent's north-south cordillera, however, and geologists seem to agree that the word that best describes its geological make-up is *mind-boggling*. It is a maze of mixed-up, topsy-turvy formations—limestones, marbles, sandstones, shales, schists, granite—jammed

Frost crystals blossom into an unusual flower.

Icicles become works of art.

together and in places shuffled like giant cards.

Earlier mountains wore away and were replaced by shallow seas. Sediments deposited in the seas hardened and rose as the Brooks Range. These mountains were crumpled up by the bulldozer action of huge plates of the earth's crust. Such vast tectonic forces triggered volcanic activity, which abetted the mountain building with intrusions of granite. Erosion has exposed and carved the volcanic material into the spires of the Arrigetch Peaks and Mount Igikpak, the highest summit in the park, at 8,510 feet above sea level. Limestone formations generally predominate in the heart of the range. Because many arctic plants prefer acidic soils, these alkaline rocks are often bare and have been weathered into crags.

The Ice Age and Its Legacy

Ice, of course, is another major sculptor, for the range was covered by a thick sheet of ice in glacial times. Because of meager precipitation, all but a few small glaciers have disappeared. A thin mantle of vegetation now softens and embellishes the raw, ice-scoured landscape, but impressive glacial features remain: U-shaped valleys, hanging valleys, cirques, tarns, moraines that often dam handsome lakes, and the sliced peaks themselves.

Although the ice has receded, permanently frozen ground extends to great depth. This permafrost seals off much of the earth's absorptive capacity. Rain runoff is therefore swift and heavy, and streams can swell dangerously in a few hours. Many places where the ground has been stripped of insulating vegetation have thawed into ponds. On some slopes, a thawed surface layer has oozed down-

Opposite: The Arrigetch Peaks are formed of volcanic material.

ward in what is termed solofluction, tipping its forest cover crazily as it slides. Permafrost can squeeze pockets of subsurface meltwater and debris into warty hillocks called pingos. And ice wedges can crystallize the ground surface into polygonal patterns.

NATURAL HISTORY

Climate

In Gates of the Arctic National Park and Preserve, summer is merely a brief respite from cold. Winter crouches everywhere, ready to end the dream of flowing water and flowering land. Temperatures in the long darkness of winter can drop to —60° or —70° F. Even in summer, snowstorms can strike, but temperatures can also approach 90° F. The weather is highly unpredictable, and ominous clouds and showers seem always to be lurking about. But the slanting arctic light produces many rainbows. Total annual precipitation in the region is so scanty that—were it not for low evaporation rates and the water retained near ground surface by the permafrost beneath—the region would be a virtual desert.

Spring break-up of the ice, when rivers are abrim, usually occurs in early June. Freeze-up generally happens soon after Labor Day. In late June and in July, daylight seems almost perpetual. So do the mosquitoes, which become more an element of climate, like rain or snow, than of natural history. In midwinter, day consists of a brief lightening of the sunless sky about noon. Early spring, when the sun has returned and the cold is less severe, attracts dog mushers, cross-country skiers, miners, and a larger number of subsistence hunters to the park.

Open Forest and Tundra

A sparse vegetation clothes the park's bony frame. In the Brooks Range, the taiga, or boreal, forest meets the treeless tundra of the arctic. On the southern flanks of the tundra, small plants share the land with an open forest of spruce, birch, and balsam poplar, interspersed with copses and bogs. Some trees here, even small ones, may be hundreds of years old; then, farther north, the forest straggles to an end. The world beyond is tundra. There are still trees, but except for shrubby thickets along waterways, they are dwarf and prostrate specimens of birch and willow woven into the tundra fabric of heaths and forbs, sedges, grasses, mosses, and lichens in ever-changing mixes. Tundra plants show exquisite adaptation to

Opposite: The arctic gyrfalcon feeds almost exclusively on ptarmigan.

the many subtle environmental changes that occur in their habitats, and many have ingenious strategies for survival. Across the lower elevations stretch miles of moist tundra, spongy to the step and often characterized by sedge tussocks. These unsteady hummocks can make walking extremely difficult and tiring. Higher on the slopes, the firmer, matlike mosaic of plants thins into stony fellfields near the ridgetops and summits.

In late June and early July, the tundra becomes brilliant with flowers that have rushed to bloom and seed in the brief period of sunflood. Most are perennials because neither time nor energy is available in sufficient quantity to allow full growth from seed to maturity in a single season. By late August, the land begins to glow with autumn hues. Bearberry leaves turn scarlet, willow becomes gold. The leaves of the dwarf birch seem bronzed, and those of the blueberry are richly purpled.

Caribou is the only deer species whose females bear antlers.

Wildlife

At first glance, the taiga and tundra seem empty of animal life. As in the case of plants, the northland has fewer animal species than do warmer climates, and populations are often low. Yet there can be local, seasonal, or cyclical abundance, as when birds come to nest and when the Western Arctic Caribou Herd makes the semiannual migration between its wintering grounds in the Yukon Basin and its summer range on the windswept Arctic Slope.

More than 130 species of birds have been observed in the park area, many of them rare, disappearing, or absent in other parts of the United States. Almost half are waders; hawks and falcons are also numerous. The gyrfalcon, a resident of the tundra, feeds almost exclusively on ptarmigan. The snowy owl, though rare, and the raven are also residents here, as are more than twenty other species. More than one hundred species nest in the park area,

including the endangered peregrine falcon. Populations of nearly half the species go even farther north. Of the many migrants, the arctic tern comes all the way from Antarctica to nest. Thrushes such as the wheatear and the bluethroat, which also nest in the park, are Asian species.

Among fish, the elegant, slender arctic grayling, flagged with a huge iridescent dorsal fin, is emblematic of pure, cold arctic waters and is found in most of the park's lakes and streams. The char inhabits some, as does the lake trout, and the northern pike is common in many of the rivers, lakes, and ponds.

The barren-ground caribou traverses the park twice yearly, often in great numbers, but the park's largest ungulate is the stately moose. Increasing numbers are evident on the north slope of the park, where the animals seek willow twigs along the rivers. While moose browse the valleys, Dall sheep graze the high meadows and are often seen as pure white dots high on cliffsides.

In treeless country, it is often difficult to gauge size, so that a fat marmot or burly wolverine loping along with its rolling gait may be mistaken for a bear. There is no mistaking the real thing for long, however: black or grizzly bear in forested country, grizzly on the barren ground. The latter is sometime discerned as a large tawny mound—until it moves. The grizzly is sovereign lord of the park. When it is near, prudent hikers retreat and take another route.

Although the bear is king, the wolf best embodies the spirit of the park: wary, secluded, wild, and free. It is seldom seen and not often heard, but its fresh pawprints can be found in the river sand, tracks perhaps made while nearby campers slept. And should the wolf give its call, those within range will hear it in their very souls.

SITES, TRAILS, AND TRIPS

Gates of the Arctic offers sustained experiences in wilderness rather than a collection of sights to see. It is one of the world's few remaining environments in which a person can regain the old perspective of being nature's humble guest. As long as the park's freshness remains, visitors can be thrilled, as Marshall was, that "beyond the most distant horizon where fact and infinity merge . . . was peace and strength and immensity and coordination and freedom."

That freedom of which Marshall wrote must be taken as a responsible freedom. The park is no place for the casual or the ill-prepared. Its stern landscape grants folly no easy reprieve. Moreover, if the park is used roughly or carelessly—if it is wounded or overworn—the bruises will not disappear.

Opposite: The granite Arrigetch Peaks crown the central Brooks Range.

The park is generally traversible despite its size and ruggedness. Smaller than Wrangell-St. Elias at "only" 8.47 million acres, Gates of the Arctic is the largest park in terms of usable wilderness. Save for the peaks and crags, the open terrain permits travelers to wander at will. Routes must vary with conditions at the time of travel, and the only trails are those that animals have worn. Any human trails could soon lead to serious erosion.

Because most of the park is wilderness, there are no facilities, no signs, and no interpretive exhibits. Visitors are on their own, just as Marshall and other explorers and adventurers were. If there were guidebooks or suggested routes and destinations, they would gainsay what Marshall saw as the park's essential mission:

> In the wilderness, with its entire freedom from the manifestations of human will, that perfect objectivity which is essential for pure aesthetic rapture can probably be achieved more readily than among any other forms of beauty.

Gates of the Arctic is almost entirely a fly-in park. To be sure, one can now drive the Dalton Highway, which is seasonally open, and walk over the passes, but to penetrate the park very deeply from the road entails a long journey.

The park headquarters is in Fairbanks, through which many visitors come, and from which many fly directly to park destinations, but closer park administration exists at Bettles Field, the usual jumping-off place for charter service in small aircraft to lake or gravel-bar landings. Scheduled air service is available to Bettles Field and on northward up the John Valley to Anaktuvuk Pass, from which visitors can disperse into the park. Visitors must be careful to respect the villagers' privacy and to make sure that traversing the village lands in the John and Anaktuvuk river valleys does not interfere with local activities.

Many beautiful lakes in the park invite camping or fishing sojourns. Backpacking opportunities seem infinite, as do possibilities for skiing and dog sledding in springtime. Many visitors seek to follow Robert Marshall's footsteps by passing through the Gates of the Arctic themselves and into the North Fork country he wrote about—but those seeking true isolation would do well to choose another route. Climbers are attracted to the granite spires of the Arrigetch Peaks. Lakes on the North Slope provide access to remote portions of the park.

Visitors also explore the park by canoe, kayak, or raft. The North Fork of the Koyukuk River, and its tributary the Tinayguk, as well as the John, Alatna, Kobuk, and Noatak rivers, are all in the National Wild and Scenic Rivers System. Access to the headwaters of some is difficult, but others, in their upper reaches or partway down, are near lakes on which aircraft can land. Experts can find challenging whitewater on upper courses and on tributaries. The major rivers present few serious difficulties to the experienced boater; however, water conditions must be carefully monitored, especially in upper watersheds, because low- or high-water conditions can develop quickly. The remoteness of the rivers, too, can make any mistake a serious one.

A number of outfitters and guides offer trips into the park. Many visitors plan their own trips, arranging with Alaskan air charter services in Fairbanks or in Bettles or other nearby villages for transportation and, if on a long trip, air drops of additional food.

Despite its location, Gates of the Arctic may be more accessible than any of the large wilderness areas in the other states. Travelers can fly in at will and reach almost any portion of the huge preserve. Because the park is one of the last places left in the United States where traditional wilderness adventuring can be enjoyed on a generous scale and because the ecology of the far north is so delicate, Gates of the Arctic was originally planned for limited and carefully monitored levels of use. In the arctic world, large though it is, people sense the presence of others and are disappointed when they find a marred landscape. Moreover, some injuries inflicted by overuse would take many decades to heal even if the park were placed off-limits to the public.

Unfortunately, a congressionally required permit and reservation system was not politically acceptable when the park was established, and people now use the park with little restriction or monitoring. Airplanes flit from lake to lake, fire rings scar shores, and trash piles accumulate. Dozens of people may be on hand at a traveler's carefully planned, long-awaited wilderness destination. Development of private in-holdings could end the wild qualities of some areas. Bright tents dot many landscapes.

In the 1930s, Robert Marshall wrote:

> The unexplored areas of the world are becoming distinctly limited. Consequently, since they are capable of giving such superb value to human beings, it is desirable that the possibility of exploration be prolonged as much as possible.

Such a prolongation—over centuries—was a central purpose of the park. Sadly and perhaps ironically, within a few years after the park was established, the region's aura of freshness, of solitude, of unspoiled, untrammeled wildness is already being compromised.

Overleaf: Sheer sides of mountains rise up from an unnamed valley near Itkillik Rim.

GLACIER BAY NATIONAL PARK AND PRESERVE

Icebergs in Glacier Bay's inlets are a sign of a continuing glacial meltback there.

GLACIER BAY NATIONAL PARK AND PRESERVE
PARK HEADQUARTERS
GUSTAVUS, ALASKA 99826
TEL.: (907) 697-2230

HIGHLIGHTS: Muir Inlet • Chilkat Range • Fairweather Range • Brady Glacier • Bartlett Cove • Margerie Glacier • Humpback Whales • Johns Hopkins Glacier • Deception Hills

ACCESS: Alaska Airlines and several air taxis, service from Juneau to Gustavus. Cruise ships enter bay but do not drop off people. Private vessel permit information at (907) 697-2627. List of air-flight companies providing service available from National Park Service.

SEASON: Open year-round.

FEES: Entrance, none; charged for boat trip to the upper bay.

GAS: Available at Bartlett Cove dock for camp stoves and boats.

FOOD: Small food store in Gustavus. Food services at Glacier Bay Lodge, Gustavus Inn, and Open Gate Cafe in Gustavus.

LODGING: Glacier Bay Lodge in the park, and several inns and bed & breakfasts in Gustavus open from mid-May to mid-September.

VISITOR CENTER: Glacier Bay Lodge; backcountry office near dock at Bartlett Cove; maps, charts, books for sale.

MUSEUM: Audio-visual presentation and exhibits at Visitor Center.

GIFT SHOP: Glacier Bay Lodge sells gift items.

PETS: Permitted on leash at Bartlett Cove, but boaters must keep pets aboard vessels.

PICNICKING: Permitted; no facilities.

HIKING: Permitted. Carry water.

BACKPACKING: Permitted. Carry water. Portable stoves necessary. Camper orientation required. Check with Bartlett Cove Ranger Station for rules, restricted areas.

CAMPGROUNDS: Bartlett Cove Campground, free. Camper orientation required on arrival. Fires only in designated areas; firewood available. Shower and laundry facilities at Glacier Bay Lodge.

TOURS: Boat trip to upper bay (9 hours); overnight available. Both accompanied by park naturalist; information and reservations at Glacier Bay Lodge. One-day to two-week canoe, kayak, raft, backpack, and ski tours with Alaska Discovery.

OTHER ACTIVITIES: Sea kayaking (rentals from Glacier Bay Sea Kayaks), chartered boat fishing, crabbing with Alaska State license. Boating in Bartlett Cove, permit required in summer. Mountain climbing, cross-country skiing.

FACILITIES FOR DISABLED: Ramp entry to lodge and 2 guest cabins, elevator to Visitor Center.

For additional information, see also Sites, Trails, and Trips on pages 123–129 and the map on pages 104–105.

GLACIER BAY EMERGES FROM THE GREAT tides of boreal ice. Primordial in their beauty, the bay and its bordering mountains were recently exhumed from thousands of years of glacial entombment. Within the past two centuries, a massive "river of ice," for reasons not fully understood, quite suddenly started to recede. Terrain once hostile to life forms became available for the building of basic, life-sustaining soils. Pioneer plant species have crept forward in the wake of the glacier's rapid retreat, and the longest-liberated sections of land are now rimmed with a forest of mature trees. Mammals, birds, and sea creatures have come to claim new habitats. Glacier Bay's terrestrial expanse reads like a chronicle written first in mosses and algae, then with bouquets of tiny but tough plants, and at last by higher forms of alder, spruce, and stout hemlock trees. But the episode has not ended, and the future can only be surmised. If cooling trends dictate, the ice age may return to the bay and surrounding mountains, as quickly as it departed, locking out wolves, whales, moose, and mountain goats. Or the work of two tectonic faults that cross this terrain could bring more radical change. Whatever the future landscape, a national park and preserve has been established to celebrate the place and the process.

The centerpiece of the park—and its main avenue of access—is a Y-shaped bay up to 15 miles wide and 65 miles long. Bedrock of

A floating ranger station, once at Goose Cove (above), is now at Blue Mouse Cove.

GLACIER
BAY
NATIONAL PARK
AND PRESERVE

Ranger Station 🇺🇸 Campground ⛺

104
GLACIER BAY

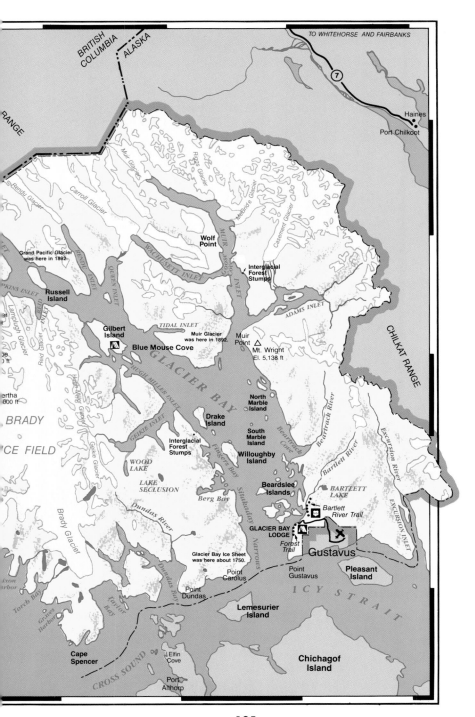

BRITISH COLUMBIA

ALASKA

TO WHITEHORSE AND FAIRBANKS

7

Haines

Port Chilkoot

RANGE

Rendu Glacier

Carroll Glacier

Muir Glaciers

Riggs Glacier

McBride Glacier

Casement Glacier

CHILKAT RANGE

Wolf Point

Grand Pacific Glacier was here in 1892.

WACHUSETT INLET

MUIR INLET (2500 ft)

Interglacial Forest Stumps

RENDU INLET

HOPKINS INLET

Russell Island

QUEEN INLET

TIDAL INLET

REID INLET

Reid Glacier

Lamplugh Glacier

ADAMS INLET

Gilbert Island

Muir Glacier was here in 1892.

Muir Point

Mt. Wright El. 5,138 ft

Blue Mouse Cove

GLACIER BAY

HUGH MILLER INLET

Hugh Miller Glacier

GEIKIE INLET

Geikie Glacier

North Marble Island

Drake Island

South Marble Island

Beartrack Cove

Beartrack River

Bartlett River

Excursion River

BRADY ICE FIELD

Interglacial Forest Stumps

Falgers Bay

Willoughby Island

WOOD LAKE

LAKE SECLUSION

Berg Bay

Dundas River

Sitakaday Narrows

Beardslee Islands

BARTLETT LAKE

EXCURSION INLET

Bartlett River Trail

Brady Glacier

GLACIER BAY LODGE

Forest Trail

Gustavus

Glacier Bay Ice Sheet was here about 1750.

Point Carolus

Point Gustavus

Pleasant Island

Dixon Harbor

Point Dundas

ICY STRAIT

Torch Bay

Taylor Bay

Dundas Bay

Lemesurier Island

Groves Harbor

Chichagof Island

Cape Spencer

Elfin Cove

CROSS SOUND

Port Althorp

this submerged valley is of startling depth—as much as 1,400 feet—below tideline. The bay is flanked by almost parallel mountain ranges. To the east and north lie the Chilkat and Alsek ranges. To the west, a peninsula dominated by the Fairweather Range separates the bay from the storm-lashed coast along the Gulf of Alaska. Summits of this range rise from 10,000 feet to the park's highest peak, Mount Fairweather, 15,320 feet above the nearby Pacific Ocean. Sweeping upward from tidewater, the range's succession of blade-like summits and steep glaciers has figured prominently in the logbooks of explorers since the first wide-eyed European exclaimed in 1741, "This must be America . . . ."

Today, an exploration by ship or kayak, or a shoreline walk, can be a strangely affecting experience. In the midst of such primeval power, speech can seem intrusive, brash. The bay's chill air carries a mix of ocean scent suffused with the gritty tang of bare rock. Moving from green stands of spruce and hemlock to frail mosses near spent glacier fronts, a visitor sees and feels a raw, postpartum landscape, upset but quietly alive. Little in Glacier Bay dispels the illusion that one's arrival is perfectly timed, with the eagles, whales, and wolves moving in for the first time.

HISTORY

Hoonah Homeland

The earliest evidence of human occupation in the Glacier Bay region dates from between 9,000 and 10,000 years ago, when the land was recovering from glaciation during the late Pleistocene epoch. Primitive stone choppers, scrapers, microblade projectile points, and fire-reddened hearth stones assigned to this period have been unearthed at archeological sites near the park's southeastern boundary. The stone tools were made from argillite and esite, a local rock, but also from such exotics as chert, quartz crystal, and obsidian. The source for the obsidian was Mount Edziza near the upper Stikine River in British Columbia, thus indicating trade between early peoples that spanned 300 miles. Yet there is scant evidence of prehistoric aboriginal people within the park. The ebb and flow of glacial ice has scattered or buried the remains of early settlements.

A Tlingit Indian people known as the Hoonah have long gleaned a living from lands and waters surrounding Glacier Bay and are today's counterpart of the early lithic culture whose stone chips have recently been found. Historical records show the Hoonah to have been semi-nomadic, moving as changing conditions of ice and

The effects of intensive sea-otter hunting during the 1700s were still felt 100 years later.

subsistence resources dictated. For example, a village site in Taylor Bay, seen by the Vancouver expedition in 1794, is now buried under the west side of Brady Glacier. They also camped at Lituya Bay on the outer coast, Icy Point, Cape Spencer, and Dundas Bay. They may also have settled near the present site of park headquarters at Bartlett Cove and at Excursion Inlet. Hoonah legends refer to the Beardslee Islands, north of Bartlett Cove, as *Klemshawshiki*, "the city on the sand at the base of the mountains." In keeping with geological evidence, the legend also holds that a great ice mountain (glacier) swept the surface of the islands clean in just one day, and then stayed for ten years. Hoonah hunters were known to use seasonal campsites near Hugh Miller Inlet, about halfway up the bay, when hunting seals and mountain goats during the 1870s. They refer to the bay by the name *Sit'ee ti geiyi*, which means "the bay in place of the glacier." This Tlingit place-name is one of the few to survive in the Glacier Bay area (though misspelled) and now identifies the bay's entrance—Sitakaday Narrows.

Exploration and Rediscovery

Alexei Ilich Tchirikov, captain of the ship *Saint Paul* and second in command to Vitus Bering, a Danish navigator in the employ of the Russian czar, sighted the coastline of Glacier Bay on July 15, 1741.

He saw the Fairweather Range and the park's highest peak, but it fell to the British navigator James Cook to describe the range in the English language for the first time. While sailing north along the archipelago of southeastern Alaska—in uncharacteristically good weather—Cook wrote in the ship's log on May 3, 1778, about "a large inlet [which he named Cross Sound] . . . lying under a very high peaked mountain, which obtained the name Mount Fair Weather." He also wrote that the mountains "were wholly covered with snow, from the highest summits down to the sea-coast; some few places excepted, where we could perceive trees."

The French explorer Jean Francois de la Perouse put ashore on July 4, 1786, along the outer coast at a windswept bay the Hoonahs called *L'tu.aa*. He named the bay Port des Français—it is now called Lituya Bay—and proceeded to record observations of Native cultural traits, geology, flora, and fauna during a 26-day stay. But the effort was marred by tragedy. In an attempt to chart the bay's entrance, officers and seamen in three boats set out during an ebb tide, when treacherous crosscurrents and tide rips form. Sucked into the bay's churning outflow, two boats were lost with all twenty-one men aboard. They were memorialized by a small monument built on an island near the center of the bay, which was named Isle du Cenotaphe. Had La Perouse and his men known of the Tlingit legend of *L'tu.aa*—a mythic monster lurking at the entrance to the bay—more caution might have been used. Such tales of warning are often based on real calamities of the past.

George Vancouver, who had sailed with Captain Cook as a midshipman, returned to Glacier Bay in 1794 as captain of H.M.S. *Discovery*. He dropped anchor in the vicinity of Port Althorp on the south side of Cross Sound and dispatched a longboat that explored the mainland shore from Cape Spencer east to Glacier Bay. Amid rafts of floating ice in Dundas Bay, the exploration party under lieutenants Whidbey and LeMesurier encountered several Native hunters manning canoes. Burial boxes containing ashes and bone fragments were also found atop constructed posts, illuminating for the first time the Tlingit culture's protocol for the dead.

Passing eastward from Point Dundas to Point Carolus (about 7 miles) in rain and fog, the party observed what was then the outlet of Glacier Bay. A sheer wall of "one compact sheet of ice" lay across the entrance of the bay—the terminus of an enormous glacier. In a cogent analysis of this important observation, author Dave Bohn, in his definitive book *Glacier Bay: The Land and the Silence*, estimates that the glacier front then lay but 6 miles north of the party's observation site at Point Carolus. Today, a boat can travel upbay unimpeded by ice for 65 miles to the terminal lobe of Grand Pacific

Glacier near the U.S.—Canadian border. Vancouver's records offer a critical benchmark for gauging the natural wonder of Glacier Bay.

Between 1796 and 1867, there is scant record of activity at Glacier Bay, though impacts on natural resources are thought to have been substantial. In 1796, an English shipwright named James Shields, in the employ of the Russian-American Company, landed 450 skin-covered bidarkas (hunting canoes) and about twice that number of Aleut hunters from Kodiak in Lituya Bay. Records show that about 1,800 sea-otter skins were secured in a matter of days. Almost 100 years later, the effects of this massive depletion would still be felt by the Hoonah.

Glacier Bay's unique blend of scenery and spectacle could not long go unrecognized. In the decades after the United States bought Alaska in 1867, a trickle of visitors began. The first American to visit the upper bay was Lieutenant Charles Wood, an adventurer and mountaineer with a keen sense of observation. In the summer of 1877, Wood and his Native guides traveled upbay by canoe and came upon Hoonah hunters at an encampment called Asonques (near Hugh Miller Inlet). He heard stories of hunting and of depleted wildlife since the coming of white men and their fur trade. Wood was also told by one of the hunters that the site of the camp had been covered by solid ice—within the hunter's own lifetime. At that moment, the main glacier's retreating snout was just uncovering Russell Island—about 17 miles upbay from the camp.

In October 1879, taunting the northern winter, the renowned naturalist John Muir, in the company of Tlingit guides and his friend the Presbyterian missionary S. Hall Young, made the first of four trips to the bay of glaciers. He traversed and explored many glaciers and their surrounding moraines, often climbing to high elevations in the wildest weather for panoramic vistas of the newborn terrain. Forest succession as an aftermath of glaciation fascinated Muir, and his discovery of a remnant interglacial spruce forest became a telling entry to his field journal:

The renowned naturalist John Muir.

"Stumps by the hundreds, three to fifteen feet high, rooted in a stream of fine blue mud on cobbles, still have their bark on." In 1880, while on his second trip, he visited the massive ice cliffs of the glacier that would soon bear his name. Muir's drawings and field sketches showed the extent and position of the retreating ice mass of the bay. One pivotal scene depicts the ice wall of the Grand Pacific Glacier uncovering a rock mass in mid-bay—Russell Island, four miles long, emerging from its icy tomb. Muir's prodigious writings about the bay heightened public awareness of its importance and helped initiate a drive among, scientists and conservationists to protect the area. Stonework remnants of the chimney of Muir's cabin, built on his third visit in 1890, still exist at Muir Inlet.

Mining

Alaska's first important mining strike occurred in 1880, when prospector Joe Juneau discovered gold not far from the site of the capital city that bears his name. In the same year, a group of miners meeting on Willoughby Island in Glacier Bay organized the Berry Mining District. The mining boom, such as it was, largely bypassed the bay of glaciers, although some small-scale mining took place early in the twentieth century.

The most prominent event in the park's mining history involves an untiring prospector named Joe Ibach. In 1924, while protection

New ice caves appear often at Glacier Bay, but they frequently collapse without warning.

for Glacier Bay was being pursued in Washington, D.C., Ibach struck gold north of Reid Inlet. Mining claims were properly filed, but the creation of the national monument in 1925 led to confusion over the status of the mining operation. Wrongly informed by government officials that the new monument prohibited work on the claims, Ibach faced the further complication of being unable to fulfill the requirements of mining law that a certain level of work must be performed before clear title can be gained. A kind of governmental gridlock ensued and lasted for almost ten years. In 1935, a friend of Ibach's, the popular writer Rex Beach, took up the cause. He went to Washington and successfully lobbied for a law opening up Glacier Bay (and several other national parks) to new mining. But the mining boom predicted by Rex Beach never materialized, and Joe Ibach's claims never quite boomed. The Mining in the Parks Act of 1976 finally closed Glacier Bay to any new mining prospects. Today, the only valid mining claim within the park (those staked before the law was passed) is one with notable potential for development—the nickel deposit along the Brady Glacier known as the Nunatak Lode. An environmental assessment of this claim and its proposed operation was submitted to Congress in 1979.

Establishment of the Park

In 1923, the Ecological Society of America took the first organized step to protect Glacier Bay. The effort was led by Dr. William S. Cooper of the University of Minnesota. Studies were conducted by the society, and a resolution was sent to Washington, D.C., calling for the creation of a national monument by presidential proclamation. More than eighty organizations, including the National Geographic Society and the American Association for the Advancement of Science, lent their support. Acting on the recommendation of the Secretary of the Interior, President Calvin Coolidge issued a temporary withdrawal of the area on April 1, 1924. The reaction among Alaskans was swift and unambiguous. The Juneau *Daily Empire*, in an incendiary editorial, called the action "a monstrous proposition"; it claimed that thousands of acres of prime "agricultural lands" would be denied development, and that mining, water-power development, and lumbering would be blocked. "It leads one to wonder if Washington has gone crazy through catering to conservation faddists," the editorial concluded. On February 26, 1925, Coolidge signed a proclamation, under the authority of the 1906 Antiquities Act, establishing Glacier Bay National Monument. The area protected then was about half the size of the present park and preserve. Another proclamation, issued in 1939, expanded the monument's boundaries and made Glacier Bay—until 1980, when Wrangell–St. Elias was established—the largest unit in the national-park system.

Passage by Congress of the Alaska National Interest Lands Conservation Act in 1980 added 523,000 acres to Glacier Bay and changed its designation from monument to national park and preserve. The statute added a 57,000-acre preserve at the mouth of the Alsek River along the park's north boundary. Sport hunting, trapping, and subsistence uses are allowed within the preserve.

GEOLOGY

Glacier Bay and surrounding regions were glaciated as early as 20 million years ago. The park's bedrock geology is complex and not well documented. Widespread folding, metamorphism, and intrusive rocks have fragmented the stratigraphic record. The most commonly exposed rocks along the park's western sector are schist, hornblende schist, biotite, and gneiss. Most mineral deposits throughout the park are associated with igneous intrusive formations.

Two major geological faults traverse the park. Margins of the continental plate and the Pacific's tectonic plate meet along the outer coast, contributing to faulting, folding of rock strata, and mountain building. The meltback of glaciers over the past 14,000 years relieved the landscape of tremendous weight and has caused a rebound, or uplift, of the landmass by some 300 to 500 feet in many locations. This continuing uplift, plus the tectonic rise along the outer coast due to movement of the Pacific plate, increases tension along fault lines, which in turn contributes to increased earthquake potential.

On July 9, 1958, the Fairweather Fault, which traverses the inland side of Lituya Bay, experienced a powerful earthquake. The steep headwall at the head of the bay sheared off the mountain and became a plummeting mass of 1.3 million cubic feet of rock and ice. The landslide hurtled to the valley floor, taking with it the snout of Lituya Glacier, then rushed up the opposing wall of mountain to heights of 1,700 feet, flinging icebergs and seals onto high ledges. The slide generated a wave of water at the head of Lituya Bay that swept toward the ocean at speeds exceeding 100 miles per hour. The wave lopped off or swept away stands of spruce trees along the edges of its path. The *Badger*, one of three fishing trollers anchored in the bay, was carried stern-first over the bay's outlet moraine and into the Gulf of Alaska; its two crew members scrambled into a dory as the boat sank. The *Sunmore* swamped and went to the bot-

Opposite: Cruise ships now visit the Bay's West Arm, but not Muir Glacier, shown here.

tom with its two crew members, while the third troller, *Edrie*, rode out the giant wave after snapping its anchor chain. The quake that caused this event registered 8 on the Richter scale and produced a 23-foot horizontal displacement along the Fairweather Fault.

Vanished Glaciers

The 3.3 million acres of the park and preserve contain fourteen active tidewater glaciers. Brady Glacier, above Taylor Bay at the south end of the Fairweather Range, is the largest glacier in the park, with an area of 188 square miles.

But the most impressive glaciers in the park are those notable for their absence. At the time of our nation's first Fourth of July in 1776, the entire length and breadth of Glacier Bay was filled to its outlet at Icy Strait with glacial ice. This ponderous mass may have been 4,000 feet thick and up to 20 miles wide. It reached upbay more than 100 miles to the St. Elias Mountains in Canada. Fed by numerous subordinate glaciers, the main trunk of the bay's ice river had barely receded into the narrows when members of the *Discovery* crew explored Icy Strait in 1794. But a meltback had begun. It signaled, we now know, a change in the glacier's basic thermal balance, or equilibrium, that had existed throughout the Little Ice Age, dating back some 4,000 years. By 1879, when Muir canoed into the bay, the glacier's length had been reduced by 48 miles! Such a retreat is without equal in recorded history and marks Glacier Bay as unique.

Glacier Bay contains countless textbook examples of landforms shaped by glacial progress and regress. High bluffs and ridgetops along the Fairweather Range that appear chiseled and jagged were above the moving ice mass that filled the bay. Slightly lower in elevation, however, the rocky bluffs have more rounded contours and are free of blade-like clefts. The smoother landscape was sculptured by overriding ice, its edges were shorn, and the rock debris was carried off as glacial rubble. The line of interface between the two zones marks the top of the great ice sheet. In lower Glacier Bay, this ice line is about 4,200 feet above tidewater. A cruise ship plying the lower bay would constitute only a minute bit of debris deep in the frozen recesses of the ice sheet that filled the bay two centuries ago.

Casement Glacier, north of Adams Inlet, displays many features of glacial retreat from tidewater. A wide outwash plain laced with braided streams now separates the glacier's terminus from the tideline of Adams Inlet. Where rubble has been piled high above the active stream, pioneer vegetation begins to take hold and greenery flecks an otherwise gray landscape. The braided stream of a young outwash plain may wander valley-wide in its course and thus defeat encroaching plant life. Stream crossings can be exceedingly dangerous. The water is gray with suspended solids, or "rock flour," the pulverized stone of mountainsides far upstream that has been ground by glaciers to a fineness approaching that of face powder. Stream depth can be deceptive. The rock flour moves and collects along the bottom in a changing, semifluid state that can easily swallow the foot of a hiker. In addition, a modest stream that can be forded with ease in the early hours of a day's hike may become an unnegotiable chute of churning water from the increased runoff of a warm afternoon, blocking a hiker's return.

Higher ground along a glacier's wake often consists of sinuous and meandering piles of mixed gravel. Known as eskers, these deposits were formed by the tunneling of meltwater within the retreating glacier and the entraining of stream gravel along the tunnel. Because eskers lie beyond the reach of eroding streams, early plant life takes hold on them, and their appearance calls to mind green tunnel mounds pushed up by a giant gopher. Eskers can also serve as a means of dating a period or an epoch of glacial activity. Some found in Glacier Bay are related to the Wisconsinian glaciation, beginning 25,000 years ago.

End moraines are also evident along the route of Casement Glacier. These high gravel deposits mark the end points of the glacier's forward advances—the bulldozer action of the moving ice provided the motive force. Marking the valley sides along glacial pathways are elongated piles of rubble known as lateral moraines. In some cases, these gravel mounds now exceed in height the top of the glacier and provide a convenient overlook for viewing the glacier's heavily crevassed surfaces. Tributary glaciers have interposed their own lateral moraines into the main trunk of Casement Glacier. These moraines now appear as long, dark ribbons of debris and rubble along the ice flow and are known as medial moraines. At its peak during the Little Ice Age, Casement Glacier was one tributary to Muir Glacier, which in turn was a tributary to the giant main ice sheet of Glacier Bay.

Snouts in the Water

The underwater terminal moraine of a tidewater glacier may act, in part, as an insulating barrier and support sill for the glacier. A well-insulated terminal snout may resist meltback. But the slightest breaching of the moraine-to-ice contact zone can lead to a rapid and spectacular loss of ice. Saltwater contact with a submerged termi-

Overleaf: Clumps of ice calved from glaciers float in quiet Muir Inlet.

nal lobe causes a high rate of melt compared to portions exposed only to air. Fluctuating tides may add mechanical stress and thus hasten the meltback by cracking loose ice calves—giant blocks and splinters of ice that can reach 200 feet in height, collapsing into the water below like toppling masonry. Viewed from a safe distance (usually half a mile or more), these watery explosions provide one of the most awe-inspiring natural scenes on our planet. Johns Hopkins Glacier calves immense volumes of ice from its towering cliffs, so the approach to it is usually halted at about 2 miles. Large blocks of ice also detach from the underwater snout and churn unexpectedly to the surface with dangerous force. These icebergs then become platforms for resting harbor seals.

The Palma lobe of Brady Glacier buries its snout in Bearhole Lake. During summer runoff the lake rises and floats the glacier upward; it falls in autumn, when the lake's volume decreases. This bobbing lobe has developed a "hinge zone" where the upper glacier is anchored to the mountainside.

NATURAL HISTORY

It is now about half past nine and raining pretty hard. . . . We have concluded that there are many infallible signs of rain in this region. If the sun shines, if the stars appear, if there are clouds, or if there are none; these are all sure indications. If the barometer falls, it will rain; if the barometer rises, it will rain; if the barometer remains steady, it will continue to rain.

So wrote Harry Fielding Reid during an expedition to Glacier Bay in 1892.

Imposing weather patterns are a dominant part of the Glacier Bay setting. Moisture-laden storms born in the Gulf of Alaska roll eastward like freight cars along the continental edge, only to collide with the park's 100-mile outer coast along the Fairweather Range. The North Pacific's Japan Current moderates temperatures year-round and brings rain, mist, and fog to lower elevations. Violent winds often accompany storms along the outer coast. Glacier Bay's annual rainfall is 55 to 125 inches, including a snowfall of 144 inches. Winter temperatures average 20° to 30° F, with extreme lows of -10° F. Cloudiness and gray mist are typical, and on average some rainfall occurs on 228 days each year. Rainfall is lightest in May and June, when clear skies brighten the scenery, but weather steadily gets wetter through autumn. "Good weather" is often said (only partly in jest) to refer to days when there is only one layer of

Opposite: A mountain goat grazes above Tidal Inlet.

clouds. Upper Glacier Bay can be as much as 20° F cooler than Bartlett Cove near the bay's outlet, where daytime summer temperatures range from 50° to 65° F. During June, a visitor can took forward to 18 hours of daylight.

From Wet Tundra to Scoured Landscapes

Four terrestrial ecosystems occur in the park. Wet tundra is found in level terrain with some standing water. Ground cover includes sedges, cottongrass, and a few woody and herbaceous plants, such as willow and Sitka alder. A thin mantle of organic material covers silty sediments and gravel. Mammals of this ecosystem include black bear, wolf, coyote, moose, and river otter. Ravens, songbirds, waterfowl, and raptors are among the avians of the wet tundra. A large number of sandhill cranes can be seen in open marshes during their spring and fall migrations. Great blue herons are found along wetlands and marshes. Bald eagles are common.

The park's hemlock and spruce forest occurs along the western, eastern, and southern borders. Shores of Glacier Bay north to Adams Inlet are primarily Sitka spruce forest less than 150 years old. Cottonwood and alder are common along streams and beach fringes. The forest understory consists of moss, blueberry, alder, devil's club, and various ferns. Mammals include black bear, wolf, coyote, porcupine, marten, and red squirrel. Birds include blue grouse, raven, hermit thrush, chestnut-backed chickadee, fox sparrow, and bald eagle. The park's major development area at Bartlett Cove lies within this environment.

Alpine tundra ecosystems are found at elevations above 2,500 feet. Barren rock is interspersed with alpine grasses, willow, dwarf blueberry, and low heath shrubs. Mammals of this region include wolverine, black and grizzly bear, mountain goat, marmot, and vole. Birds include ptarmigan, raven, water pipit, and junco.

Glaciers and ice fields are associated with algae, while adjacent morainal material gives rise to lichens, mosses, horsetail, willow, fireweed, and dryas. These early plants are followed in successional growth by alder, willow, soapberry, and cottonwood. The Sitka alder is an important species in reestablishing the fertility of glacier-scoured landscapes because of its high capacity to fix nitrogen in the soil. Snowfields are an important source of relief from summer insects for mountain goats and other mammals.

Of Whale Songs and Throbbing Engines

The marine ecosystems of Glacier Bay contain a wide variety of species. Pelagic birds common in the park's waters include tufted puffin, Arctic tern, and kittiwake. Sea mammals include orca (killer whale), harbor seal, and harbor porpoise. But Glacier Bay is honored most by the ponderous grace of the humpback whale. Following winters spent off the Hawaiian Islands, humpback whales enter the bay each summer for periods of intense feeding. The humpback is classified as an endangered species. Populations in the North Pacific Ocean have declined from 15,000 to 1,450. The latter figure, however, represents a rebound from a low of 1,200. About 500 to 600 humpback whales forage in southeast Alaskan waters each summer for herring, capelin, and krill, a minute shrimp-like sea invertebrate. Summer feeding cycles are of critical importance because the nourishment they provide must carry the whale through long winter months when no feeding takes place.

Before 1977, ten to twenty-four humpbacks foraged within Glacier Bay each year. Their magnificent breachings, tail-lobbings, and feeding activities provide an incomparable visitor experience in a setting of spectacular mountain scenery. During 1978, the number of whales entering and feeding in Glacier Bay declined—while the number of commercial tour ships, fishing vessels, and private pleasure craft operating in the bay increased. Some change in forage availability and location was also noted. A limit was imposed by the National Park Service on the number of vessels that could enter the bay during the June-to-August whale season. Speed and traffic patterns for watercraft were also regulated. The objective was to reduce, or at least hold level, any human impact on the whales, pending an analysis of the problem. A research program begun in 1981 has examined whale behavior in relation to the movement of boats and also the hydroacoustics of boats in the bay and the effects of unnatural sounds on feeding and resting whales.

Recent observations of whale behavior have resulted in a heightened appreciation for these gentle giants. Whales display distinct individual markings, much like fingerprints, on their dorsal fins and on the underside of their tail flukes. Through photo-identifications, comparisons can be made of the use by individual whales of different areas of the bay. The duration of "residence" in the bay for one whale was determined to be 54 days, but others made shorter visits. The whales appear to be most sensitive to disturbance by watercraft when first establishing a feeding zone in the bay. This suggests a kind of "investment economics" by which the whale will show higher resistance to disturbance after a productive investment of time and energy in a particular feeding zone.

Disturbed whales show a telltale change in breathing pattern—shorter breath cycles on the surface, for example—easily observed by the animal's vapor plume and the audible "whoosh" of its megabreath. Whales respond to both the noise and proximity of approaching vessels. Chris Gabriele, NPS whale biologist, notes, "Vessels moving in a straight line transit are less disturbing than ones doing erratic patterns." Reactions by the whales include, in order of intensity, movement away from the approaching vessel; longer dive periods; aerial behavior, such as tail-lobbing and breaching; and, finally, temporary abandonment of the feeding area.

The humpback whale possesses both keen intelligence and formidable grace. A feeding humpback will circle a concentration of krill or capelin to confine its size and increase its density. Then, filling its lungs with a fresh charge of air, the whale will follow a spiral path in its dive while releasing a curtain of rising bubbles from its air spout. The narrow, tube-like formation created by the bubble net, or lariat, further confines the krill and helps guide the whale upward—with its elastic mouth agape. Its furrowed lower jaw can expand the capacity of its mouth to hold about 150 gallons of water and prey. As the whale closes its mouth around the mass of krill and water, its head often can be seen broaching the surface. With its tongue and jaw muscles acting as a piston, it then expels the sea water through a fine-mesh baleen until only the krill remain. The humpback has considerable body mass to nourish. An adult whale may be 50 feet long and weigh 34 tons. One ton of krill or other prey is required to fill the stomach of an adult humpback whale.

The most musical of whales, the humpback has a repertoire of songs that varies seasonally and in different oceans of the world. Cetologists find that humpback bulls do most of the singing, and that their vocalizations will change each year within an oceanic region. Covering a range from piercing trumpetings to bassoon-like groans, the song is thought to emanate from resonating chambers deep in the whale's head. The voice box, or larynx, may also play a part. Yet there is no external passage of air, as breath flows in human speech. In quiet ocean, the humpback's sound may carry for tens of miles. There are also quiet periods. Pods of humpbacks gather in placid coves during summer nights; they lull the dark hours away without moan or motion, their breathing rates reduced to sleepy rhythmic puffs.

These swimming giants also use sound and hearing to navigate. But the humpback's medley of sounds falls outside the frequency range best suited for sonar effect, or echolocation, as compared, for example, to that of the bottle-nosed dolphin, which has an uncanny echolocating ability. Though poorly understood, the humpback's audio-perception appears to rely on an array of background sounds of very low frequency and broad wavelength, well below the human audible range and sometimes referred to as "infrasound." An audio-picture is gathered from a vast scramble of oceanic noise—from schools of clicking shrimp to grunts of various bottom-feeding fish to the sibilant hiss of distant wave wash and tidal flow across sub-surface landforms. Infrasound creates a kind of spatial map monitored by the humpback whale. Navigational signs and warning signals are selected. But when the churn of high-speed propellers, sonar signals from boats, and the throb of ocean-going diesel engines are introduced to the same waters, the humpback whale could be forced out. Park regulations and ongoing research will help ensure that whales remain at home in Glacier Bay.

SITES, TRAILS, AND TRIPS

Generally, the visitor season for Glacier Bay runs from mid-May through mid-September. Accommodations consist of the well-appointed Glacier Bay Lodge and a campground, both at the Bartlett Cove headquarters site. Access is by commercial or charter air service between Juneau and Gustavus, a distance of 53 miles. The National Park Service conducts a wide variety of naturalist programs at Bartlett Cove. Tour boats are available for daily trips upbay to see wildlife, birds, and glaciers. Hikers can be dropped off and picked up in several areas of the upper bay, via the scheduled tour boat. Charter float-plane tours are also available from Bartlett Cove. There are no established trails except at Bartlett Cove.

Trips to the Ice Age

The majority of those who visit Glacier Bay experience the park from the decks of large, ocean-going cruise ships. Tidewater glaciers of the West Arm are the most frequent destination; occasionally, ships go into Muir Inlet. The calving of glaciers and the passing parade of magnificent scenery are the main attractions. Interpretive presentations are given throughout the passage in park waters by on-board National Park Service rangers.

Smaller tour vessels offer a more intimate view of park resources. The *Spirit of Adventure*, an 85-foot, 300-passenger vessel, takes visitors daily to Margerie and Grand Pacific glaciers, 55 miles from Bartlett Cove. This tour boat also serves as the principal camper shuttle, dropping campers at three designated sites within the bay. Tour-boat service originates both in Juneau and at Bartlett Cove near park headquarters. Interpretive services are

Overleaf: A moist climate and sandy soil are perfect for wild strawberries.

supplied by the National Park Service. Humpback whales are occasionally sighted during transits of the bay.

An overnight campsite near the snout of a massive glacier will bring an explorer to the doorstep of the ice age. Typically, amid a moonscape of ice-hewn rock and an active glacial front, a thin strand of beach will accommodate campers in an ambience of raw Pleistocene beauty. Thunder from toppling pillars of ice will echo from rock walls and mingle day and night with the sound of rushing veils of meltwater and the groans, pops, and squeals of a separating mass of ice. The exposed bedrock will be steep and the hiking arduous. Rapid retreat of the glaciers has allowed little time for pioneer plants to take hold. One may find patches of mosses and lichens, along with some fireweed and a few timid sprigs of willow.

Kayak transit of Muir Inlet, north to south, offers an exceptional view of vegetational succession matching a human lifespan, or about 70 years. From McConnell Ridge near Riggs Glacier to Muir Point, a distance of 28 miles represents the Muir Glacier's retreat between 1890 and 1960. During the three-day transit, kayakers paddle from bare bedrock to the green habitats of moose, black bear, and mountain goat sauntering along alpine pastures of Mount Wright. Hardy redpolls will be seen along the advancing edge of willow and alder, along with ptarmigan and rosy finches; warblers and fox sparrows will follow, and ducks and geese may be seen near Muir Point.

Congress has designated five saltwater wilderness areas in the park. Unique in the national-park system, they are intended for the use of self-propelled boats only.

Glacier Bay and its inlets and fjords provide access corridors into the backcountry for all types of vessels, from kayaks to sailboats to 30,000-ton cruise ships. At present levels of use, the countless bays and coves offer seclusion for those seeking to depart from major waterways. But, due to a diverse shoreline and varying bottom topography, the region's tidal characteristics are complex. Tidal range averages 15 feet between mean low and high tides. Tide rips and currents in Sitakaday Narrows have been measured in excess of six knots, and in Adams Inlet in excess of 10 knots. Anchor holds are often prevented by extreme depth. These factors can present serious problems to inexperienced boaters.

Destination: Dry Bay

Canadian and American outfitters provide float trips on the Tatshenshini and Alsek river systems, with launch points at

Opposite: Puffins can catch and carry up to ten small fish in their bills at once.

Dalton Post on the Haines Highway in the Yukon Territory. The fast-flowing and roily Tatshenshini crosses into British Columbia, where it joins the glacier-fed Alsek River, which then crosses the international boundary into Glacier Bay National Park. The lower Alsek River Valley constitutes a natural gateway, or migration path, for moose, bears, and wolves bypassing coastal glacier systems to reach habitats along the outer coastline of Glacier Bay. The float trip requires about one week and ends within the preserve at Dry Bay, where commercial salmon fishing is a summer activity and sport hunting for moose and bear takes place during late summer and fall. Near Dry Bay are the Deception Hills; intimate "tea cup" lakes occupy their northern slopes. A small airstrip at Dry Bay provides egress via charter aircraft to transportation centers at Yakutat and Juneau.

In the early 1990s, the wildness of the Alsek–Tatshenshini river system was threatened by the plan of Geddes Resources Ltd. to build the world's largest open-pit copper mine above the confluence of the rivers. Windy Craggy Mountain would have been excavated, and the runoff of sulfuric acid would have degraded water quality. In 1992, the United Nations declared Glacier Bay a World Heritage Site, pressuring Canada on the proposed mine. In 1993, British Columbia established the Tatshenshini-Alsek Wilderness Park, which killed the mine plan. Glacier Bay and the Alsek-Tatshenshini parks are contiguous with Canada's Kluane National Park and Alaska's Wrangell-St. Elias National Park and Preserve; their total area—nearly 21,000,000 acres—represents the largest protected expanse in the world.

Dry Bay is also the departure point (or end point) for one of the park's more challenging and remote backpacking routes. The outer coast between Lituya Bay and Dry Bay is a wild and windswept region requiring a transit time of 8 to 10 days. The route, generally along the beachline with numerous stream crossings varying in degree of hazard, traverses the outwash plain of Fairweather Glacier and Grand Plateau Glacier. Short hikes to high promontories of the coastal mountains offer spectacular vistas of Desolation Valley, Sea Otter Glacier, and many small and unnamed lakes along valleys of the outer foothills. Moose, grizzly and black bears, and wolves may be found on this route, along with a wide variety of migratory birds. Access to Lituya Bay is by floatplane from Gustavus or Yakutat.

Blackwater Pond lies at the center of a boggy area.

TRAILS OF GLACIER BAY
NATIONAL PARK AND PRESERVE

The park has no trails or established campsites, other than at Bartlett Cove. Two trails begin at Glacier Bay Lodge:

FOREST TRAIL: Starts at the lodge; ends at the Cove dock; 1 mile round trip; 1 hour; winds through pond-studded spruce-hemlock forest for first .5 mile, and then descends to the beach; June and July are best months for wildflowers.

BARTLETT RIVER TRAIL: Starts at the lodge; ends at Bartlett River estuary; 4 miles round trip; 2-3 hours; meanders along a tidal lagoon, through forest, then emerges and ends at the estuary; wildlife along shore and in forest; salmon run upriver in late summer.

KATMAI
NATIONAL PARK
AND PRESERVE

Brown bears prepare for winter hibernation by gorging on spawning salmon.

KATMAI NATIONAL PARK AND PRESERVE
BOX 7, KING SALMON, ALASKA 99613
TEL.: (907) 246-3305

HIGHLIGHTS: Valley of Ten Thousand Smokes • Mount Katmai • Novarupta • Naknek Lake • Lake Brooks • Mount Griggs • Fumaroles • Shelikof Strait • Brown Bears • Brooks River

ACCESS: Jet flights connect Anchorage and King Salmon. Travel from King Salmon to Brooks Camp is by bush aircraft, or by boat from local boat charter. Package tours available through a concessionaire-run visitor camp.

SEASON: Park is accessible from early June to early September only.

FEES: None.

PARKING: Space for 5-10 cars at Lake Camp.

GAS: At King Salmon, outside park.

FOOD AND LODGING: At Brooks Lodge and Grosvenor Camp, as well as Kulik Lodge, Cry of the Loon Lodge, Enchanted Lake. Limited freeze-dried food available at "trading post" at Brooks. Make reservations well in advance for summer.

VISITOR CENTER: Administrative office in King Salmon. Summer Visitor Center at Brooks Camp. Interagency Visitor Center at airport in King Salmon (year-round).

GIFT SHOP: At Brooks Lodge.

PETS: Not allowed.

HIKING: Permitted throughout park; boil water.

BACKPACKING: Permit and itinerary submission requested. Streams, lakes, and snow provide water; boil water.

CAMPGROUNDS: At Brooks Camp, reservations by lottery; 17 sites; lottery deadline in mid-February. White gas and propane may be purchased at lodge. Meals may be purchased at lodge with 12 hours' notice; tents, cots, and stoves may be rented. Showers available.

OTHER ACTIVITIES: Boating, permit required; fishing, Alaska State license required; float trips, canoeing, and kayaking.

TOURS: Air tours, all-day fishing charters, and drop-offs at remote locations available through concessionaire, as is all-day bus tour to Valley of Ten Thousand Smokes. Park Service conducts daily nature walk at Brooks Camp.

FACILITIES FOR DISABLED: Bear-viewing platform, auditorium.

For additional information, see also Sites, Trails, and Trips on pages 156–161 and the map on pages 134–135.

"Dwarf" fireweed grows out of the way of Katmai's incessant winds.

THE KATMAI MOUNTAIN BLOW UP WITH LOTS OF fire, and fire come down trail from Katmai with lots of smoke. We go fast Savonoski. Everybody get in bidarka [skin boat]. Helluva job. We come Naknek one day, dark, no could see. Hot ash fall. Work like hell." With these words American Pete, chief of Savonoski village, told of one of the greatest eruptions in recorded history. On June 6 and 7, 1912, the earth shuddered, convulsed, and gaped, spewing forth 7 cubic miles of incandescent sand and gas that inundated a valley 15 miles long and 3 to 6 miles wide, burying it up to 700 feet deep. Volcanic dust fell 1,500 miles away, and fine particles in the atmosphere so obscured the sun that the entire Northern Hemisphere experienced an unusually cool summer.

Robert Fiske Griggs, who led most of the early expeditions into the Katmai area and who called for the creation of a park there, described his discoveries in *National Geographic Magazine* and in his fascinating book *The Valley of Ten Thousand Smokes*. He wrote:

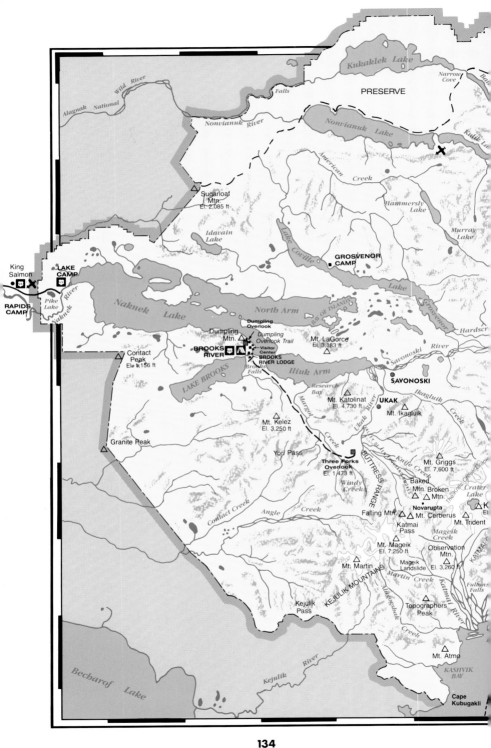

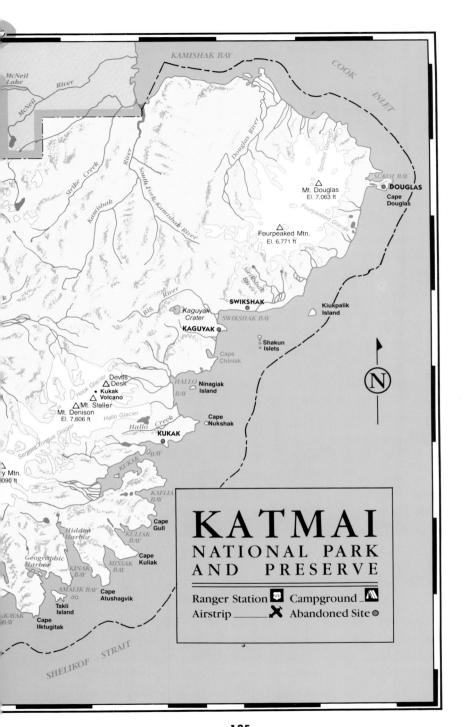

KAMISHAK BAY

COOK INLET

McNeil Lake

McNeil River

River

Strike Creek

Kamishak River

South Fork Kamishak River

Douglas River

Spotted Glacier

SUKOI BAY

Mt. Douglas
El. 7,063 ft

△ Mt. Douglas

● DOUGLAS
Cape
Douglas

Fourpeaked Glacier

Fourpeaked Mtn.
El. 6,771 ft

Sukoi River

Big River

Kaguyak
Crater

SWIKSHAK

Kiukpalik
Island

SWIKSHAK BAY

KAGUYAK

Shakun
Islets

Cape
Chiniak

Hook Glacier

Devils
Desk
△ ● Kukak
△ Volcano
△ Mt. Steller

Mt. Denison
El. 7,606 ft

Hallo Glacier

Sergeant Tongue Glacier

Hallo Creek

HALLO
BAY

Ninagiak
Island

Cape
Nukshak

KUKAK

Hallo

y Mtn.
090 ft

KUKAK BAY

KAFLIA
BAY

Cape
Gull

Hidden
Harbor

KULIAK
BAY

Cape
Kuliak

Geographic
Harbor

MISSAK
BAY

KINAK
BAY

AMALIK BAY

Cape
Atushagvik

Takli
Island

Cape
Ilktugitak

KAVAK
BAY

SHELIKOF STRAIT

N

KATMAI
NATIONAL PARK
AND PRESERVE

Ranger Station 🅄🅂 Campground ⛺

Airstrip ✕ Abandoned Site ●

If such an eruption should occur on Manhattan Island, the column of steam would be conspicuous as far as Albany. The sounds of the explosions would be plainly audible in Chicago. The fumes would sweep over all the states east of the Rocky Mountains. In Denver they would tarnish exposed brass, and even linen hung out on the line to dry would be so eaten by the sulphuric acid content as to fall to pieces on the ironing board. As far away as Toronto, the acid raindrops would cause stinging burns wherever they fell on face or hands. Ash would accumulate in Philadelphia a foot deep. To add to the terrors of the catastrophe, that city would grope for sixty hours in total darkness—darkness blacker than anything imaginable, so thick that a lantern held at arm's length could not be seen. As for the horrors that would be enacted along the lower Hudson, no detailed picture may be drawn. There would be no survivors. The whole of Manhattan Island, and an equal area besides, would open in great yawning chasms, and fiery fountains of molten lava would issue from every crack. This, disrupted by the escaping gases, would be changed into red hot sand, which, consuming everything it touched, would run like wildfire through the town. The flow of incandescent sand would effectually destroy all evidence of the former city.

Brooks River, near Brooks Camp, is a favorite fishing spot for humans and bears alike.

But in the Katmai eruption there was no loss of life; Katmai was a wilderness. Few people lived in the area, and most of them, heeding the forewarning earthquakes, had fled.

And a wilderness Katmai remains—an incomparable wilderness, the essence of wildness. The magnitude and importance of the eruption are somehow eclipsed by the rivers teeming with salmon, by the commanding brown bear, elusive lynx, and wolverine, by towering peaks that descend abruptly into deep blue lakes or coastal fjords, and by the feeling—that indescribable feeling—one has when traveling alone and unarmed through raw, rugged, unpeopled country.

Visitors come to Katmai to fish for rainbow trout, to hike through the Valley of Ten Thousand Smokes, and to experience, photograph, and study a truly wild and wonderful land. Originally set aside as a scientific classroom, Katmai has other important lessons to teach, lessons about ourselves. As Katmai activates, energizes, and exhilarates our senses, it also soothes and calms our souls, adds perspective, and leads us to philosophize about the nature of humanity and our relationship with our environment.

History

Early Peoples of the Coast and Lakes

In the distant past, the peoples of the coast and of the interior were effectively separated by the high, stormy, glaciated peaks that form the northern part of the Aleutian Range. Coastal sites dating to 4000 B.C. have revealed projectile points, knives, and other tools of people who hunted the sea mammals. Until about A.D. 1000, these tools differed markedly from those of interior cultures.

In the Brooks River area, twenty-two sites containing 750 house depressions have yielded artifacts enabling archeologists to piece together the human story in Katmai's interior. The sites line terraces that mark previous levels of the lakes and river. The postglacial lakes were once 86 feet higher than the current 32-foot level.

Scholars have divided the prehistory of the Brooks area into four periods. The earliest peoples, who were there by 2500 B.C., left large ground or chipped lance and knife blades, suggesting a life more dependent on hunting caribou than on fishing. About 1900 B.C., Eskimo-related people, whose lives centered more on fishing for salmon, appeared. Members of the Arctic Small Tool Tradition, they used a variety of small, delicate points and blades on their implements and weapons. The latter people may have completely displaced the former. In any case, from this time forward, the general influence was Eskimoan—although there is no evidence of habitation between 1000 and 200 B.C. Around the latter date, however, the Brooks site became the home of people who used slate-rubbing techniques to polish their tools and who introduced pottery to the area. Pots from this era tend to be thin and relatively plain. These gave way to the stronger pottery of the Naknek Period, which persisted from A.D. 1000 until the eruption. People of the Naknek Period refined their tools, increasing the ratio of polished slate to chipped tools; they also crossed the Aleutian Range to the coast more often. Professor Don Dumond has written that during this period there was "open communication" across the peninsula and that the cultures became technologically similar.

The Russianization

During the late 1700s, the Russians pursued the sea otter, prized for its fur pelt, up the Aleutian Islands and the Alaska Peninsula, subduing all Native peoples they encountered. Grigory Ivanovich Shelikov sailed to Kodiak in 1784 to found the first permanent Russian settlement in Alaska. From that base, his agents plied the waters of Shelikof Strait, trading with the coastal villages and trying to force the villagers to hunt for the Shelikov-Golikov Company.

The Russian-American Company, which succeeded Shelikov's company, used Katmai village, on Katmai Bay, as a major trading post. A trail over Katmai Pass connected the post with the interior villages of Savonoski, at the mouth of the Savonoski River, and Pauwik (Naknek), at the mouth of the Naknek River. By 1845 missionaries had also reached these villages. Although coastal people were more dependent on the Russians than people of the interior were, Russian influence in both regions permeated every phase of village life. Thanks to a directive from Shelikov, however, local Native names rather than Russian names appeared on many early Russian charts, and many Native names have survived.

The Searchers

After the United States purchased Alaska in 1867, fierce and unscrupulous competition among American fur companies led to the rapid decline of the sea otter. Conservation measures that had been introduced by the Russians were abandoned, and some companies used liquor to gain Native loyalty. Although sale of liquor to the Natives was illegal, sale of supplies to make the powerful home brew known as kvass was not. The use of larger boats and more guns, as well as bigger payments to hunters, produced annual sea-otter slaughters four times as great as those conducted by the Russians. By 1890, the sea otter was near extinction and former

In 1915, the botanist Robert Fiske Griggs studied revegetation near Katmai volcano.

sea-otter hunters were nearly destitute. The village of Katmai, previously an important trading post, declined as well.

The route over Katmai Pass, from the village to the western slope of the Aleutian Range, had already begun to attract other travelers. Census takers Ivan Petroff (1880) and William Greenfeld (1890) both crossed the pass, an undertaking so hazardous that the Natives would attempt it only on clear summer days. They were followed by E. Hazard Wells and Alfred Schanz, whose articles in *Frank Leslie's Illustrated Newspaper* helped introduce the Katmai region to a large audience. The Nome gold rush drew prospectors through the pass, and some lingered in the area to try their luck. One disenchanted prospector, Rex Beach, struck gold in a literary vein, using Katmai as the background for his book *The Silver Horde*.

Scientists also probed Katmai, in search of coal, oil, and gold, but they found no deposits that would warrant commercial enterprise. Josiah Spurr of the U.S. Geological Survey team of 1898 provided the first scientific descriptions of the peninsula. In 1899 the privately funded Harriman Expedition—twenty-five scientists, plus photographers and artists—landed in Kukak Bay to conduct botanical research. They collected plant and fossil-plant specimens and returned home full of praise for the beauty of the area.

The Katmai region did not gain much recognition, however, until 1912, when volcanic activity claimed the attention of the world.

". . . awaiting death at any moment . . ."

Although minor earthquakes had caused the earth to tremble throughout the preceding week, the clear, calm morning of June 6, 1912, gave no warning that night would fall just after noon. About 1 P.M., thunderous explosions—heard in Juneau, 700 miles away—rocked the area. From the head of a valley, masses of incandescent sand and gas flowed downhill, instantly engulfing all forms of life. A searing wind accompanying the flow carbonized trees on the flanks of the adjacent mountains.

A towering cloud of volcanic ash filled the sky and spread toward the town of Kodiak, 100 miles southeast of Mount Katmai, on the prevailing northwesterly winds. As ash began to fall, sulfur-laden fumes and razor-sharp particles of volcanic glass assaulted the nostrils and throat, making breathing difficult. The ash choked rivers and contaminated drinking water. Birds, unable to fly, fell to the ground. Additional explosions at 11 P.M. on June 6 and at 10:40 P.M. on June 7 kept the air filled with ash and the waters with floating pumice. Darkness prevailed for 60 hours, broken only by flash-

A photo of the 1915 National Geographic Society's expedition, taken by Robert F. Griggs.

es of lightning.

Ivan Orloff, who was visiting a fishing camp in Kaflia Bay, 30 miles east of Mount Katmai, wrote to his wife, "We are awaiting death at any moment. . . . A mountain has burst near here, so that we are covered by ashes, in some places 10 feet and 6 feet deep . . . and we have no water. Here are darkness and hell, thunder and noise. I do not know whether it is day or night."

Captain William Perry on the U.S. Coast Guard cutter *Manning* directed rescue and recovery operations for the town of Kodiak. At one point, 500 residents crowded onto the *Manning*, prepared to escape to sea if necessary. When the volcanic activity subsided, Kodiak lay under a foot of ash; Katmai village was uninhabitable.

Villagers from Katmai and Douglas fled south or to Kaflia Bay for rescue by Lieutenant W. K. Thompson on the tug *Redondo*. Captain Perry directed relocation efforts farther south on the peninsula, and the new village was named Perryville in his honor. The former residents of Savonoski moved to a site they called New Savonoski on the south bank of the Naknek River. (The population of New Savonoski numbered 54 and of Perryville 94 before an influenza epidemic swept the peninsula in 1918. Although Perryville has survived as a village, no one remains in New Savonoski.)

From Katmai Pass, a Vision of Hell

News of the eruption spread, drawing scientists and entrepreneurs to Katmai. On behalf of the National Geographic Society and the U.S. Geological Survey, George Martin visited the deserted village of Katmai in August 1912. He did not approach the volcano, but he did collect firsthand accounts of the eruption and publish an article in *National Geographic Magazine.* In 1913, William Hesse and M. A. Horner, two enterprising Alaskans, entered the area hoping to produce a documentary film. The insidious volcanic dust ruined their motion-picture cameras and film, but they climbed and photographed nearby Mount Martin. Fake post cards printed from their film were later labeled "Katmai Volcano" and sold in Seward.

Public and scientific reaction to Martin's article encouraged the National Geographic Society to sponsor additional expeditions. In 1915, Robert Fiske Griggs, a botanist, led a small party to Kodiak Island to study the process of revegetation. To their surprise, lush stands of grass had already grown in recently barren, ash-covered areas. Griggs then moved his base closer to the volcano. He observed the effects of a tremendous flood in the Katmai village area that had occurred a few days earlier, and scouted the Katmai River Valley to the lower slopes of the volcano. The going was slow. Griggs's account refers repeatedly to "ankle-deep, soft sticky mud," the "omnipresent mud" that was of more concern to the group than were the bears.

Returning in 1916, Griggs and two colleagues ascended Katmai volcano for the first time on July 19. En route, they discovered that the 1915 flood had been caused by the collapse of a natural dam, which had been created by the ashflow but which proved unable to resist the increasing pressure of a vast lake. When they first reached the volcano rim, steam blocked their view, but then it parted and they were "struck speechless" by the sight below. Griggs continued, "We found ourselves hanging over the brink of an abyss of such immensity that, as the event proved, we were powerless even to guess its size. . . . In the bottom lay a wonderful lake, of a weird vitriolic robin's-egg blue, milky . . . set with a horseshoe island. . . . Around the margin hissed columns of steam, issuing from every crevice."

Griggs's excitement on viewing the crater was surpassed by his astonishment twelve days later when he climbed up to Katmai Pass and looked to the northwest. "The sight that flashed into view as we surmounted the hillock was one of the most amazing visions ever beheld by mortal eye. The whole valley as far as the eye could reach was full of hundreds, no thousands—literally tens of thousands—of smokes curling up from its fissured floor." And as it released its ash-laden steam, all the valley hissed and roared.

J. W. Shipley, the chemist for the 1917 expedition, wrote:

On first entering the valley from between the two guardian volcanic cones, I experienced the same sensation as the man who on seeing a giraffe for the first time exclaimed, "There ain't no such animal." Hot streams issue from beneath banks of snow; extensive glaciers hobnob with steaming fumaroles; icebergs and hot water are found in the same little lake. Enormous mud flows appear to have run uphill. A stick chars when thrust into a jet of steam. It is uncannily unreal. But the unreality suddenly vanishes when one's foot breaks through the crust and hot volcanic gases rush out.

Establishment of the Park

Griggs set out to persuade the National Geographic Society and the National Park Service to establish a park in this valley of vapors. The society sent a small expedition to Katmai in 1918 to monitor the smokes and record temperatures for some of the fumaroles. The highest temperature recorded was 645° C., nearly 1,200° F. Activity seemed to be stable—an assessment that proved to be too optimistic—so proposals were drawn up for a park. Using the executive power created by the Antiquities Act of 1906, President Woodrow Wilson established Katmai National Monument on September 24, 1918.

Successive expeditions, particularly Griggs's in 1930, exposed the tremendous beauty of the lakes area and its potential as a wildlife sanctuary. Concern for the preservation of brown-bear habitat led President Herbert Hoover to double the size of the monument in 1931. Additional proclamations expanded it in 1942, 1969, and 1978. Finally, Congress passed the Alaska National Interest Lands Conservation Act (ANILCA) in 1980, transforming the monument into a 4,090,000-acre national park and preserve, 3,473,000 acres of which were designated as wilderness.

The *Exxon Valdez* oil spill in 1989 had a heavy negative impact on some coastal wildlife populations. All kittiwake colonies failed in 1989—no young were produced. Nearly 20 percent of the bald eagle nests failed to produce young. Peale's peregrine falcon, common historically on the Katmai coast, was rarely seen in the five years after the spill. Nearly 8,000 sea bird carcasses were recovered from the Katmai coast after the spill. The accident also exacerbated the decline of the Steller sea lions.

The geological story of Katmai is largely one of volcanism, glacial activity, wind, and erosion. Lying at the head of the Aleutian Range, the 7,000-foot Katmai volcanoes belong to the Ring of Fire, which encircles much of the Pacific. The theory of plate tectonics postulates that the earth's crust, divided into a series of plates, floats on a subterranean sea of magma. Where the plates meet, friction results. The friction generates heat, melting rock and creating more magma, which fuels the volcanoes. Frequently one plate overrides the other. The subduction of the overridden plate produces intense thermal activity, faults, and earthquakes. Such is the case in the Katmai area. The Bruin Bay Fault parallels the mountains and separates the mountainous coastal region from the lowlands to the west. The entire volcanic district in Katmai remains very active. Mount Trident expelled steam, ash, or lava every year between 1957 and 1965 and did so again in 1968. The steaming plumes of Mount Martin, which may be seen on a clear day from King Salmon more than 60 miles away, are daily reminders of the tremendous forces underlying the park. Mount Mageik steams intermittently.

The Foundation

Although older volcanic and metamorphic rocks dating to the Triassic period, 180 to 225 million years ago, are found in the lowlands west of the Bruin Bay Fault, most of the volcanic ejecta in the park represent the newest rocks, materials spewed forth in vents through older layers. The oldest rocks in the main portion of the park, those of the Aleutian Batholith, were formed by consolidation of molten materials beneath the earth's surface in early to mid-Jurassic times, 140 to 155 million years ago. Later, they were uplifted and then eroded by streams 130 million years ago. This same period saw the deposition of the sedimentary materials—the siltstones, sandstones, and shales—of the Naknek Formation, which underlies much of the park, including most of the volcanic area.

A Cretaceous sea (60 million years ago) was the source of another major mass of sediment. This came to be known as the Kaguyak Formation; heavy erosion of exposed sedimentary materials has left only spotty evidence of this period, however. Nonetheless, fossils—including those of mollusks, snails, and leaves—do remain in places, and those from the two sedimentary formations differ con-

Opposite: Swiftly running rivers and fierce pumice-laden winds have eroded these ash deposits.

siderably. Sedimentary layers were raised above sea level with remarkably little deformation and topped with volcanic material produced during the Eocene epoch, 40 to 60 million years ago. Recent volcanism contributes to the geological story as well.

Glaciers Old and New

Two glacial advances and retreats scoured the major lake basins of the region and left moraines, U-shaped valleys, and rolling hills in their wake. Ice that receded during the Wisconsinan age, about 10,000 years ago, left Naknek, ldavain, Brooks, and Coville as postglacial lakes. The land separating Lake Grosvenor from Lake Coville and the pair of narrow peninsulas separating the Iliuk Arm from the rest of Naknek Lake are believed to be terminal moraines of a less extensive period of glaciation that ended about 6,000 years ago. Many active glaciers remain in the mountainous area of the park.

The interaction of volcanic activity and glaciers in the Katmai caldera is particularly intriguing to scientists because the glaciers that have formed there since 1912 are the first ones ever to be observed from their beginnings. Studies of the movement of the ash-covered glaciers on Mount Griggs indicate that the ash acts as an excellent warm-weather insulator, much like "sawdust in an ice house," allowing less than normal seasonal recession.

Fire in the Valley

Robert Griggs's original theories about the eruptions of 1912 and the "ten thousand smokes" have been revised, refined, and redefined in an effort to unravel the true sequence of events. Although many mysteries and points of contention remain unresolved, the explanation presented by Garniss Curtis of the University of California, Berkeley, is generally accepted. He contends that the major eruption occurred not from Mount Katmai but from Novarupta and fissures at the head of the valley. "Within a few moments, no less than 2.5 cubic miles of ash were expelled, and the incandescent mass, acting like a fiery-hot liquid, swept down the valley with incredible swiftness."

While material was being ejected from Novarupta, a lava conduit connecting Novarupta and Katmai volcano drained magma from the latter, causing the dome of Katmai to collapse. The molten andesite beneath Katmai mixed with the rhyolite of Novarupta to produce a "hybrid" banded pumice. As a rhyolitic plug formed in Novarupta, the andesite was forced back up through Katmai's

Opposite: A shifting layer of ash from the 1912 eruption still covers the valley floor.

vent, forming a small cone on the caldera floor. As the huge caldera (measuring 3 miles long and 2 miles wide, with a depth of 3,700 feet) began to fill with water, the cone stood as a small island. By 1922, the lake had disappeared, enabling geologists Charles Yori and Clarence Fenner to descend to the floor of the caldera and examine the andesite, mud geysers, and boiling springs. Later, the waters rose again, eventually submerging the island cone.

Climbers who venture to Katmai volcano's rim today see a peaceful turquoise take framed by two glaciers that cascade over steeply sloping walls of a massive caldera. Hikers on the valley floor encounter a 200-foot-high dome of jumbled blocks of volcanic rock, a "pimple" that measures barely 800 feet in diameter; this is Novarupta. It is difficult to imagine that such an unpretentious volcano could have spewed forth such an enormous amount of material. It is encircled, though, by steam vents that still produce enough

A fossil from sedimentary rock that lies under most of the volcanic areas in the park.

heat and moisture to foster luxuriant growths of moss and sedges.

Volcanologists have examined the placement and proportions of rhyolite, dacite, and andesite—volcanic rocks that vary in silica content and mineralization—in the ejecta in order to gain a better understanding of the conduit system that lies beneath the volcanoes. Novarupta is semiencircled by andesitic volcanoes, including Griggs, Katmai, Mageik, and Trident, and all of these may be sitting atop a single, massive magma reservoir. However, current theory espoused by Dr. Wes Hildreth favors the idea of a "complex injection zone" that feeds a few "discrete reservoirs," some of which are probably hydraulically connected.

According to Curtis, as the fiery ashflow of 1912 consolidated in the valley, "hot gases, mostly steam derived from buried rivers and feeding springs, began to rise to the surface through myriads of small holes and cracks." Although most of the fumaroles were probably formed in this manner, some may vent from deeper sources. Fumaroles on the flanks of surrounding mountains escaped the ashflow, and their origin consequently requires a different explanation. Venting of gases from subsurface hot areas is generally accepted as the most likely cause.

Griggs's "ten thousand smokes," which were primarily associated with the ashflow, fizzled out over a thirty-year period as the ash cooled. Visitors to the valley today see steam only from those few vents that are connected to deeper heat sources.

Pebbles of Pumice

"Everywhere throughout the region one is made to feel the importance of wind action on the landscape. Almost every part of the surface of the country shows the effect of wind, being either eroded away by the powerful blasts or built up by deposits of wind-borne sand." Written in 1922, Griggs's words are still true today. Winds at speeds approaching 100 miles per hour funnel through Katmai Pass, abrading everything they encounter with ash and bits of pumice, a featherweight, light-colored, highly porous, gas-blown lava that will float on water. After any sizable storm, the lakeshores are awash with pebbles of pumice.

Rivers, too, have cut deeply into the ash-laden valley and carried detritus to the lakes beyond. In their march to the sea, rivers have cut through ancient moraines and connected the major lakes. Perhaps Father Bernard Hubbard best summed up this ever-changing landscape in his book *Cradle of the Storms*: "The real trouble [is] that Nature has never appeared satisfied with the Valley of Ten Thousand Smokes region. She is always making radical changes in her handiwork."

"Always the Wind"

"To wait for good weather here, before trying to reach an objective, simply means not reaching it at all, for the good weather doesn't come. . . . In the Alaska-Peninsula-Aleutian-Island cradle of the tempests, it seemed that we were always fighting storms. They were worthy foes." Visitors to the park should heed Father Hubbard's words and be prepared for inclement weather. In Katmai, weather systems from the Gulf of Alaska and from the Bering Sea meet, and the meeting is not always cordial. Warmed by these bodies of water, temperatures do not dip as low as they do in the interior, but the rain and winds generate impressive chill factors. Daytime summer temperatures average in the 50s and 60s, but the 30s and 40s are common in the evenings. Rain may fall frequently during the summer. Victor Cahalane, who conducted biological research in the 1940s and 1950s, wrote, "Occasionally a driving rain may continue for many hours, but most of the summer precipitation occurs as prolonged drizzle or showers alternating with periods of complete cessation. The effect is to keep the vegetation wet and the traveler complaining."

Writing two decades later, Dave Bohn added, "Wind. Always the wind." Three-day blows packing winds of 30 to 50 miles per hour occur and may commence with little warning. Violent windstorms are known locally as williwaws. Within minutes, gusts racing down the lakes turn ripples into 5- to 7-foot crests. However grim this may sound, Katmai's weather, like its bears and volcanoes, is highly unpredictable, and visitors might be treated to several days of cloudless sunshine. Wind and rain also greatly affect the distribution of flora and fauna throughout the parklands.

Vegetation

On the slopes above 2,000 feet, where the winds try continually to rip soils bare, plants dig in and lie low to survive. In this treeless area known as alpine tundra, "dwarf" varieties of many plants are the rule. Dwarf alpine birch, low-growing willows, tiny Kamchatka rhododendrons, saxifrages, and mountain avens mingle with club moss, rock-growing lichens, sedges, and grasses. These sturdy plants possess branching root systems, which help secure them against the wind's tirades and enable them to draw more nutrients from the poor soil.

The winds and rains of the high country wash soil and nutrients

Opposite: Katmai's netted willow grows to a mature height of only about 3 inches.

to lower elevations. Protected from the intense gales by surrounding hills, the richer soils of the lowlands are able to support the relatively lush boreal forests of the lakes area and the coastal forests to the east. Moss- or wildflower-carpeted floors underlie canopies of spruce and birch. Stands of balsam poplar add texture to low-lying areas, while thickets of alder and willow line drainages and persist at the tree line. Lower, more poorly drained areas produce grasslands, marshes, and the moist tundra that covers much of the western part of the peninsula.

The revegetation of the Valley of Ten Thousand Smokes and the regrowth of plant life in outlying areas covered by ash provide the most interesting botanical stories in the park. The ash-blanketed land recovered more rapidly than botanists had anticipated. Within two or three years, shoots from the old roots of sturdier plants had thrust through the ash layer on Kodiak Island "in such profusion," Griggs wrote, "as to upset completely even the most optimistic of predictions." The ash appeared to work as a mulch, holding back weaker plants and allowing stronger ones to proliferate. Cross cuts of trees revealed increased rates of growth after the mantle of ash was deposited.

Closer to the scene of the eruption, the deeper ash and the wind-blown pumice shifted about constantly. The field horsetail—the one plant Griggs found that proved able to pierce 36 inches of ash—spread rapidly and stabilized the barren surface in many areas. Another important pioneer plant that Griggs noted in Katmai Valley is the lupine. Its large seeds lodge easily and supply considerable food to the young plants, enabling them to establish themselves and grow rapidly. Because lupines are legumes—members of the bean family—they have the characteristic bacterial root tubercles that permit them to use free nitrogen from the air. Such plants help enrich the soil so that it can support other species.

The valley itself is still far from being revegetated. The old growth was obliterated by the fiery mass that descended upon it. Even if it had survived the initial onslaught, it could not possibly have pierced the several hundred feet of ash and pumice above. Revegetation here must rely wholly on seeds or on encroachment from valley margins. Given the winds and the abrasive action of the windblown pumice, it is amazing that anything has managed to take hold and survive. Conditions allow at best only a precarious existence, but here and there, where erosion created a semiprotected cranny, a few hardy plants such as dwarf fireweed, sedges, grasses, willows, oxytropes, and Arctic poppies began the struggle. Each year sees more pockets of life emerge. In time, it may once again be a green valley in which, as Ivan Petroff recounted in 1880, reindeer, fox, land otter, marten, and mink are "plentiful throughout."

Wildlife

Bears and Other Mammals. On anyone's list, the most notable species in Katmai is the awesome brown bear. Katmai has the world's greatest population of unhunted brown bears. Billed as the world's largest land carnivore, Katmai's brownies rarely fail to impress. Visitors walking trails or lakeshores may come upon 12- or 13-inch hind footprints, which become yet more impressive if they are still oozing water. Boars (males) attain maximum size by age ten, and their prehibernation weights may reach 1,000 pounds; the smaller sows (females) mature in 6 to 8 years and may weigh 650 pounds. Although they belong to the same species as the grizzly, the brown bears of Katmai weigh more because of their high-protein diet. Despite their weight and bulk, bears are surprisingly agile. They run easily across hummocks that cause many a hiker to stumble, and they catch fish from streams with timely swipes of their racquet-sized paws.

The original national monument was expanded primarily in order to protect the habitat of the bears throughout their yearly cycle. Bears tend to hibernate from November to April, choosing denning sites on the flanks of the higher hills and mountains, especially those that surround the lakes. Cubs (usually two) are born during hibernation and generally stay with the sow for 2 to 3 years. Upon emerging from their dens, coastal bears forage on tidal flats for marine mammal carcasses, marine invertebrates, sea-bird eggs, and algae, and they graze the grasses and sedges of the fields and marshlands. Inland bears seek grasses, roots, and the remainder of last season's berries. Omnivorous, bears also claim carrion, prey on moose calves, and attempt to dig ground squirrels out of their tundra dens. Once the spawning salmon return in July, bears concentrate on the streams and rivers, building up reserves of fat that will see them through the winter. Midsummer visitors to Brooks Camp are likely to encounter bears munching berries along a trail, fishing in Brooks River, or in front of the campground on Naknek Lake. Katmai affords an outstanding opportunity to watch bears in their natural habitat, but it is not a zoo; the bears are wild and unpredictable, and must be respected so they will keep returning to Brooks.

Bears share their domain with a variety of other mammals, including caribou, wolf, fox, lynx, hare, marten, otter, beaver, porcupine, wolverine, weasel, squirrels, and voles. A conspicuous resident of Katmai is the largest member of the deer family, the Alaskan moose. Moose are imposing creatures whose weights rival those of the bears—and they appear to have been designed by a committee. Visitors should give moose the same respect they

would a bear, especially if encountering a bull moose in autumn or a cow and her calf anytime.

Marine mammals frequent the fjords, bays, and inlets of the coast. Steller sea lions and harbor seals haul themselves out of the water to sun on rocky islands. The sea otter, once nearly extinct, rolls in the surf in replenished numbers, feeding on mollusks and seeking protection from predators in the kelp beds of the bays and shallow areas. Beluga whales occasionally navigate the strait in sizable pods, feeding along river mouths; seaward-bound salmon are their principal food.

Birds. During the summer, birds occupy every niche of Katmai's habitat. Rock ptarmigan, gray-crowned rosy finches, Lapland longspurs, and snow buntings scratch for dinner among the high tundra plants, while overhead gyrfalcons, short-eared owls, and other raptors search for small birds or for mice and ground squirrels that burrow in the hillsides. In the forests and forest margins live varied, hermit, and Swainson's thrushes; white-crowned and golden-crowned sparrows; yellow, orange-crowned, and blackpoll warblers; olive-sided flycatchers; northern three-toed and downy woodpeckers; great horned owls; and many other species. Marsh hawks and rough-legged hawks skim the grasslands and brushy areas. Swallows nest in the riverbanks, while water ouzels test the currents below. Yellowlegs, sandpipers, and plovers wander shorelines, while kingfishers, gulls, and Arctic terns fish from above. Bald eagles and ospreys perch on trees overlooking marshes and streams. Katmai's many ponds, marshes, and bays provide nesting sites for loons, grebes, mergansers, mallards, goldeneyes, and whistling swans. Coastal bays and islands are frequented by cormorants and puffins, the colorful, half-comic creatures that never fail to brighten a gray day. From the tundra to the coast, Katmai's birdwatchers are richly rewarded.

Fish. The waters of the park's lake and river system provide extensive spawning grounds for salmon, particularly the sockeye, or red, salmon, the fish prized by both bear and the commercial fisheries in Bristol Bay. Returning to the place of their birth, salmon seem to pave the streams with their red backs. During the months of July and August, they crowd the rainbow trout and grayling out of their habitual eddies. The rainbows, too, enjoy world renown. Sharing park waters with these celebrities are arctic char, lake trout, northern pike, and two dozen other fresh-water species.

Opposite: Each summer more than a million salmon spawn in the Naknek Lake system.

Katmai's vistas, animals, and auras provide incomparable rewards for hikers. A bit of planning ensures a memorable visit. Hiking before mid-June often proves difficult because of patches of snow and swollen streams. From mid-June to mid-August, insect repellent is a must. Biting insects depart by mid-August, and by that time the bears are focusing on the fish in the rivers and streams. Katmai in winter can be incredibly beautiful, but no facilities are open and weather conditions limit entrance to the experienced and hardy. Others wishing to see Katmai during the winter may arrange for scenic flights from King Salmon, Homer, or Kodiak. A backcountry hiking permit is strongly recommended for any overnight trip and may be obtained free of charge from the rangers.

Brooks Camp Area

Katmai's summer headquarters, the area's largest concession operation, and a campground are all located at Brooks Camp, which is accessible by air from Anchorage via King Salmon. Brooks Camp is adjacent to Brooks River, a favorite fishing area of bears and humans alike. Unfortunately, as visitation increases (the campground saw a fivefold increase in use between 1970 and 1984), the potential for undesirable human-bear encounters and for unfavorable human effect on the bear population becomes disturbing. For this reason some facilities may be moved or limitations may be imposed on use. In any event, however, the following attractions will remain park highlights:

Salmon fry hatch in springs, then swim into lakes, and finally find their way to the sea.

Brooks Falls. During July, the sockeye salmon gyrate high in the air in their attempts to leap the 6-foot falls and proceed upriver to spawn. As many as six fish may be in the air at once. Although it may seem that few are successful, their patient persistence hour after hour sends thousands on to the smaller streams entering Brooks Lake to continue the species. On the trail to the falls, hikers may find bear trails deeply embedded in the moss on the forest floor and perhaps carcasses of fish that bears have hauled into the woods for dinner. Bears may appear at any time. Their different fishing habits are intriguing: some take a single swipe; others prefer the two-paw method; still others lunge in on all fours, mouth agape. Then there are the snorkelers, who swim serenely down the river or at the river mouth where newly arriving fish bunch up.

Dumpling Overlook. The overlook, 1.5 miles up a moderately steep trail from the campground, affords a magnificent view of the Brooks River area, Mount Katolinat, and the Iliuk Arm. The trail leads through a variety of bird habitats and is used by man and beast alike. Make noise to avoid surprising a bear. An early morning or evening walk offers the best chance to see animals and frequently provides some moody views from above. Beyond the overlook, the trail continues a more gradual 2.5-mile ascent to the summit of Dumpling. Along the way, the trees and thickets give way to alpine tundra, horizons expand, and the likelihood of seeing moose and bears increases, especially in early summer. The trail may be skied in the winter; the views of late February and March add a new dimension to the park, but skill is required for the run from the overlook to the campground.

Barabara. A level half-mile walk from Brooks Camp leads to a partially reconstructed pit house, a reminder of the subsistence life style that persisted in the lakes area for forty centuries.

In the Valley of the Smokes

By bus or van or on foot, visitors may follow a 23-mile road from Brooks Camp that leads across streams and past a ghost forest devastated in 1912. The road ends at a cabin overlooking the Valley of Ten Thousand Smokes. To understand better the special nature of this valley and its formation, a visitor must venture into it with either a short walk to the valley floor or an extended camping trip.

Overlook Cabin to the Valley Floor. A 1.5-mile trail leads through alder-willow thickets and brush to the valley floor 400 feet below

Boaters especially enjoy the serene fall colors of Naknek Lake.

the cabin. There visitors walk on the consolidated ash and pumice of the 1912 eruption or, where the processes of erosion have once again exposed them, on the underlying, fossil-filled rocks of Jurassic origin. Several bridges built across the Ukak River have been swept away by spring torrents, reminders of the exceptional power of all the valley-shaping forces. The waters of Knife Creek, the River Lethe, and Windy Creek join to form the Ukak, a surging river that has sliced through nearly 200 feet of consolidated ash, leaving impressive, nearly vertical cliffs. Hikers gazing across the rapids at these tremendous, desolate escarpments may picture the fiery fury that engulfed the valley in June 1912. Pockets of new vegetation that increase in size each year speak of the ever-changing nature of the valley.

Overlook Cabin to the Head of the Valley. The impact of volcanism and the powers of wind and water quickly become apparent during a hike up the valley. This sea of volcanic ash produced such a lunar-like landscape that astronauts trained in the valley in preparation for flights to the moon. Knife Creek and the River Lethe roar through deep, lightning-like gashes in the valley floor. River crossings can be lethal. The wind can sandblast exposed skin with bits of pumice and can riddle tents with holes or send them careening down the valley. Although the hike is not especially difficult, weather conditions can make it an exhilarating challenge. In Longfellow's words, it can be very, very good or horrid. For those who are both competent and prepared, the hike affords the opportunity to experience some of the same awe the original explorers felt. Although the heat and the volume of steam have subsided, "paint-splotched" rocks dyed hues of ocher, pink, white, red, and rust still mark the vents of fumaroles. Some vents far up the valley continue to emit the rotten-egg smell characteristic of sulfur fumes. The jumbled plug of Novarupta and the ash-covered glaciers of Mount Griggs intrigue the adventurous. After Robert Griggs and his wife died in the 1960s, their son and grandson placed their ashes in a cairn atop Mount Griggs.

Access to the valley begins in a small gravel pit .5 mile west of the overlook cabin. An animal trail descends through alder and willow to Windy Creek. The distance to Novarupta is about 12 miles. The best course after crossing the creek is to ascend the flanks of the Buttress Range and maintain altitude to avoid gullies. For the first 6 miles, the trail is continuous as it follows the base of vegetation on the Buttress Range. Except during periods of high water, the River Lethe may be forded near its widest point, but hikers should exercise extreme caution and probe before stepping. The research cabin on Baked Mountain, constructed by the U.S. Geophysical Institute of the University of Alaska, is not available for overnight stays except in emergencies. Plan on camping out. Drinking water is scarce and wood, nonexistent. From the cabin, short hikes lead to Novarupta and to a few active fumaroles; the superheated steam can burn skin severely.

Routes Leading from the Valley

Katmai Pass to the Coast. The pass was used historically by mail carriers, fur traders, and gold seekers, but volcanism, rock slides, and the massive 1915 flood have obliterated any resemblance the ancient trail may have had to the present route. It is unmarked, uncharted, and beset with "quick-mud," alder thrashes, hummocky marshes, and other obstacles. When 100-mile-per-hour winds funnel through Katmai Pass, walking and camping are impossible. In good weather, a backpacker in the valley can reach Observation Mountain fairly easily for good views of the coast and the scenic canyon of the Katmai River. Visitors who have the necessary time, patience, experience, skills, and courage should consult the rangers.

Yori Pass. From midway on the valley road, a route channels experienced hikers through Yori Pass into the Angle Creek and Takayoto Creek drainages, a wild and open area beneath the spires of the Kejulik Mountains in the southwest corner of the park. The broad vistas offer the park's best opportunity for viewing the migratory caribou and good possibilities for watching bears. There are no trails, no campgrounds, and no guidelines. Consult rangers for route information and permits.

Beyond the Beyond

Only in a few places in this world can one still be alone, free to test personal resourcefulness and to learn nature's lessons in an unstructured manner. Although not for the novice, such places entice the experienced hiker skilled in cross-country travel and survival. They should remain undelineated for future generations to discover on their own; written guides would be a disservice.

Visitors should obtain a permit, carry topographical maps, use a stove rather than fires, and limit traveling-party size to protect the environment. Experienced hikers always carry extra food and anticipate bad-weather delays. Raingear and extra clothes are essential items. In Katmai's damp climate, a sleeping bag filled with synthetic material is better than one filled with down. A tent with a rainfly is indispensable.

Climbing. Many of Katmai's volcanoes and lesser peaks have been climbed. Of special interest is the tremendous caldera in the 6,715-foot summit of Mount Katmai. The main route to the summit is relatively easy for climbers who are experienced in glacier travel.

Lakes and Rivers. Katmai's extensive lake and river system and coastal inlets offer fantastic opportunities for exploring by canoe, kayak, and raft. For everything from short paddles along

Moose range over most of Alaska and can be seen near streams and ponds in summer.

lakeshores to extended trips, the waterways are impressive. When the weather cooperates, Brooks, Naknek, Coville, and Grosvenor lakes offer idyllic paddling and opportunities to view wildlife and the results of past glaciation. Trips of a few hours or a few days are delightful, especially in late summer, when the yellows of the birch play against the deep green of the spruce.

A popular 5- to 7-day (70- to 75-mile) trip starts from Brooks Camp. From there visitors paddle to the Bay of Islands, a miniature wonderland of myriad islets. Near Fure's cabin, a well-constructed trapper's cabin on the northern shore, a portage leads to Lake Grosvenor, a narrow, deep, blue lake. Paddling southeasterly past hills rounded by glacial action, boaters come to the picturesque Grosvenor River, which drains into the open country of the wide and braided Savonoski. In late summer and fall, when the fish are running, eagles dot the trees and bears line the sand bars. Campsites should be established at a distance from bear trails and areas where bears have slept or fed. The park requests that all camps be located on the lakes. The class I and II water (riffles and small rapids) of the Savonoski empties into Iliuk Arm, milky turquoise from glacial silt, and leads past Mount Katolinat, the islands of Research Bay, and the narrows en route to Brooks Camp. Although the trip can be completed in a week with favorable weather, extra days should be allowed for side trips and weather delays. The infamous three-day blows will halt a trip for the duration.

More experienced boaters may enjoy the stark beauty of the Ukak River or the views offered by the Alagnak and Nonvianuk rivers—both a part of the National Wild and Scenic Rivers System. These two require flying in from King Salmon or Brooks Camp. Boaters should write to the park superintendent for information.

The Battle Lake area and the high tundra near Murray and Hammersly lakes are accessible by air. Both areas offer opportunities for cross-country wilderness hiking.

The Coast. The bays and inlets of Katmai's coast offer unparalleled wilderness paddling and camping in a domain where seals, sea otters, sea lions, and puffins hold sway. The beauty of Geographic Harbor makes it a favorite destination. Boaters should be aware that the Cook Inlet waters are known for tremendous tidal and wind changes that vary with the seasons and time of month. Camps should be pitched well above the high-water line. Shelikof Strait has been called one of the most treacherous stretches of water in the world; boaters should stay close to shore and watch for signs of inclement weather.

Overleaf: Amalik Bay is the domain of sea otters, sea lions, seals, and puffins.

KENAI FJORDS
NATIONAL PARK

Coleman Bay is one of the many inlets and coves found along the Kenai coast.

KENAI FJORDS NATIONAL PARK
P.O. BOX 1727, SEWARD, ALASKA 99664
TEL.: (907) 224-3175

HIGHLIGHTS: Harding Ice Field • Exit Glacier • Bear Glacier • Resurrection Bay • Marine Bird Colonies • Nuka Bay/McCarty Fjord • Harris Bay/Northwestern Lagoon • Aialik Bay

ACCESS: Turn off Seward Highway (Alaska 9) at mile 3.7, onto 9-mile gravel road that ends at Exit Glacier in park.

SEASON: Open year-round; Seward Visitor Center open 7 days a week during summer, Monday through Friday thereafter. Exit Glacier Ranger Station open 7 days a week during summer, closed in winter.

FEES: None.

PARKING: At Seward Visitor Center and Exit Glacier.

GAS, FOOD, LODGING: None in park; available in Seward.

VISITOR CENTER: Slide programs and evening programs at Seward Visitor Center; guided walks at Exit Glacier.

PETS: Not permitted beyond Exit Glacier parking area.

HIKING: Unrestricted, but some terrain is difficult to traverse because of brush and incline. Air charter is only means of access for coastal ridge hiking. Contact ranger for current information and to register plans for extended trips in backcountry.

BACKPACKING: Unrestricted; water available in most areas, but treat it.

CAMPGROUNDS: Designated walk-in campsites for tent camping at Exit Glacier. Fires permitted. No showers. Backcountry camping permitted park-wide. No trailer camping.

CABINS: Four available for summer rental on coast; one at Exit Glacier for winter use. Reservation only.

TOURS: During summer, ranger-led hikes to Harding Ice Field, weekends only. Daily nature trail hikes at Exit Glacier.

OTHER ACTIVITIES: Winter cross-country skiing, dog-mushing, and snowmobiling at Exit Glacier; boat launching in Seward; fishing in Resurrection Bay with Alaska State license; advanced mountain climbing at Harding Ice Field; daily boat charters for wildlife viewing along coast, May 15–Sept. 15 .

FACILITIES FOR DISABLED: Trail for handicapped from Exit Glacier Ranger Station to within .25 mile of glacier.

For additional information, see also Sites, Trails, and Trips on page 183 and the map on pages 168–169.

The indolent Steller sea lions may reach 10 feet in length and weigh 2,000 pounds.

SELECTING A PARKLAND THAT WOULD SAMPLE Alaska's coastline was no small challenge. The state's point-to-point perimeter exceeds 6,640 miles; and if countless islands and bays are considered, its coastal edge increases to 33,904 miles. Yet one stretch of mountainous seafront along the Kenai Peninsula has long stirred the interest of explorers, miners, trappers, cartographers, and naturalists who have wandered its wild and picturesque shores. It is a landscape where high alpine ridges reach far to seaward. Deep blue fingers of the Pacific probe far inland to meet with snouts of glaciers. And pods of cruising whales swim high above drowned valleys. Kenai Fjords is an ice-capped mountain range tilting into the sea.

Landscapes surrounding the area's fjords and bays form a steep-sided terrain sandwiched between tidewater and the mile-high Harding Ice Field. The shoreline is sinuous and convoluted, with numerous bays, islands, and sea stacks. Landforms have largely been shaped by movement of glacial ice. Cirques and cusped bays mark the granite formations along oceanward ridgelines, while U-shaped sedimentary basins sweep upward to active glaciers. Water and land intersplice like the fingers of folded hands.

The 300-square-mile Harding Ice Field defines the landward

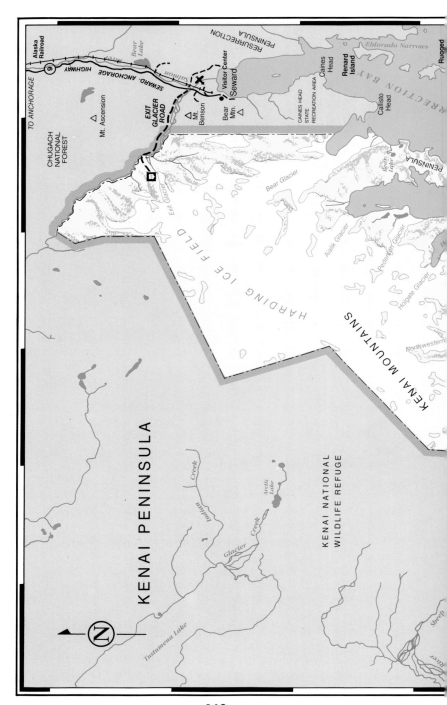

KENAI
FJORDS
NATIONAL PARK

Ranger Station [US] Airstrip ✈

Unpaved Road − − −

MILES

0   5   10   15

BERING SOUND

Chat Island
Harbor Island
Natoa Island
Chiswell Islands
Granite Island
Dora Passage
Cliff Cape
Harris Bay
PENINSULA

ALASKA MARITIME
NATIONAL WILDLIFE
REFUGE

Sandy Bay
Paguna Arm
Two Arm Bay
Taroka Arm
Cloudy Mtn.
Cloudy Cape
Thunder Bay
Black Mtn.
Black Bay
McCarty Fjord
James Lagoon
McCarty Lagoon
Moonlight Bay
Palisade Peak
Hoof Point
Rabbit Island
Outer Island
Pye Islands
Harrington Point

ALASKA MARITIME
NATIONAL WILDLIFE
REFUGE

GULF OF ALASKA

North Arm
Storm Mtn.
Nuka River
Mt. Diablo
Beaver Bay
West Arm
Yalik Bay
Yalik Glacier
Petrol Glacier
NUKA BAY

Nuka Island
STATE OWNED
Nuka Point
NUKA PASSAGE

perimeter of the fjords. This vestige of a vast Pleistocene ice sheet is sustained today by 400 to 600 inches of annual snowfall. The ice field feeds more than thirty active glaciers, seven of which reach down to tidewater. Across its high plain, the ice field lies like a sea of whipped cream unmarred by fissures or crevasses. Only the few summits of buried mountains, known as *nunataks*, or "lone peaks," rise hundreds of feet above the surrounding ice. Turbulent snow squalls occur year-round and can be seen for miles as they approach.

One of the earliest appraisals of Alaska's central coastline may prove to be the most lastingly accurate. "There are glaciers, mountains and fjords elsewhere," wrote geographer Henry Gannett after seeing the Kenai Peninsula's southern coast in 1899, "but no where else on earth is there such an abundance and magnificence of mountains, fjords and glacier scenery."

HISTORY

Little is known of the early aboriginal settlement and occupation of the Kenai Fjords coast. The steep and rugged terrain, proximity to glaciers, and exposure to maritime storms discouraged major settlements. Some archeological evidence suggests use by Chugachigmiut, an early Eskimo-Aleut people, and by a related but distinct subgroup known as the Unixkugmiut, which did not survive into modern times. Massive ice fields and the Kenai Mountains formed a barrier between the fjord-dwellers and the more northerly Tanaina Athapaskans of Cook Inlet. The last Native settlement of the area, along the coast of Aialik Bay, was abandoned about 1880. The name Kenai (KEY-nigh) derives from the Russian adaptation of *Knaiakhotana*, the Athapaskan word meaning "non-Eskimo people," referring to the Kenaitze Indian tribe still living on the peninsula.

Exploration and Exploitation

The Danish navigator Vitus Bering is thought to be the first European to sight the Kenai Peninsula during his historic voyage of exploration for the Russian czar in 1741. In 1778, the British Captain James Cook sailed by the area en route to the large inlet that now bears his name. But the rock-strewn coast of Kenai Fjords held little attraction for early navigators. Entrances to some bays and fjords are hidden by outer islands, while others open wide to storms and high seas and offer only sheer walls and no reachable bottom for anchorage. Mixed seas and echo waves from islands and headlands could spell disaster for a lumbering sail ship of the eighteenth century.

As part of the fur-trading activities of the Russian-American Company and its Siberian *promyshleniki*, or hired fur hunters, the port of Alexandrovski was established in 1785 at the present site of the English Bay, 30 miles west of the park. Seven years later, Alexander Baranov named Resurrection Bay (*Voskressenski*, or "Resurrection Sunday," Harbor) and constructed a ship-building facility in 1792. The location is thought to be near the present site of Seward, where ample supplies of hemlock and Sitka spruce were found. With the help of James Shields, an English shipwright in Russian employ, the first European-style vessel built in Alaska was completed in 1794—a twin-deck craft of 23-foot beam, 73-foot length, and 180-ton displacement. Early records suggest that countless tons of wood were burned in making charcoal for forging bolts and nails. The vessel that emerged from all of these ashes was given a particularly apt name, *Phoenix*.

Alaska's first coal mine was started in 1855 under the Russian-

A ship sails into Coal Harbor, on the west side of the Kenai Peninsula, in 1789.

American Company at the present location of Port Graham, 30 miles west of the park. Miners were brought from Germany. Some evidence suggests the use as well of Tanaina Indians, under conditions of forced labor. Although the venture was a financial failure, the mine continued to produce coal until the United States acquired Alaska in 1867. The nearby coastal town of Homer was founded in 1895 by coal and gold prospectors.

Development of the gold-mining center named Sunrise on Turnagain Arm near Cook Inlet brought interest in constructing a railroad to tidewater at Resurrection Bay. Construction began in 1904 from the community of Seward under a company called the Alaska Central Railroad. With 41 miles of rail completed, however, the company went into financial receivership in 1908. Under new ownership, the track was extended to Turnagain Arm, a distance of 71 miles. Purchased by the federal government in 1915, the line became part of the Alaska Railroad. By 1923, Seward's population had reached 1,500.

Mineralized zones of the Kenai Mountains stirred some mining interest during the twentieth century, but little profit resulted. Some gold-bearing quartz veins were discovered in 1918 along the steeply walled fjords at Nuka Bay, and several small mines operated in the area between 1920 and 1940. The veins of white quartz were relatively abundant, but gold, pyrite, and other sulfides were found only in minor quantities and in irregular masses or pods. The Nukalaska Mine at Nuka Bay was opened in 1926, with some production from 1934 to 1940. After World War II, a group of Hawaiians tried to revive the mine, but the short-lived venture ended in the 1950s.

Another notable property in the Nuka Bay region was the Sonny Fox Mines in the amphitheater-shaped valley at the head of Surprise Bay. In a surrounding rock of graywacke and dark slate, a gold-bearing quartz fissure from 6 inches to 18 inches wide was evaluated by territorial mining engineers in 1925 and yielded assay samples of both gold and silver. Through 1940, the five known gold-producing ventures of the Nuka Bay region had a total yield of $166,000, according to U.S. Geological Survey reports.

The Good Friday Earthquake of March 27, 1964, badly battered the town of Seward. Earth shocks, followed by widespread fire, wrecked many structures. And then came inundation by an ocean seismic wave. Thirteen persons died and more than 90 percent of the city's industry was destroyed. The firm of Dun & Bradstreet estimated the city's loss to be total. Yet only one year later, after extensive rebuilding, Seward was given an All-American City award. Its remarkable recovery from wreckage and ashes recalls again the legendary symbol of the phoenix.

Seward in the 1940s.

Establishment of the Park

Long recognized as one of Alaska's most scenic coastal regions, Kenai Fjords came under study for possible national-park classification as a result of the Alaska Native Claims Settlement Act (1971), which directed such studies of public lands in the state. Seven years later, in December 1978, Kenai Fjords was designated as a national monument by presidential proclamation. In December 1980, Congress passed the Alaska National Interest Lands Conservation Act, which redesignated the area's 580,000 acres as Kenai Fjords National Park. Except in the case of valid preexisting rights to mining claims and other privately owned lands, the park is closed to all new mineral development, consistent with policy in other units of the national-park system. The park is closed to subsistence uses.

Disaster struck southern Alaska on March 24, 1989, when the supertanker *Exxon Valdez* struck a reef in Prince William Sound and spilled 10.8 million gallons of crude oil into one of the world's most bountiful and diverse marine ecosystems. The sound lies northeast of the Kenai Peninsula, and the data that follow do not apply to this park alone, where only 20 of 464 miles of the coast felt the impact. The overall devastation to wildlife was appalling. Some 500,000 birds may have died. As feathers became matted with oil, cold water soaked the birds' skin, causing hypothermia. Animals ingested oil in the course of preening and grooming. Bald eagles, their plumage heavily oiled, were unable to fly; more than 150 were found dead. Birds that spend most of their time on the water's surface were especially at risk. These included the common murre and marbled murrelet. Among marine mammals, sea otters also suffered from a lack of insulation caused by oil matting their fur. The oil slicks spreading southward from the spill washed over haulouts for hundreds of harbor seals just as the pupping season was about to begin. Many seals died, and survivors had elevated levels of oil compounds in their internal organs. Scavengers feeding on carcasses beame poisoned as well. Declines in the populations of fish, including salmon and herring, were also reported.

GEOLOGY

The presence of metamorphosed marine sedimentary rock indicates that the park's mountainous landscapes were formed by erosional and uplifting forces during Jurassic to late Cretaceous times. Major rock types are graywacke and slate, with some greenstone, chert, and limestone, occasionally interspersed with conglomerate. The graywacke is erosion-resistant sandstone whose faces form slopes of 70 degrees or greater. Highly faulted rocks have been infused with granitic flows. Glacial and fluvial (river-borne) deposits overlie the bedrock except on steep slopes.

The White Sculptor

Scenic headlands along the seaward ends of the Aialik and Harris peninsulas, along with their related offshore islands, are largely composed of massive granite intrusive rock dating to late Cretaceous and early Tertiary times of 120 to 65 million years ago. Major landforms of the Kenai Fjords' sedimentary and granite rock were shaped by glacial and stream erosion. Scouring action of glaciers during the Pleistocene epoch tended to deepen valley troughs and thus accentuated the earlier, preglacial relief of the region. Secondary processes shaping the landscape include avalanching and repeated cycles of frost cracking.

The Harding Ice Field is a vestige of a massive continental ice sheet that covered lands bordering the Gulf of Alaska during Pleistocene and probably late Pliocene times. Ice-field elevations range between 4,000 feet and 6,000 feet above sea level. The Bear Glacier, some 16 miles long at the east end of the ice field, displays numerous ice falls, where the moving river of ice flows over steep slopes. Several glaciers fed by the Harding Ice Field are undergoing a period of meltback, or retreat.

Opposite: The Harding Ice Field is a remnant of a massive continental ice sheet.

A Restless Earth

The fjord landscape is Alaska's most pronounced example of a global process of land formation and reduction. The North Pacific rim is an earthquake zone near the midpoint arc of the "Ring of Fire"—a geological term that describes the continent's interface with a tectonic plate under the North Pacific Ocean. The moving plate, which forms a crustal segment of the earth's surface, reaches depths as great as 60 miles below the ocean floor. Its edge, the Ring of Fire, stretches in a great arc from Oregon and Washington to Japan.

Movement of the Pacific's tectonic plate in the Gulf of Alaska is generally toward the northwest. This brings the plate into its most direct contact with Alaska's continental margin. The energy expended is the mountain-building force that, across eons of time, produced the Coast Range and, if theory holds, lifted the great arc of the Alaska Range which crowns the continent with its highest peak, Mount McKinley, at 20,320 feet. But the tectonic collision also produces mountain shrinkage. Along the Kenai Peninsula's outer coast, the plate angles downward and creates a subduction zone. As it underslides the coastal rim, the plate pulls down crustal material along its path and thus diminishes the surface landmass. Mountains lower into the sea, sometimes abruptly.

On Friday, March 27, 1964, at 5:36 P.M. the subduction plate lurched downward and created North America's most notable earthquake. The energy released was twice that of the San Francisco quake of 1906—reaching 8.6 on the Richter scale. The earth's crust quivered far from the epicenter. Water in underground aquifers and wells oscillated as far away as Puerto Rico and Denmark. A seismic sea wave (tsunami) hit the coast of California hours later. It damaged property along San Francisco Bay and swept four blocks deep into downtown Crescent City near the Oregon border. According to a U.S. Geological Survey report, "The entire earth vibrated like a tuning fork."

Radiating out from its epicenter near College Fjord in Prince William Sound (100 miles northeast of Kenai Fjords), the 3-minute temblor changed the configuration of more than 100,000 square miles of land through either uplift or subsidence. Across a 600-mile coastal arc in the Gulf of Alaska—with Kenai Fjords lying about mid-arc—the land in numerous areas sank more than 6 feet. Kenai Fjords' shoreline was dramatically altered, and its mountains and islands took another step down into the sea. It is by this process that an alpine cirque of the Kenai Mountains can become a quiet cove at tideline. Evidence of canyons submerged 300 feet below sea level attests to the longstanding nature of the subduction and movement of the Pacific's tectonic plate.

Climate

Kenai Fjords National Park lies in a maritime climate zone characterized by moderate temperatures and high precipitation. It is an area of Alaska influenced by the North Pacific Drift, which draws warm ocean currents into the Gulf of Alaska. Spring is usually the driest time of the year, and fall and winter are the wettest. Mean annual rainfall for Resurrection Bay is about 60 inches. Snowfall is common at sea level from November through April. Summer mean temperatures are in the high 50s (F), and winter lows range from 0° F to 20° F. Summer and fall contain many days of high overcast. Temperatures of ocean waters in bays and fjords vary from summer highs of 55° F to 38° F in winter.

Some fjords, such as Nuka Bay, are wide open to ocean storms, with few sheltered beaches or backwaters for protection. Within narrow passages, echo waves and crosscurrents can create a choppy wave action too severe for light watercraft. The Harding Ice Field should also be approached with caution. One attempted summer crossing of the ice field was stopped when a storm dropped 12 feet of snow in three days and then leveled the travelers' tents with winds reaching 100 miles per hour. Scenic grandeur should never be allowed to induce visitors to forsake caution.

Mussels anchor themselves by means of a group of silky filaments called a "byssus."

A Sparse but Hardy Vegetation

More than 90 percent of the Kenai Fjords landscape is unvegetated. Soils are shallow and acidic along higher slopes; at lower elevations a stony loam is prevalent. Older glacial moraines contain small deposits of loamy and acidic soils, while recent moraines are made up of gravelly till with little or no organic matter. A variety of grasses and sedges occur where decomposed peat has accumulated.

The fjord's narrow forest belt is dominated by western hemlock and Sitka spruce. Breast-high diameter of 3 or 4 feet is a maximum for spruce in this region. Coastal stands of the more salt-tolerant western hemlock commonly have diameters of 2 to 3 feet. Black cottonwood and mountain hemlock are found sporadically in the park. Along riverbanks and terraces, white spruce and cottonwood are dominant species. Dense brush in lower elevations, primarily alder, willow, and devil's club, often limits foot travel to well-used trails. Along the Kenai fjords, alder can survive at elevations of 2,000 feet. The highest vegetational community approaching glaciers and ice fields is made up of a low carpet of tough alpine species, such as mountain avens, dwarf birch, and a variety of grasses. The driest areas, talus slopes and rock screes, support such plants as arctic willow, sedges, and arctic wormwood

Left: Amanita mushroom. Right: The arctic willow.
Opposite: Black-legged Kittiwakes.

in individual pockets of soil, while adjacent areas are covered by prostrate forms, including diapensia and a variety of lichens.

Alpine meadows, or "herbmats," occur where well-drained soils are fed by water from snowdrifts or cirque glaciers. Herbmat vegetation is lush with grasses and sedges, along with such species as Ross avens, wormwood, Alaska spirea, and several forms of lousewort. On clear days above timberline, these colorful floral patches can be seen for miles. In areas where rock outcrops have intruded into alder and timber stands, the break in the shade canopy gives rise to serviceberry, red-berried alder, red currant, highbush cranberry, and mountain ash.

The Seashore

Ocean waters of Kenai Fjords support twenty-three species of marine mammals, including humpback whales, minke and gray whales, various porpoises and dolphins, sea lions, and fur seals. Harbor seals can often be seen floating on icebergs calved from tidewater glaciers. Sea otters, once hunted nearly to extinction, now populate the waters of Kenai Fjords in relative abundance. The luxurious nut-brown fur of the sea otter was the Russian-American Company's primary commodity and Russia's main

Overleaf, left: Gray wolves are present in parts of Kenai, but are furtive enough that sightings are rare. Right: Grizzly bear (Ursus arctos horribilis).

export item to the Orient during the eighteenth and nineteenth centuries. Were it not for the decline in sea-otter pelts, and the associated faltering of the Russian trade economy, it is arguable that the offer by the United States to purchase Russian America in 1867 for $7 million would have been rejected. History aside, an encounter with one of these charming, bewhiskered sea mammals can be the highlight of a visit to Kenai Fjords. They are often seen along quiet lagoons grooming their rich fur coats, or floating on their backs and clapping a stone to a sea urchin in preparation for a meal.

Black bears are found throughout most of the coastal area, and brown bears in the Resurrection River and Nuka Bay areas. Wolves, wolverines, and coyotes occur in the park, along with hoary marmots (at higher elevations), lynx, martens, and weasels. Mountain goats are found along higher ridges during summer. The Kenai Peninsula is the western-most extension of the goat's natural range in North America (Kodiak Island, farther west, has a transplanted population of mountain goats).

The most impressive spectacle of Kenai Fjords and nearby islands is provided by the great horde of marine birds that find nesting and rearing habitat along rock bluffs and sea stacks. Thirty species of sea birds—with total numbers exceeding 174,000—occupy discrete nesting habitats, in terms of both space and time. Crepuscular, or twilight, species such as the marbled murrelet can be heard more easily than seen as they repair to well-hidden nests in the wee hours before dawn. According to a 1976 survey, the colorful tufted puffin accounted for more than half of the 53,000 breeding pairs of sea birds. Entire cliff faces are taken over by squealing black-legged kittiwakes, which ranked second in numbers. Common murres, horned puffins, and glaucous-winged gulls ranked third through fifth among nesting species. The surf scoter is the most abundant sea duck along the Kenai fjords. The Chiswell and Pye islands hold the area's greatest concentration and diversity of breeding birds (including Alaska's northernmost colony of rhinoceros auklets), along with remarkable offshore scenery of sheer cliffs and surging waves. These two island groups are managed as part of the Alaska Maritime National Wildlife Refuge and are under the jurisdiction of the U.S. Fish and Wildlife Service.

Joining the whirling colonies of marine birds are numerous bald eagles that nest along island ledges and headlands. A coastal variety of the peregrine falcon also nests along cliffs in the outer islands. Chiswell Island, with its tilting slabs of rock, harbors the offshore islands' largest kittiwake colony, and Outer Island of the Pye Islands provides the largest sea-lion rookery of the fjord islands. More than 900 adult sea lions were counted there in one survey. And nearby, on a lone rock less than three acres in size, is the only habitat in the northern Gulf of Alaska used by nesting pairs of smoky-gray northern fulmars, possibly the outer limit of their oceanic range. In sum, the Kenai fjords and the offshore islands constitute one of the richest marine environments in the Gulf of Alaska.

SITES, TRAILS, AND TRIPS

Exit Glacier is the most accessible area of the park. The visitor access point is 13 miles by road northwest of Seward and along the Resurrection River Road. A .25-mile trail with wayside exhibits offers access to within .3 mile of Exit Glacier. For those desiring a closer approach, the trail continues across moraines and scoured bedrock to the glacier. From near the snout of the glacier, a steep trail climbs approximately 3,000 feet to the edge of the Harding Ice Field. The trail's steep switchbacks climb along the north edge of the glacier and offer overlook points and an occasional view of mountain goats in their upland environs. At the very top of the trail a spectacular view can be had of the sweeping expanse of the Harding Ice Field.

Charter-plane flights, most of which originate in Seward, are available for scenic flights over the beautiful Harding Ice Field. Flights may be scheduled for accession to the ice field for day cross-country skiing or for overnight excursions. The ice field is generally flat and appears to be free of crevasses except at the tops of glaciers. Explorers who climb the nunataks, the peaks isolated above the snow and ice, are rewarded with sweeping views. Even if one does not plan to venture far from the airplane, proper attire and precautions are required. Any extended trip on the ice field is hazardous, requires appropriate outdoor skills and equipment, and must be well planned.

Guided boat tours of the Kenai fjords, for either sightseeing or fishing, are available. The nutrient-rich North Pacific produces an abundance of salmon that spawn in the coastal streams. Dolly Varden, bottomfish, crabs, and shrimp are also sought. Kayakers can paddle past ice floes crowded with seals to the snouts of tidewater glaciers and to beaches suitable for camping. Both air-taxi and charter-boat services provide access to the coast. Guided backpacking and kayak trips are available. There are no established trails in the fjords. However, with a map and a desire to hike, several areas may be explored. Anyone attempting these trips, especially without guides, must be aware of the isolation and multiple hazards of these areas. Information on access is available through Kenai Fjords National Park headquarters.

KOBUK
VALLEY
NATIONAL PARK

Driftwood, dunes, the mighty Kobuk River, and the Jade Mountains.

KOBUK VALLEY NATIONAL PARK
P.O. BOX 287, KOTZEBUE, ALASKA 99752
TEL.:(907) 442-3890

HIGHLIGHTS: Great Kobuk Sand Dunes • Little Kobuk Sand Dunes • Kavet Creek • Onion Portage • Baird and Waring Mountains • Kobuk Valley and River • Salmon River • Caribou Herd

ACCESS: Commercial jet from Anchorage to Kotzebue; scheduled airlines to Kiana and Ambler; charter air service to landing areas in park.

SEASON: Summer season is June through September. Winter travel in March and April.

FEES: None.

FOOD AND LODGING: Available in Kotzebue, Kiana, Shungnak, and Ambler. Supplies are available in Kiana.

VISITOR CENTER: In Kotzebue at park headquarters; films shown in summer.

GIFT SHOP: Alaska Natural History Association outlet at park headquarters in Kotzebue.

PETS: Strongly discouraged.

PICNICKING: No designated areas.

HIKING: Unrestricted hiking; respect private property. Treat water from rivers and ponds.

BACKPACKING: Unrestricted, with some natural restrictions relating to arctic conditions.

CAMPGROUNDS: No designated campgrounds. Campers choose own sites; avoid private property and practice minimum-impact techniques. Portable stove necessary.

TOURS: Concessionaire-led floating, fishing, and backpacking trips. Aerial sightseeing by charter aircraft.

OTHER ACTIVITIES: Floating and fishing, with Alaska State license, in Kobuk River and its tributaries; bird-watching is especially good at Kobuk.

FACILITIES FOR DISABLED: None.

Note: Kobuk Valley National Park is north of the Arctic Circle. Prepare for severe arctic weather and isolation. Communications not available in park.

For additional information, see also Sites, Trails, and Trips on pages 203–206 and map on pages 188–189.

The unstable nature of the dunes discourages all but the most persistent plants.

PALE JADE WATERS OF THE KOBUK RIVER FLOW westward above the Arctic Circle for 200 miles before entering a mountain-rimmed basin where tundra and boreal forest blend with an unusual cultural history. The land between the gentle crests of the Baird Mountains to the north and the southerly Waring Mountains contains an improbable mix of biotic and geological anomalies, relict flora from a time when Asia and our continent were joined, and an arctic people who have made peace with one of the earth's most austere environments. A visitor may walk through living plant communities of ancient steppe tundra, and come to know landforms described not by mapper's jargon but by a language honed sharp by thousands of years of survival in arctic environs.

Some 300 square miles of sand cover about 11 percent of the basin's area. A thin mantle of vegetation has covered and stabilized most of the sandy substrate. Riverbanks along the valley's eastern third, near the confluence of the Kobuk and Hunt rivers, show open facings of gold-yellow sand where plant life has yielded to wind or water erosion. But midway in the Kobuk River's 50-mile course through the valley, a startling landscape emerges. Rolling sand dunes have held off encroaching vegetation and shift and swirl with seasonal winds much like their counterparts in desert regions of the world. The Great Kobuk Sand Dunes lie 40 miles above the Arctic Circle, and their 25 square miles represent the largest active sand-dune field in arctic latitudes. The meeting of stunted spruce trees gnarled by polar blasts and balmy yellow sand dunes where summer temperatures can soar to 100° F stands as one of Alaska's natural oddities. Near the valley's eastern edge, the Little Kobuk Sand Dunes cover an area of 5 square miles in a setting of rich herbaceous vegetation.

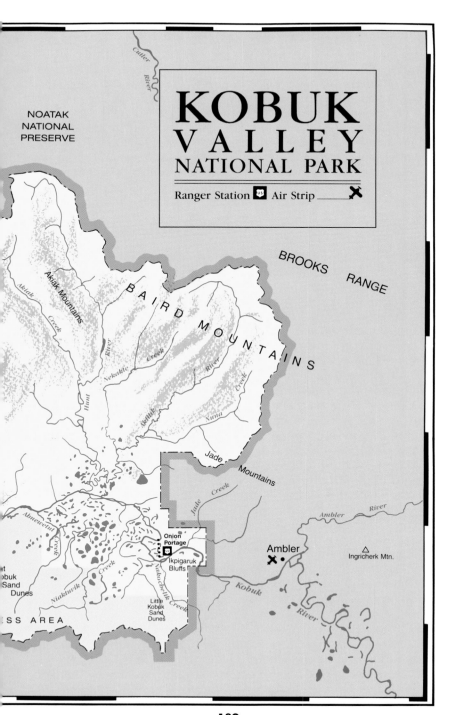

KOBUK
VALLEY
NATIONAL PARK

Ranger Station 🅄🅂 Air Strip ✈

NOATAK
NATIONAL
PRESERVE

BROOKS RANGE

Cutter River

Akak Mountains

Aklak Creek

BAIRD MOUNTAINS

Nekakte Creek

River

Creek

Hunt

River

Bettib

Nuna

Creek

Jade
Mountains

Jade Creek

Ambler River

Ambler
✈ •

Ingricherk Mtn.

Abnewetut Creek

Onion
Portage

Ikpigaruk
Bluffs

Nakochelia Creek

Niaktuvik Creek

obuk
Sand
Dunes

Little
Kobuk
Sand
Dunes

Kobuk

River

SS AREA

During late Pleistocene times, much of the continent north of Wisconsin lay buried beneath a glacial ice sheet. But the Kobuk Valley remained part of an unglaciated refugium, an area of relatively unaltered climate. The lower ocean levels of this period also exposed lowlands that linked the Asian landmass to Alaska. This now-submerged terrain is known as the Bering Land Bridge; it extended north to south a distance of 900 miles. The tying of the two continents made the Kobuk Valley an eastern extension of Siberia, and part of "Beringia" with respect to flora and fauna. It also provided a pathway to the New World for ancient nomadic peoples.

14,000 Years of Human Habitation

Our knowledge of the earliest established human culture in the Kobuk region rests on a combination of geological evidence, animal fossils, worked stone tools, and cautious surmise. When rising sea levels broke through the Bering Land Bridge about 14,000 years ago, the bands of nomadic hunters in the area used tools quite similar to those found across Alaska and as far west as northern Japan. The similarities in worked stone indicate widespread contact and trade. Hunters attacked with antler- and stone-tipped spears, and they butchered game with large stone cleavers. Though primitive and crude, the stonework was marked by a sophisticated chipping technique. Forebears of the Kobuk River Eskimos were part of this American Paleo Arctic cultural tradition.

By 6,500 years ago, people of the Northern Archaic Culture were using obsidian scrapers, oval knives, and side-notched projectile points—all markedly different from the slender spear points of the Paleo Arctic people. By this time limited forests had moved onto previously open grasslands, so wood for tools, dwellings, and fire enhanced survival. Bison and horse had become extinct and moose had not yet appeared. Caribou became a main staple. Evidence of fishing from lakes and streams emerged for the first time.

The Kobuk Valley of 4,000 years ago witnessed the flourishing of the widespread Denbigh Flint Culture. These successful hunters, who produced small, finely chipped stone blades for weapons and tools, have been ranked by specialists as the world's foremost lithic craftsmen. They spread as far south as Alaska's Bristol Bay region and soon combined coastal sea-mammal hunting with techniques for hunting caribou and fishing, thus broadening their subsistence survival base. Some anthropologists consider the Denbigh Flint people to be the first representatives of early Eskimo culture.

Amid abundant resources of the Kobuk Valley, certain influences began to give the people of the region a distinctive character. The Arctic Woodland Culture, as it has come to be known, evolved around a riverine environment. People of this culture migrated yearly to coastal areas around Kotzebue Sound, where they also engaged in trade. The presence of exotic materials such as obsidian (used to fashion tools and weapons) among the artifacts of these people indicates contact with Athapaskans of the interior. The Woodland Eskimos of the Kobuk prospered. Just below the mouth of the Hunt River, at a bend in the Kobuk River called *Ahteut,* more than 100 dwellings have been discovered along with artifacts and tools that date to as recently as A.D. 1250. These neo-Eskimo people are believed to be the precursors of today's Kuuvangmiit, the "people of the Kobuk."

Onion Portage, a caribou-lookout point, has been used by hunters for 12,500 years.

Exploration and Discovery

European contact came relatively late to this region of Alaska. In 1816, a German-Estonian officer in the Russian Navy, Otto von Kotzebue, sailed his ship *Rurik* into the sound that now bears his name. He was seeking a "northeast passage" to the Atlantic and did not find the narrow channel leading to the Kobuk delta. Ten years later, Fredrick Beechey, a young English lieutenant in command of the *Blossom*, discovered Hotham Inlet adjoining the Kobuk delta and established trade relations with some of the Eskimos of Kotzebue Sound. Some trade items from Russia were noted among the Eskimos. Rifles and gunpowder soon found their way into the Eskimo life style, along with liquor supplied by whaling ships stopping en route to arctic hunting grounds. However, in part because of rumors of hostile Natives along inland rivers, casual explorers avoided the Kobuk River.

In 1849, John Simpson, surgeon of the British naval ship *Plover*, saw the delta of the river Eskimos called *Kuuvuk* (big river), measured its width, and heard tales of villages far upstream. The year 1884 marked the beginning of American contact throughout the Kobuk River Valley. Two competing expeditions—led by Lieutenant J. C. Cantwell of the Revenue Cutter Service and by navy Lieutenant George Stoney—explored virtually the entire length of the watershed. Cantwell, using a steam-powered river boat, made it upstream to the outlet of Lake Selby. Stoney remained through the winter in the upper reaches and established Fort Cosmos, named for a favorite club in San Francisco.

Eskimo place-names of long standing began to give way to names provided by the newcomers. Explorers had a penchant for naming landforms after prominent people of the day. The north-rimming mountains of the Kobuk were named by Stoney in honor of Spencer F. Baird, secretary of the Smithsonian Institution. The Ambler River took its name from an American navy surgeon, James Ambler, who died after the *Jeanette* sank during its polar expedition in 1881. The Ambler River, an important tributary of the Kobuk, had a useful and descriptive Inupiaq (Eskimo) name for centuries that somehow was overlooked in the fever of exploration. Its original name, *Natmaaqtuak*, means "route for backpacking." This warns a winter traveler that the river's headwaters are too steep for a dog sled and that one should pack only what can be carried over the pass. Geographical features of the Kobuk Valley commonly bear rich and meaningful Eskimo place-names. Visitors floating the Kobuk's quiet waters might enjoy a summer stop along the bluffs downstream of Onion Portage called *Paungagtaugrug*—if they knew the name meant "place for wild blackberries."

Gold and Jade

Lured by rumors of pay dirt along the Kobuk, disappointed miners in the Klondike goldfields and Alaska's upper Yukon River moved westward in 1898. More than 1,500 miners briefly invaded the valley, establishing more than thirty camps. Ill-prepared for the valley's isolation from supply routes, and hard pressed to find a nugget, 80 miners died and many suffered badly from scurvy and phlebitis. Most moved on to better diggings to the southwest at Nome and Council. In 1909, marginal gold discoveries were made on the Squirrel River and Klery Creek, but production remained below $1,000 during the entire year. A town perhaps appropriately named Squirrel City emerged at the confluence of the Kobuk and Squirrel rivers. The name was changed to Kiana.

Jade, or greenstone, has long been part of Eskimo tradition in northwest Alaska as a raw material for tools, weapons, and ornamentation. Today, jade boulders weighing 20 tons are mined in the Jade Mountains near the village of Ambler, which is at the confluence of the Ambler and the Kobuk. The Kobuk's nephrite jade comes in a variety of colors, but thus far it has not gained the type of international market enjoyed by gemstone-quality jadeite from Burma. The Jade Mountains greenstone is not the type from which copper ore is extracted; it contains more magnesium and iron than the greenstone in Wrangell-St. Elias National Park, a major source of copper.

Establishment of the Park

After Congress passed the Alaska Native Claims Settlement Act in 1971, the opportunity came to evaluate the many cultural and natural resources on publicly owned lands along the Kobuk River. The area's outstanding archeological value has long been recognized, and the Onion Portage site has been declared part of an Archeological District. The area's landscapes and wildlife were preserved in essentially pristine condition, despite centuries of intense use by Native people. After almost eight years of study and planning, Kobuk Valley was declared a national monument in December 1978 by presidential proclamation. In December 1980, Congress passed the Alaska National Interest Lands Conservation Act, which redesignated the area's 1.75 million acres as Kobuk Valley National Park. The legislation specifically allows for nonwasteful use of subsistence resources by local Native and non-Native people, and calls for protection of these resources. The statute also defines as one of the purposes of the park the protection and interpretation of archeological sites associated with Native cultures in cooperation with Eskimo people of the area.

The landscape of the Kobuk Valley gained much of its present form from an ancient glacial advance that extended down the Kobuk Valley from the central Brooks Range to what is now tidewater at Kotzebue Sound. The terminal moraine left by the glacier's forward thrust forms the Baldwin Peninsula, on which the town of Kotzebue stands. A line of glacial drift found along the Waring Mountains indicates that at one point ice was piled up 800 feet above sea level.

The south flank of the Baird Mountains is formed of Paleozoic metamorphic rock with an east-to-west structural trend. This rock is composed mainly of phyllite—a lustrous slaty rock—and quartz-mica schist. Some greenstone, calcareous schist, and limestone are also present. The Jade Mountains are of Jurassic age with local serpentine bodies, along with deposits of asbestos and jade. Upper slopes of the Waring Mountains comprise stratified basaltic rocks in a matrix of mudstone and graywacke, a poorly sorted "dirty" sandstone. Well-preserved plant fossils are found in the Waring uplands, and a small vein of bituminous coal occurs near the Kallarichuk tributary of the Kobuk River.

Radiocarbon dating of underlying peat strata reveals that the Great Kobuk Sand Dunes have been active within the last 24,000 years. On the basis of his studies, Thomas D. Hamilton of the United States Geological Survey believes that the sand was first brought into the general area about 150,000 years ago by glacial-

The Great Kobuk Sand Dunes along Kavet Creek.

outwash streams that emptied into a large lake in the central Kobuk Valley. The medium-to-fine sand grains have a mean size of about 0.25 millimeter. Most grains are well rounded and frosted and are composed of quartz, phyllosilicates, and feldspar, with minor fractions of calcite. Under close inspection, the grains also reveal the wavy shatter lines (shell-shaped conchoidal fractures), ripple marks, and striations typical of glaciofluvial movement. Carbonate grains, constituting 2.5 percent of the sands by weight, also play a special role in the dunes' overall character. Recent research has shown that carbonates have leached out of the sand over time and formed rigid and compact sheets, now known as a relict calcium-carbonate crust. Largely composed of fine-grain carbonates and calcite crystals, this grayish surface mass ranges from 2 to 10 centimeters in thickness and appears as hard as street pavement. The relict crust covers the central and eastern portions of the dune fields.

The Great Kobuk dunes display a sequence of forms from U-shaped, concave dunes to the crescent-like barchan dunes identified with some of the world's most arid climates. Dune crests rise like ocean waves to heights of 100 feet. The valley's easterly winds of winter have heightened the sand field toward its western perimeter along Kavet Creek. Dunes pushed by the wind have inched the path of this stream westward and have buried several tributary springs. *Kavet*, an Inupiaq (Eskimo) place-name, means "moving sand," and serves warning that a traveler attempting a summer crossing on foot can sink in a mire of quicksand-like ooze.

NATURAL HISTORY

Climate

The visitor season might best be determined by reference to the Eskimo calendar. *Sikuvik* (October) is "ice time" as well as the breeding time for caribou. The river usually freezes in mid-October, and days grow short and nights cold. *Sikuigvik* (May) is "ice break-up time" and marks the start of spring (and a short period of mud and of rivers swollen with sediment). Between break-up and ice time, the valley has some of the finest weather in Alaska—except for the rainstorms of late August. Throughout a few weeks of June and early July, the arctic sun does not set. *Sikinaatchiak* (December), by contrast, is "no sun time."

The span of temperature along the Kobuk goes from winter lows of -55° F to summer highs of 85° F, though temperatures of

Overleaf: Shifting sand dunes first covered live spruce, then passed, leaving skeletons.

more than 100° F have been recorded on the sand dunes. Annual rainfall ranges from 10 inches near the river's delta to 20 inches along mountain headwaters. The area's annual mean temperature of 22.5° F assures a continuous zone of permafrost beneath a 1-to-5-foot layer of summer-thawed soil. The depth of the permafrost layer is unknown.

Life on the Dunes

The cold, arid climate and the well-drained, sandy soils of the region continue to approximate conditions that existed when the Bering Land Bridge joined Asia and Alaska. Remnants of the arctic steppe biome—sagebrush, sedges, and grasslands that continued to flourish in the corridor that was not covered by ice—are found today in the Kobuk Valley. Surviving among this flora—and found nowhere else—is a unique and colorful pea of the legume family: *Oxytropis kobukensis*. This purple-flowered, stalky oxytrope decorates the edges of the sand dunes and is distinguished from other peas by a purplish leaf base densely covered with silky white hairs. Such relict plants of the Kobuk were contemporaries of the long-horned bison, the saber-toothed cat, and the woolly mammoth—creatures that faded along with the last ice age.

Several colorful plants share with *Oxytropis* the open, sandy environs along the Kobuk River. Beach rye grass, common along arctic ocean-fronts, seems a striking anomaly on these inland sand dunes. Shifting winds bow the stalks of rye and scribe perfect circles in the sand. The thigh-high stalks of brome grass show their fuzzy purplish spikelets in early July. A pink-to-reddish carnation shares the sandy terrain with a wallflower having four-petaled, purplish blossoms that are some of the first to appear in June. The yellowish short-horned grasshopper of the family Acrididae hops among these tough and stalky plants. And neighboring creek bottoms and bogs provide habitat for the Kobuk's lone amphibian, the brownish-green wood frog. A reminder of the terrain's wild remoteness is close at hand in the splayed and ranging tracks of a passing wolf. The sand dunes, like a giant tablet, register the marks of their community members, from nodding grass stems to hunting carnivores.

Forest and Tundra

Radiating northward from the valley floor is a broad vegetational zone where two of the continent's biotic provinces—the boreal forest and arctic tundra—meet in an epochal shoving match along the

Arctic bell heather grows on rocky, dry tundra to elevations of about 2,200 feet.

northern treeline. This interface, or ecotone, consists of a shifting stress zone between competing adaptive forces, both driven by climatic change. As warming trends prevail in global weather, such species as birch, alder, and spruce begin advancing into tundra zones occupied by low-growing, leathery plant forms. Then, as cooling trends begin, the trees give ground to those same winter-hardened tundra species, which include mountain avens, heather, and rosebay. Elsewhere in the arctic, this change occurs abruptly, but in the Kobuk Valley the actively contested area ranges across several miles, north to south.

Core drill samples taken near the Ikpigaruk Bluffs along the Kobuk River indicate that successional layers of fossil pollen, or "pollen rain," have been laid down over the past 12,000 years. Spruce trees, common in the valley today, first appeared along the Kobuk a scant 7,000 years ago. Profiles of fossil pollen have also shown that, while Alaska's interior steppe tundra held several species of sagebrush, only one species (*Artemisia borealis*) was present among the Kobuk Valley's early flora. This tough, sweet-smelling sage continues to thrive today.

The diverse habitats of the area support an array of arctic wildlife. Small populations of Dall sheep are found along uplands of the Baird Mountains. River otter, beaver, and muskrat are common along streams flowing north from the Waring Mountains and along sloughs and oxbow lakes. Additional furbearers are red fox, marten, lynx, and the highly prized *kapvik*, or wolverine, whose pelts are utilized in traditional winter dress of Kobuk Eskimos. Marshes and meander scrolls along the river provide habitat for moose, waterfowl, ptarmigan, and shore birds. Chum salmon, arctic char, pike, and four species of whitefish are found in waterways and lakes. One unusual resident is the sheefish (*Stenodus leucichthus*), a highly prized subsistence and game fish found in only a few rivers of western Alaska and eastern Siberia. A predator of smaller fish, it can range up to 60 pounds. Eskimos call the fish *sii*.

Caribou: A Resource of the Ages

But the epic wildlife spectacle of northwestern Alaska that is shared by the Kobuk Valley is the restless, tide-like migrations of barren-ground caribou. Twice yearly they cross the Kobuk on their way between wintering grounds in the neighboring Selawik Valley and traditional calving grounds near the arctic coastline. Seasonal clocks are set by their movement. The Inupiaq (Eskimo) word for August, *Amigaiksivik*, means "the time for caribou to lose antler velvet." This creature holds a special place in the Kobuk Valley's panoply of resources.

The single trait that has best guided the caribou along its path of survival is its synchrony, the precise timing of behavior, movement, and physiology among individuals. This mechanism begins with the gathering of the herds on the winter range for the rutting, or breeding, period. Soon, during the lengthening days of early spring, the change in the photoperiod (the interval of exposure to light) brings on a shift in metabolism and the urge and energy to move. As though a signal had been given, widely scattered bands join and begin their northward trek. Once started, the annual migration gains in pace and concentrates into still larger herds. But along the route another influence is at work—the quality of snow, its texture, density, and hardness. Caribou instinctively avoid the brittle and sharp-edged crust that forms on spring snow. Instead, they seek out the softer and lighter snow that lies just to the north. In effect, they are herded toward ancestral calving grounds by a wave of changing snow texture that flows north with the advance of spring. This movement, synchronized with the fall rutting season and the ongoing gestation of unborn calves, inevitably leads the caribou to their tundra calving grounds just in time for fawning. Bands of cows scattered across the arctic give

Opposite: Caribou are the American members of the species that Europeans call reindeer.

birth to the greatest number of calves within a ten-day period in early June.

Tuttu is the Eskimo word for "caribou"—along with fifty-eight subtly shaded terms of description. From the traditional fur footwear of winter (*tuttulik*) to ancient bone and antler artifacts found in archeological excavations, the barren-ground caribou forms an elemental link between the Kuuvangmiit and their valley homeland. An example of the longstanding nature of this tie came to light on a gentle birch-covered hilltop along a major river bend known as Onion Portage. The high ground is an important lookout point used by today's hunters to watch for the first bands of caribou filing through passes in the Baird Mountains during fall migration. In July 1961, archeologist J. Louis Giddings of Brown University uncovered a stratified site at Onion Portage revealing consistent use by hunters of caribou over the past 12,500 years. Covering two acres and yielding thirty artifact-bearing layers, Onion Portage has been called by Henry Collins of the Smithsonian Institution "the most important archeological site ever found in the arctic." It is the benchmark by which other sites in the north are measured.

SITES, TRAILS, AND TRIPS

Prospective visitors are cautioned that the Kobuk Valley is in a remote part of Alaska surrounded by thousands of square miles of uninhabited land. There are no maintained trails or developed river crossings. Many of the safeguards and facilities common to parks in the contiguous forty-eight states will not be found here. Careful planning that involves the National Park Service is the key to a safe and rewarding visit.

Hiking on the ridges or lowlands is excellent. Stream crossings and wet tundra add "spice" to any trip, but the area has many fine routes. Most are unused. Park Service employees in the park or at the Kotzebue headquarters can give suggestions.

The Kobuk and Salmon Rivers

The length of a float trip on the Kobuk River is a matter of choice. The most ambitious plan would be to begin at Walker Lake in Gates of the Arctic National Park. From the lake, a tributary leads to the upper Kobuk at the boundary of the "Gates" Preserve. On a trip of 5 to 7 days, depending on the weather, the river route crosses the preserve and Native land between the parks and then

Opposite: The lynx uses its large, padded feet to move quickly over the snow.

enters Kobuk Valley National Park downstream of the village of Ambler. To a canoeist or kayaker on the Kobuk, the river appears to be a series of placid lakes. The river gradient is a drop of 2 to 3 inches per mile; at a point 150 miles upstream, the river is only 50 feet above sea level. While riverbanks are generally low, certain bends are marked by steep bluffs reaching more than 100 feet in height. Eroding faces of the bluffs often exhibit ice wedges and sometimes reveal fossilized remains of Pleistocene animals, grasses, and woody shrubs. The area near the confluence of the Hunt and Kobuk rivers offers a composite view of valley resources, including examples of wet and dry tundra, spruce and birch forest, and active sand dunes.

The downstream portage route at Onion Portage provides an interesting river stop. A series of small ponds and marshes align to form a shortcut that saves several miles of river travel. Now a winter snowmobile and dog-sled route, it was once an important summer portage route for Eskimo hunters and fishermen traveling up the Kobuk in traditional birch-bark canoes. In springtime, bouquets of a stalky wild chive with bright magenta blossoms grow in profusion on the gravel banks. This pungent relative of the onion has flavored Eskimo food over countless centuries, and its perky name, *paatitak*, long ago identified the portage from which the modern place-name derives. The internationally recognized archeological site at the upstream end of the portage lies mainly on Native-owned land within the park boundary.

One of the park's main tributaries to the Kobuk, the Salmon, flows south from high valleys in the central Baird Mountains. This picturesque waterway has been designated as part of the U.S. National Wild and Scenic Rivers System. Gyrfalcons and golden eagles nest along the steep walls of its upper reaches. Farther downstream, the sand bars often show clawed prints the size of pie plates left by wandering grizzly bears. Small pebbles of jade are found mixed in river gravel along the Salmon's mid-reaches, and by midsummer the sweet water takes on a delicate azure color. The flash of arctic char and chum salmon on upstream spawning runs can be seen in deeper pools. Arctic grayling with rainbow-colored dorsal fins are found throughout the waterway. The area below the Salmon River mouth is a favored resort of the Kobuk's husky sheefish, which use the river during summer runs from Hotham Inlet to their spawning grounds in the upper Kobuk watershed.

The remote Salmon River flowed into national consciousness in 1976 with the publication of *Coming into the Country* by John McPhee. McPhee describes a typical summer setting for August

The red fox often sleeps in the open, protected from the cold by its bushy coat.

18, 1975: the water temperature of the Salmon River is 44° F; the air temperature is 56° F at 7 A.M., and "the sky blue and clear—an Indian-summer morning. . . ." Three other tributaries of the Kobuk, less frequently floated than the Salmon is, offer as much or more to wild-river travelers.

The ancient Eskimo place-name *Kaqliikuuvik* offers some clue to what lies south of the Kobuk's banks near the outlet of Kavet Creek. The term means "the place to take off your waterproof skin boots." And it marks one of the access routes to the Great Kobuk Sand Dunes (where waterproof footwear would offer little advantage). However, caution should be used in this locale. Native-owned allotment land and a subsistence fishing area lie next to the creek mouth and along the east bank. The recommended route from the river to the sand dunes begins below the mouth of Kavet Creek. A low bankside bluff provides access to a gentle shoulder of open spruce forest that parallels the creek's west side and leads to the most scenic section of the dune fields. The walk through a mixed flora of reindeer moss, blueberries, and Labrador tea takes about one hour.

Park Service ranger stations along the Kobuk are at Onion Portage near the east boundary and at Kallarichuk Camp near the west boundary. The name for the latter campsite derives from the original Eskimo term *Qalukraitchiaq*, which means "place for big fish." Presumably this bit of information had little to do with the choice of Kallarichuk for a Park Service Camp. The stations are staffed full-time from June to September and intermittently the rest of the year.

Whether they have come via the upper Kobuk or the Salmon, most parties leave the lower Kobuk at Kiana, west of the park, or arrange for a bush plane on floats to pick them up somewhere along the river.

The Native Presence

Schoolchildren come from Kotzebue and other river villages to study Inupiaq culture at Onion Portage and other locations along the river. Eskimo village elders accompany the classes, along with teachers from local schools and National Park Service field personnel. The program was initiated by the regional Eskimo community to expand knowledge of Inupiaq culture and its rich history and to teach traditional survival skills.

Local subsistence activities vary with the season, but all harvest practices are of great importance to people who depend on such yields. These practices can be disrupted easily. The main caribou hunt takes place during late August and early September, at the time of fall migration. Traditional hunting locations at Onion Portage and Hunt River are especially sensitive then, just before the annual freeze-up. Most fishing camps are on private land within the park. The sixty-four private land parcels along both banks of the Kobuk River range in size up to 160 acres. A map showing Native allotments and other private lands is available from the National Park Service.

Along the Kobuk, the Park Service administers two other units from its headquarters at Kotzebue. Cape Krusenstern National Monument lies along the coast of the Chukchi Sea and Kotzebue Sound northwest of Kotzebue. In 114 lateral beach ridges, formed over a period of 5,000 years, are preserved artifacts representing every major period of Eskimo occupation of North America. The giant (6.5-million-acre) Noatak National Preserve, which abuts Kobuk Valley National Park on the north, contains the largest untouched river system in the United States. Each summer, the hardy fly far north of the Arctic Circle to fish or float a portion of its 425-mile course. Selawik National Wildlife Refuge abuts Kobuk Valley on the south.

Opposite: In Kobuk Valley, low-growing boreal forest and delicate arctic tundra occur together over the same terrain.

LAKE CLARK
NATIONAL PARK
AND PRESERVE

Autumn hikers in the Twin Lakes region encounter dramatic terrain

Lake Clark National Park and Preserve
4230 University Drive, Suite 311, Anchorage, Alaska 99508 or General Delivery, Port Alsworth, Alaska 99653
Tel.: (907) 271-3751 or (907) 781-2218

Highlights: Lake Clark • Chigmit Mountains • Mulchatna River • Mount Redoubt • Mount Iliamna • Tanalian Falls • Turquoise Lake • Portage Lake • Tlikakila River

Access: Air charter via Anchorage, Homer, Kenai. Commercial flights from Anchorage to Iliamna, 48 miles outside park.

Season: Best time is from early June to the end of September.

Fees: None.

Food, Lodging: At privately run lodges. An extensive business directory is available.

Visitor Center: At field headquarters in Port Alsworth and administration office in Anchorage. Orientation programs given in summer.

Pets: Permitted on leash.

Hiking: Wherever accessible, though private property and Native allotments are not open to the public. Carry water. Best in western preserve.

Backpacking: No permit needed for backpacking, but registration with ranger station strongly encouraged.

Campgrounds: No established campgrounds. Contained fires permitted. Showers available at lodges.

Tours: Lodges provide scenic tours. Aerial tours.

Other Activities: Climbing, rafting, kayaking, fishing with Alaska State license, and boating. Hunting in preserve.

Facilities for Disabled: None.

For additional information, see also Sites, Trails, and Trips on pages 232–242 and the map on pages 212–213.

JAGGED SPIRES AND STEAMING VOLCANOES towering above expansive glaciers that could seemingly swallow small states; waterfalls plummeting from hanging glaciers to wild and roaring rivers far below; dark, brooding forests; jewel lakes; rolling hills of alpine tundra where migrating caribou come to calve; shore birds and seals, bears and salmon: this is Lake Clark National Park and Preserve. It has been called the "essence of Alaska" and "Alaska's epitome"—and so it is. Here, all of the symbols and feelings of The Great Land are within reach. Vistas are at once awesome and intimate, complex yet understandable. Each tundra-lined pocket valley brings a smile, a feeling of joy and belonging, and a mute prayer of thanks.

Although much of the precipitous, ice-blanketed terrain remains incomparable, untrammeled wilderness, humans do belong and have lived in the lowlands in small numbers for thousands of years. Few others have come to know the park well, even though it is only 100 miles southwest of Anchorage, an hour's flight in a small plane. Lake Clark's Chigmit Mountains join the Alaska and Aleutian ranges and divide the park into two distinct sections: the coastal region bordering Cook Inlet to the east, and the lake and tundra country to the west. Although the Chigmits appear nearly impenetrable, they are slashed by Merrill, Telaquana, and Lake Clark passes. Small planes provide the only access to the interior of this roadless wilderness; once aground, visitors must travel by foot or boat.

Tanalian Mountain, above an outlet of Hardenburg Bay.

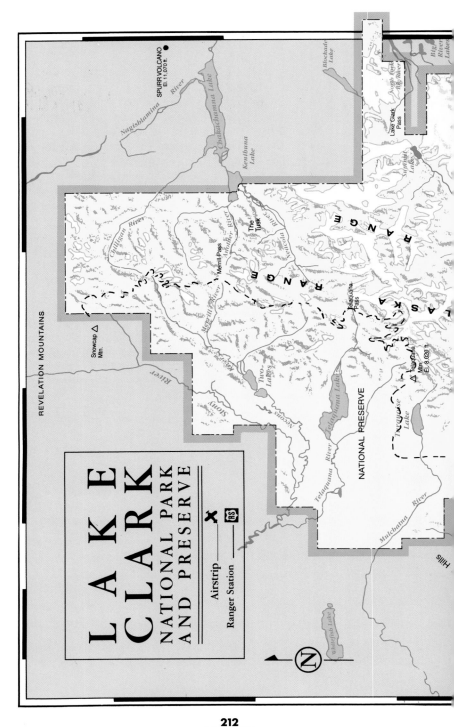

LAKE
CLARK
NATIONAL PARK
AND PRESERVE

Airstrip ✗

Ranger Station Ⓡ

REVELATION MOUNTAINS

SPURR VOLCANO ●
El. 11,070 ft.

Nagishlamina River

Chilikadrotna Lake

Kenibuna Lake

Blockade Lake

Lake Clark Pass

Big River Lakes

Arnch Park Big River

Summit Lake

Chilligan River

Merrill Pass

The Tusk

Amalik River

Neacola River

RANGE

RANGE

A L A S K A

RANGE

Telaquana Pass

Snowcap Mtn. △

Two Lakes

Stony River

Necons

Telaquana Lake

Turquoise Lake

Telaquana River

Mulchatna River

Hills

Whitefish Lake

NATIONAL PRESERVE

△ Telaquana Mtn.
El. 8,020 ft.

Ⓝ

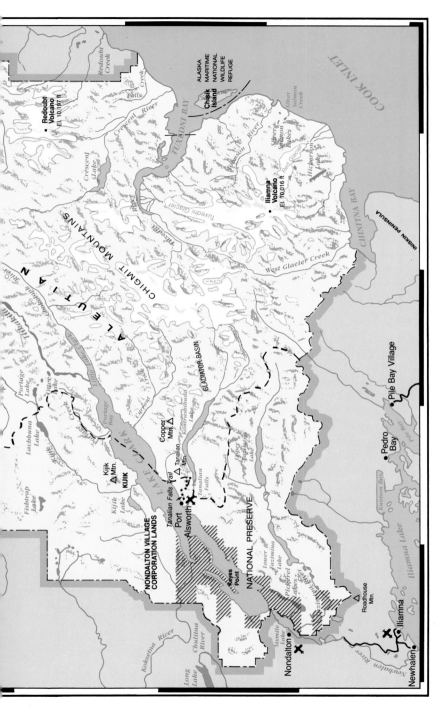

ALASKA
MARITIME
NATIONAL
WILDLIFE
REFUGE

Chisik
Island

COOK INLET

Redoubt
Volcano
EL 10,197 ft

Redoubt
Creek

Polly
Creek

Crescent
Lake

Crescent River

TUXEDNI BAY

Tuxedni Glacier

Johnson River

Silver Salmon
Lakes

Silver Salmon Creek

Iliamna
Volcano
EL 10,016 ft

Hickerson Lake

Red Glacier

CHINITNA BAY

West Glacier Creek

INISKIN PENINSULA

CHIGMIT MOUNTAINS

Big Mountain

A L E U T I A N

Tlikakila River

Tlikakila River

Neacola River

Little River

Lachbuna
Lake

Portage
Lake

Silver Salmon
Creek

Portage
Bay

Currant Creek

LAKE CLARK

GLADIATOR BASIN

Kontrashibuna
Lake

Kijik
Mtn.

KIJIK

Copper
Mtn.

Tanalian
Mtn.

Upper
Tazimina
Lake

Fishtrap
Lake

Kijik
Lake

Tanalian Falls Trail

Tanalian
Falls

Port
Alsworth

NONDALTON VILLAGE
CORPORATION LANDS

Keyes
Point

NATIONAL PRESERVE

Lower Tazimina
Lake

Pickerel
Lakes

Pile Bay Village

Pedro
Bay

Pile Bay

Knutson Bay

Iliamna Lake

Roadhouse
Mtn.

Kvichak River

Kokbsena River

Chulitna River

Long
Lake

Sixmile
Lake

Nondalton

Newhalen River

Iliamna

Newhalen

Early Cultures

Archeologists and historians are still piecing together the history of the ancient peoples of the Lake Clark area, but evidence indicates that humans have probably lived in the lake country, at least intermittently, for 6,000 to 8,000 years. The early people moved in after the glaciers retreated at the close of the Pleistocene epoch. People of the Northern Archaic Tradition left behind double-notched projectile heads that indicate that the culture was oriented toward hunting large animals. Living in temporary camps, they followed their game and left little trace of their passage.

Successors left miniature tools that seem to show a slight change in life style and an increasing reliance on sockeye salmon. Although several different cultures lived in the area through the ages, by the dawn of the Christian era the people were primarily Eskimoan.

The Tanaina

Three major cultural groups come together at the head of the Alaska Peninsula: the Eskimoan people from the northwest, the Aleuts from the southern peninsula and the Aleutian chain, and the Athapaskans from the interior. In the not-so-distant past, frequent clashes among the groups led to shifting territorial borders. By the 1700s, the Tanaina (pronounced duh-NI-nuh), people of Athapaskan culture, had become firmly established in the lake country and coastal areas of the park, although they frequently hid their villages to protect them from raiding parties of Eskimo-speaking peoples who lived to the west and south along the shores of Lake Iliamna. Other Tanaina lived around Cook Inlet on the Kenai Peninsula. Despite the distances and treacherous passes, trade routes were well established.

Unlike the Athapaskans of the interior, who had to move frequently to find food, the Tanaina of Lake Clark could depend on rich salmon runs and relatively abundant wildlife. This enabled them to build semi-permanent villages of "winter houses"—called *barabaras* by the Russians and *nichil* by the Tanaina. A barabara consisted of a living chamber dug out of the ground, log walls that extended above ground level, and a roof of sod and birch bark. Dirt and sod were heaped against the walls for added protection. They varied in size, but the largest might at times have housed ten to fifteen families. During the summer, families moved to "fish camps" and lived in tent-type dwellings.

Salmon, the summertime pulse of village life, were prepared for winter storage in several ways. Then, as now, dried and smoked

A fumarole on Mount Iliamna is active almost continuously.

fish were favorites. Sometimes the dried salmon were pounded to meal, immersed in bear fat, and kept in an airtight dried bear intestine. Another delicacy was *chuqilin,* or "soured fish," which was made by placing the salmon in spruce- or birch-bark-lined holes in the ground, covering them with grass and birch bark, and allowing them to ferment. As summer passed, the women gathered berries and put up "fall fish," while the men turned their attention to hunting bear, moose, caribou, sheep, porcupine, and migrating waterfowl. During winter months, people jigged for lingcod, trout, pike, and grayling through holes in the ice; trapped; and eagerly awaited the lengthening days that would bring the returning birds, the ice break-up, and eventually the salmon.

Kijik, the primary historic village area in the park, is near the mouth of the Kijik River on the northern shore of Lake Clark. Included in the several sites are an old village that contains pit remnants of barabaras and ground caches, and the more recent settlement of Kijik, which archeologists believe dates from the late 1700s or early 1800s.

Natives have long relied on hunting and fishing, which they may still do in the parks.

The Russians: Fur Traders and Missionaries

Following Vitus Bering's explorations in 1741, Russian fur traders (*promyshleniki*) ventured up the Aleutian chain and the Alaska Peninsula. In 1783, the Shelikov-Golikov Company was established on Kodiak Island, and in 1799 it was expanded and renamed the Russian-American Company. The Tanaina had a long history of trading with other people, so they adapted fairly easily to the idea of trading with the Russians.

The Russians often mistreated the Natives in these dealings; finally, in retaliation, the Tanaina obliterated a trading outpost on Lake Iliamna. Trade with posts on the Kenai Peninsula continued, however, and in 1818 members of the Korsakovsky expedition, which explored the northern Alaska Peninsula, found that the Tanaina of Lake Clark were accustomed to Russian trade goods.

Father Yakov Juvenal, a Russian missionary, entered the Iliamna-Lake Clark area in the 1790s to spread the Russian Orthodox faith and elements of Russian culture. He was executed by the Tanaina in 1796, possibly at Kijik. His opposition to the Tanaina practice of polygamy may have been a factor. Missionary activities in the area did not resume until the mid-1800s. The church at Kijik, one wall of which is still standing, was built in 1884.

Russian influence was apparent in several ways in the village of Kijik. The church played an important role in village life. Many villagers were baptized and men were obliged to cut their hair for the ceremonies. Burial customs changed from exposure of the body on an elevated open platform, followed by cremation of the remains, to interment. Barabaras gave way to log houses, and more single-family dwellings were built that reflected the new emphasis on the European concept of the family. Archeologists excavating Kijik found that the people had used a large variety of trade goods, a further expression of quiet cultural assimilation.

Copper, Gold, and Salmon

The Lake Country. The purchase of Alaska by the United States in 1867 brought no immediate change for the people of the Lake Clark region. The Russian-American Company was purchased by Hutchinson-Kohl and Company and reorganized in 1869 as the Alaska Commercial Company. Fur trading continued, but as fur prices declined interest turned toward the Bristol Bay canneries that opened in the late 1880s.

In 1891, *Frank Leslie's Illustrated Newspaper* sponsored the first known American expedition into the Lake Clark area. Alfred Schanz, the leader, was accompanied by John Clark, an agent of the

Alaska Commercial Company. Their mission was to explore the territory and gather data for the eleventh national census. Surviving on "hardtack, tea and tobacco," they faced bitter cold and near-starvation as they struggled up the wrong river. Realizing their error, they cut overland to a "mountain pot" in the distance, which proved to be the lake they sought. Schanz named the lake in Clark's honor, and they pressed on to find Kijik and food. Clark expressed surprise at the friendliness of the Tanaina and at the fact that they were wearing blue jeans!

Gold fever brought prospectors to the lake country. Efforts were concentrated on Portage Creek, which drains into Lake Clark, and on the Mulchatna River and Bonanza Creek to the west. In 1906, Charles Brooks and Charles von Hardenberg staked several copper claims along Kasna Creek above Kontrashibuna Lake. No one struck it rich, but mining activity increased trade in the area and brought the first long-term non-Native residents. One of them, Brown Carlson, married a Tanaina woman and lived at Kijik for a while before building his own place near Portage Creek. His wintertime solo treks to tend his 100-mile trapline made him a legend in the area.

The new arrivals brought more than a lust for gold; they brought disease. The Tanaina, unaccustomed to measles, smallpox, and influenza, were hit by a series of epidemics that decimated village populations. The epidemics, coupled with a desire to be closer to the trading post at Iliamna, caused the Tanaina to leave the village of Kijik between 1900 and 1910 and start the village of Old Nondalton on Sixmile Lake. When they left, they dismantled their log houses but left the church standing in memory of those who lay in the cemetery beside it. In the 1940s, the village was moved again to its present site at Nondalton.

Most miners left the area during World War I, and mining activity did not resume until the 1930s. Babe Alsworth, a pilot for Northern Consolidated, built an airstrip in the 1940s and began the present community of Port Alsworth.

The Coastal Plains. The story of the coastal plains area is similar, yet unique. Furs and minerals first drew fur traders and miners to the area. By 1890, the Alaska Commercial Company was using schooners or steamers to transport 100 to 200 canoe-loads of Native hunters to Chinitna Bay for the annual sea-otter slaughter. For years it was the richest hunting ground in the area. The Alaskan Petroleum Company staked claims and by 1896 had started drilling for oil just south of Chinitna Bay. Although that round of drilling ceased during World War I, visitors en route to the park today will see numerous, active offshore oil rigs.

Trapper, Tanalian Point, c.1939; he traveled with dogs, skis, traps, and two sleds.

The Cook Inlet salmon fishery grew in the late 1800s, but the lack of good harbors on the west coast restricted most canneries to the Kenai Peninsula and Kodiak Island. In 1909, a cannery was established on Chisik Island, which is just outside the park near the outlet of Tuxedni Bay. Operated as a cannery until the 1960s, it is now used as a support facility for commercial fishermen based on the Kenai. Visitors will also see set-net fishing at many points along the shore.

Lumber attracted settlers, and in the late 1930s sawmills were erected at Tuxedni Bay, near Polly Creek, and near the outlet of Red Glacier above Chinitna Bay. Many private in-holdings in the coastal plains area of the park date from this period.

Establishment of the Park and Preserve

Questions of land ownership and usage continue to be complex issues that affect the nature of Alaska's parks. The Alaska Native Claims Settlement Act (1971) entitled Native corporations to select a number of parcels of federal land for conveyance at a future date. One such corporation, the Cook Inlet Region, Inc. (CIRI), initially selected both coastal and interior parcels in the Lake Clark area, the heartland of the current park. However, in the Cook Inlet Land Exchange, CIRI agreed to relinquish interior selections, thus paving the way for the establishment of the park. President Jimmy Carter gave national-monument status to Lake Clark in 1978. On December 2, 1980, Congress passed the Alaska National Interest Lands Conservation Act, which changed Lake Clark's status from monument to park and preserve. The legislators recognized the needs of the Native and non-Native residents and provided for subsistence use in the park and preserve. The approximately 2.6 million acres of parkland include nearly all of the rugged Chigmits, the coastal plain from Polly Creek to Chinitna Bay, and part of the lake country on the western flank of the mountains. The 1.4-million-acre preserve encompasses the remainder of the lake country and the low rolling tundra west of the park.

Some questions of land ownership, however, were not resolved quickly. In addition to patented in-holdings, Alaskan Natives were entitled to select sites called "Native allotments." Although conveyance was not completed immediately, a number of prime locations, including most of the shoreline of Lake Clark itself, were selected. Large-scale development, whether residential or recreational, would entirely change the nature of the park and the experience it offers visitors.

GEOLOGY

It is impossible to fly over the jumbled, apparently endless mass of peaks known as the Chigmits without marveling at their complexity and wondering about how they were formed. So many geological processes have been involved that it is not a simple story. Intrusion, folding, uplifting, underthrusting, volcanism, earthquakes, faulting, and glaciation have all played roles in shaping the landscape.

Early Formations

The great mass of the Chigmits is primarily granitic and was formed sometime during the Jurassic period, 135 to 180 million years ago, when molten rock (magma) was forced up (intruded) into older rocks of the Paleozoic and early Mesozoic eras. In the process, the older rocks were often folded or flexed and tilted. In the Tuxedni Bay area, visitors can see sedimentary rocks from the Jurassic that appear to be diving into the sea. The Chinitna Shale beds are especially visible on the west shore of Chisik Island and the shores of Chinitna Bay. The marine fossils in the underlying Tuxedni Sandstone bespeak a time before uplifting, when the seas covered the coastal plains. On Fossil Point, visitors may discover

A glacier-carried rock bears the image of a fault caused by tectonic activity.

fossil remnants of various mollusks that resemble clams.

Tectonic Activity

According to the theory of plate tectonics, the earth's crust is not a continuous, even mass, but is divided into a number of sections, or "plates." The areas where different plates come into contact with each other are often characterized by violent activity. The Chigmits are such an area. Here, the oceanic crust of the Pacific plate dives under (subducts) the North American plate, creating powerful stresses in the crustal material. This area, or subduction zone, which lies only 30 miles beneath the Kenai Peninsula, dives to more than 100 miles beneath the eastern portion of the park. Volcanoes, earthquakes, and faults provide visible, bone-shaking evidence of the underlying stresses.

Mount Spurr (11,070 feet), which lies northeast of the park, Mount Redoubt (10,197 feet), and Mount Iliamna (10,016 feet) top a string of more than eighty volcanoes that extends 1,600 miles along the Aleutian chain. Iliamna has sent steam and volcanic gas skyward more than half a dozen times since 1768, and active fumaroles on the summit attest to continuing thermal activity at the volcano. Redoubt erupted in 1966, spewing tumultuous clouds of ash to heights of 40,000 feet. A major series of eruptions in 1989 and 1990

Overleaf: This boulder-strewn moraine marks the former length of Shamrock Glacier.

began after earthquakes struck beneath the volcano. Billowing ash clouds from Redoubt disrupted air travel in southern Alaska and damaged four commercial jets. In the most dangerous incident, December 15, 1989, a jetliner carrying 231 passengers entered an ash cloud, lost power in all four engines, and dropped 4,000 feet in altitude before the pilot was able to restart the engines. Mount Spurr erupted in 1992 and 1993.

Earthquakes are commonplace in the park. The center of earthquake activity lies 55 to 110 miles beneath the surface, reflecting the subterranean stresses created by the movement of the crustal plate.

Geological stresses also result in faults, and the most obvious fault in the area lies along a line beneath Lake Clark itself and then proceeds through Lake Clark Pass. Geologists have found that rock beds on the north side of the lake are fully 8 miles east of the corresponding beds on the south side. The fault appears to be a relatively late development because volcanic rocks from the Tertiary period (3 to 65 million years ago), as well as the Mesozoic granites and the slates, cherts, limestones, gneisses, and schists from the Paleozoic, have been displaced to the same extent.

Glaciation

On the western flank of the Chigmits, beautiful glacier-polished walls of granite rise above the head of Little Lake Clark, silently testifying to the major role glaciers played in carving the park landscape. Only the serrated ridges, spires, and peaks of higher elevations escaped glaciation during the ice age, as the ice, following existing drainages and fault lines, flowed into the lowlands. Large tongues of ice from the Tlikakila, Chokotonk, and Currant Creek drainages converged to scour the great area that is now Lake Clark. In 1891, Albert Schanz tried to measure the depth of the lake and was astonished to find that he ran out of line at 101 fathoms (606 feet) without reaching the bottom. The deepest area has since been measured at 852 feet.

During the height of the late Wisconsinan glacial age, some 18,000 years ago, ponderous masses of glacial ice from the Alaska, Chigmit, and Aleutian ranges flowed not only westward into the lowlands, but also eastward into the Gulf of Alaska. Glacial activity fluctuated considerably during this time, and the Lake Clark area saw at least three major advances and retreats, the last major retreat beginning 6,000 to 10,000 years ago.

Current glaciers are receding, leaving characteristic U-shaped valleys and other reminders of their passage. Hikers enjoying the park area's smooth, tundra-covered alpine meadows occasionally encounter house-sized granite boulders and may pause to consider

the power of the glaciers that carried and deposited such behe-
moths. Terminal moraines deposited by retreating glaciers form
the southwestern shores of the many lakes. Lateral moraines composed of material that accumulated on the sides of advancing
glaciers can be found high on mountainsides, indicating the thickness of the ice in ages past. Churning rivers, murky with glacial
silt, turn lakes milky and change their color from deep blue to
turquoise or green. Visitors cannot pass through the park without
feeling the presence of the glaciers.

One remnant of a settlement on Lake Clark dating from early in the twentieth century.

The water world of glaciers, lakes, and rivers is ruled by the Chigmit Mountains, which force clouds from the Gulf of Alaska and Bristol Bay to rise and release their moisture. Frequently enshrouded, the 5,000- to 7,000-foot peaks may gather snow during any month. Their mass creates a weather wall that divides the park into two major climatic areas. The southeastern coastal corner, which bears the brunt of many storms, receives far greater rainfall and snowfall than the interior lake country. The maritime temperatures are more consistent and have a smaller range than the record Port Alsworth high of 86° F and low of -55° F.

The differences in temperature, precipitation, and landscape create a variety of ecosystems and impose latitudinal boundaries for some species. Sitka spruce grow no farther northwest than the Chigmits, while Dall sheep and black bears rarely venture farther southwest. Certain species of alpine tundra plants cling to the western slopes of the Chigmits but are found no farther south on the peninsula.

The Coastal Flank

Noted for annual precipitation of 40 to 80 inches, the southern coastal area produces mature stands of Sitka spruce and luxuriant growths of the hiker's banes, alder thickets and devil's club. Steep, rocky cliffs provide protection for rookeries of cormorants, kittiwakes, and other sea birds, while the tidal basins offer playgrounds and feeding areas for harbor seals and beluga whales. Rivers teeming with summer runs of red, pink, chum, king, and coho salmon attract bears, eagles, and osprey. Farther up the coast, the cliffs give way to tidal salt marshes and grasslands of bent grass, fireweed, and ferns. Precipitation diminishes, forests thin and change from Sitka to white spruce, and the country seems to open up, providing better browse for moose. Above the marshes, grasslands, forests, and alder thickets rise the higher slopes of alpine tundra.

The Lake Country: Boreal Forests and Tundra

Low-lying lakes in rain-rich areas are fringed with boreal forests of black and white spruce, paper birch, balsam poplar, and some aspen, which provide homes for many creatures. Moose browsing birch and willow wander river drainages and forest margins seeking out the plentiful lowland pools and marshes where they dine on *Equisetum* (horsetail), pond weeds, sedges, and grasses. Spruce and birch bark are gustatory delights for porcupines. Beavers sup-

Two shy maiden plants.

plement a bark diet with aquatic plants, roots, and grasses. Hares, too, eat spruce twigs, needles, and bark as well as grasses and hardwood buds. Chattering red squirrels run the pathways of spruce limbs to gather cones they will store for the winter in the middens beneath the trees. They are joined on the wildflower-carpeted forest floor by voles and shrews that harvest grass seeds and dig homes among the roots.

The forests offer shelter, food, and nesting areas for many migrating birds. During the early summer, the ruby-crowned kinglet holds forth from the treetops, while varied and hermit thrushes, white-crowned sparrows, dark-eyed juncos, and others join in song from below. Haunting cries of loons and grebes pierce the evening stillness. As night falls, the tireless Swainson's thrush sings the world to sleep.

The plant-eating animals and birds are prey for the park's carnivores. Lynx, wolves, fox, mink, weasels, wolverines, martens, and black and brown bears roam the woodlands, although not all subsist entirely on meat. Bears feed regularly on grasses, roots, and berries; they also feast at the annual banquet of spawning salmon, sometimes carrying the carcasses well back into the trees before dining. Bears and other large carnivores leave the woodlands to scour the high slopes and tundra for other sources of food.

The high-lake country offers different habitats. Less precipitation and colder temperatures encourage smaller, tougher plants that are adapted to such conditions. Spruce and hardwood forests blend into rolling tundra-covered hills. Dwarf birch, shrubby and mat willow, sedges, grasses, and lichens of the tundra are the favored food of the caribou. A portion of the Mulchatna herd (which numbers 160,000) migrates to the Turquoise-Telaquana lakes area to calve each spring. With increasing elevation, the tundra becomes drier and supports shorter, more mat-like vegetation—highly

Overleaf, left: Alpine blueberry. Right: Red alpine bearberry and lingonberry leaves.

desirable habitat for ground squirrels and Dall sheep. The sheep generally roam the ridges in small bands, but spring-time may find ninety or more converged on a mineral lick.

The Sockeye

Assembling glacier-fed rivers and nutrient-rich creeks, Lake Clark channels the headwaters of the Kvichak drainage, the world's finest spawning ground for the sockeye, or red, salmon. During one ten-year period, this system provided 55 percent of the sockeye caught in Bristol Bay, 33 percent of those caught in the United States, and 16 percent of the world catch. (Some 30 to 35 million sockeye made the "run" in Bristol Bay in 1981.) So important are salmon to the Bristol Bay fishery and local subsistence users that protection of the waters for the perpetuation of this species was one of the primary reasons the park was established. Although important, the waters that feed the Kvichak constitute only a small part of the living rivers of the lake country. The Mulchatna, Chilikadrotna, Koksetna, Telaquana, and Stony rivers of the Nushagak and Kuskokwim drainages swell with runs of king, silver, pink, and chum salmon as well as sockeye. Still, it is the sockeye that dominates not only Lake Clark but also the entire Bristol Bay area. *Sockeye* is a corruption of a southern British Columbia Indian word for this fish, *sukkai*.

Sockeye salmon are anadromous: after spending 4 to 8 years at sea and traveling thousands of miles, salmon instinctively return to

Trumpeter swans, threatened in the lower forty-eight states, range into Alaska.

The weasel-like marten lives in fallen logs or holes in trees.

the streams of their youth. By the time the sockeye reach the fresh-water lakes, they have stopped feeding and rely on stored body oils, fat, and minerals to sustain them through spawning. A red pigment called carotene, which is found in salmon prey, is stored in the fat. As the fat is absorbed, the blue-black backs and silvery sides characteristic of salt-water sockeye change to a fluorescent red trimmed with iridescent olive-green head, tail, and fins. The sleek body of the male contorts to a humpbacked, hook-jawed, long-toothed fighting physique that helps him battle rival males and fish of other species that try to devour the eggs.

Most salmon proceed through the lake to rivers and streams to spawn, but a few use lakeshores. After entering the spawning area, the female slaps the gravel with her tail to build a nest, or "redd." Males fight to join her and cover the deposited eggs with a secretion called milt. The female continues upstream, slapping the gravel so that it will cover the newly laid eggs and extend the redd for additional egg deposits. Within two weeks after spawning, both the male and female die. By spring, the eggs develop into fry, which leave the protective gravels of the streams to venture into the lakes. There they stay for a year or two before heading to sea as smolts, 3- to 5-inch youngsters.

Of the 3,000 or more eggs each female may lay, only a few will return to the sea. The eggs and fry fall prey to mergansers, grebes, and other birds, as well as to other fish. Lake and rainbow trout, grayling, whitefish, and candlefish, among others, also inhabit the lakes. Survival is not an easy matter.

Sites, Trails, and Trips

In spite of thousands of years of habitation, Lake Clark is essentially a wilderness area, and the mountainous region is most decidedly so. There are no roads to lead visitors briskly and passively through the park, no campgrounds, and only one short developed trail. The general management plan for the park and preserve calls for a systematic study of trail needs, followed by the preparation of a trail development and maintenance program. For the short term, no actual trails are planned. In areas of heavy use, such as popular camping sites on major rivers and lakes, pathways will be established in order to minimize erosion. Longer trails will be designated and information will be placed at trail heads, but hikers will continue to select their own routes.

Visitors skilled in wilderness travel will find extraordinary hiking, climbing, kayaking, and rafting opportunities. Others will prefer aircraft tours of the area and guided photographic, fishing, and hunting (in the preserve only) trips offered by private lodges. Most visitors prefer to explore the park between late June and the end of August, when temperatures and climatic conditions are most benign. But September offers the glory of golden birch trees playing against the dark conifers. Lake Clark itself is a most beautiful view. Lodges and campsites are available at the lake.

The Developed Trail

Visitors to the park's field headquarters at Port Alsworth on Lake Clark will enjoy the easy 5-mile round-trip hike to exquisite Tanalian Falls. Spectacular on either clear or misty days, the Tanalian River thunders into pools rich in grayling before continuing its rapids-choked descent to the lake. The trail begins on the southern side of Hardenburg Bay, past the end of the second airstrip. Its meanderings through black spruce–hardwood forest and past bogs and ponds offer visitors a good opportunity for spotting a moose dipping its muzzle into the water in search of succulent aquatic plants. Looking up from time to time, one may sight Dall sheep on the slopes of Tanalian Mountain, which rises on the northeast side of the trail. Visitors should always be alert for bears. Although traveling quietly does allow a hiker to see more animals, it is also desirable to make some noise to let the bears know that someone is coming. Generally, they will move away when not startled.

Cross-Country Hiking

Although there is only one regular trail, much of the terrain lends itself to exciting cross-country hiking. Coastal beaches, lakeshores, peaks, ridges, and the expanses of rolling tundra hills beckon those who would know the park. Most of the hikes are not for neophytes. Adequate preparations for all of the following situations are essential: enduring rapid, unpredictable changes in weather, including long periods of rain with high, gusty winds; fording high-water streams and rivers; managing scree slopes, tundra tussocks, quicksand, batallions of bugs, and crawls through alder thickets; encountering bears and other animals; and patiently awaiting overdue pickups. The routes suggested are just that—suggestions, not detailed plans to be followed to the letter. Each hiker may take a different route through unnamed valleys past unnamed peaks; that is what wilderness hiking is all about. Hikers should always carry topographic maps, avoid privately held land, and check with rangers for current conditions.

Tanalian Mountain. Rising east of Port Alsworth, the mountain

Overleaf: Headwaters of the Telaquana River, near the crest of the Alaska Range.

provides an excellent vantage point for views of Lake Clark, Kontrashibuna Lake, Tanalian Falls and River, and surrounding peaks. Sights are likely to include moose, bears, sheep, or eagles. Hikers should take lunch and water and plan to spend the day. In August, wild blueberries and cranberries make excellent snacks along the way. From headquarters, there are several ways to approach the peak. A frequently used route begins on the trail that leads to Tanalian Falls and heads up a likely ridge along the way. Alternatively, one can walk the beach to a suitable ridge. Traveling along ridges is advisable in order to avoid as much alder-thrashing as possible. Once above the alder, the going becomes much easier. The approximate distance is 7 miles round trip, with a 3,600-foot gain in elevation.

Telaquana Lake to Lake Clark. A number of excellent, short hikes from base camps on Telaquana, Turquoise, Twin, or Portage lakes provide good vantage points for observing the work of the glaciers and scanning the hills for wildlife. Each lake is unique, delightful, and easily worthy of an entire vacation. Experienced hikers may wish to get a better feel for the country by hiking from lake to lake, traveling through distinctive vegetation zones, seeing different animal habitats, and watching the terrain change. The trip may easily be broken into four sections and hikers may choose to do one or all, depending on the time available and their level of expertise. The first two sections described below are easier than the latter two. Assuming no long detours, the total length for all four sections is about 57 to 60 miles, one way. (A hiker's guide to the historic Telaquana Trail—actually a route—was scheduled for printing in 1995. The approximate route is also shown on USGS topographical maps. There is an NPS ranger station at Telaquana Lake.)

Telaquana Lake to Turquoise Lake. While trekking through wet and alpine tundra, hikers may see hundreds of caribou as well as bears and sheep. Starting from the southernmost bay of Telaquana Lake, the 16-mile route leads upward through thick willow and spruce vegetation to timberline at the 1,700-foot level. Plenty of insect repellent or netting may be needed. Above timberline, the terrain is still steep, but the alpine tundra makes walking considerably easier. From this slope there are excellent views of Telaquana Lake and the Revelation Mountains to the northwest. Once atop the ridge, hikers face only a fairly short hike down to Trail Creek and good campsites. Visitors planning to camp before Trail Creek should carry water. High water often makes it neccessary to head east to where the stream braids in order to cross safely. Once across, hikers should head southwest again, climbing and crossing two streams. The second is the last good source for water before Turquoise Lake. The caribou trail can be followed through the notch in the hill to a flat, moist plateau of hummocks and small pools. By traveling at the 3,500-foot level after reaching this plateau, hikers can avoid major stream crossings and continue to a rocky hillside overlooking Turquoise Lake. There, the land dries out again and there are some decent campsites. Once the lake is in view, the easiest descent involves heading east and staying high until northeast of the major point of land on the south shore.

Turquoise Lake to Twin Lakes. Heavy doses of glacial silt give Turquoise Lake its vivid, unforgettable color. Visitors, captivated by this aesthetic amphitheater, often find themselves reluctant to depart for new territory. From the head of the lake, this 13-mile route begins with a walk up the drainages to the receding glaciers. Climbs of surrounding peaks offer extraordinary views. Visitors should keep in mind, however, that Turquoise Lake has a well-deserved reputation for extremely strong winds that rise with no warning and funnel down the valleys. Campsites must be chosen with care, as there are no trees and few windbreaks. From the northwestern shore of Turquoise Lake, it is usually possible to cross the Mulchatna River right at the outlet or downstream 400 to 500 yards, but it is very likely to be at least knee-deep. After crossing and thawing out, hikers should invest the effort to climb the ridge and see the views rather than simply skirting the base to Twin Lakes. Maintaining elevation also means easier hiking on dry tundra, less brush, and less harrowing stream crossings.

Twin Lakes to Portage Lake. Twin Lakes country is hikers' heaven. A narrow margin of trees along much of the lakeshore protects picturesque campsites. The trees give way quickly to alpine valleys and scree slopes. (An NPS ranger station is situated at the southwest cove of the lower lake, 1 mile south of the outlet.) Most of the day hikes are fairly straightforward, but distances can be deceptive, and plenty of time should be allowed. During low water, the Chilikadrotna can be forded about half a mile below lower Twin Lake. The channel connecting upper and lower Twin is usually fordable through late June, but caution is advised. During high water, it is simply better to have a boat. From the southern shore, Portage Lake may be reached in 17 miles either by skirting the ridge southwest of lower Twin Lake and following it southeast to the Kijik River or by climbing through the low pass just southeast of the connecting channel and dropping down steeply to the Kijik. The Kijik River is swift and crossings may prove difficult. During low water, it can be crossed just west of Portage Lake. High water may require an easterly walk toward the river's source for safe crossing.

Portage Lake to Lake Clark. Portage Lake, a small tarn tucked high in an alpine valley, is a classic gem. There are good sites for base camps at the east and west ends of the lake. Animal trails connect the two and lead through spruce-birch forests interspersed with tall grass, alders, and willows. Currants and the watermelon-flavored berries of twisted stalk are much in evidence, but hikers must beware of the baneberry, the only poisonous berry in the park. A climb to the rim of the waterfall gorge southwest of the lake or a hike to the ridge overlooking Otter Lake offers unsurpassed alpine views. The routes from Portage Lake to Lake Clark involve thicker vegetation and more demanding travel than most of

Forests thrive on the banks of Lake Clark.

the previous hikes. Again there are several possibilities, but the 11-mile preferred route is to walk down the south shore to the west end of Lachbuna Lake. Hikers must be careful fording the Kijik and must beware of quicksand at the east end of Lachbuna. The route then moves up the drainage to the south, perpendicular to the outlet of Lachbuna. It should be followed south over the ridge until it drops into alder-banked Portage Creek. After doing battle with the alders, hikers eventually emerge on the shores of Lake Clark.

More Primitive and Demanding Hiking Routes

It is both impossible and undesirable to delineate all of the exciting routes in the park. Part of the thrill lies in finding a new, undescribed place. However, a few routes are so spectacular that they demand

mention. They are frequently difficult and lined with boulder fields, bogs, or quicksand, but they allow entrance into the inner sanctum, the mountains of Lake Clark. From Telaquana Lake through Telaquana Pass, down the Neacola River to Kenibuna Lake is one such route. Up Another River is another. The hike through Merrill Pass to the Tusk, a geological formation, is beautiful. Rangers should be consulted before any of these routes is attempted.

The Coastal Area

Cook Inlet beaches offer good day hiking and, in some areas, good clamming. Hiking the slopes is generally less enticing, however, because of thick walls of devil's club and alder. Hikers willing to brave the brush will find good views from the ridges behind Tuxedni and Chinitna bays. The hike up Middle Glacier Creek to Middle Glacier on Mount Iliamna is passable and affords tidewater access to one of the two active volcanoes in the park. It is possible to traverse the park via Tuxedni River, over the glaciers, to Kontrashibuna Lake, but this route requires technical glacier work and rock climbing.

Lodges at Silver Salmon Creek, Chinitna Bay, and Crescent Lake provide a support base for sport fishing, hiking, and boating. Camping sites are plentiful, but particular precautions for brown bears must be taken. All visitors should take care to respect private property and the rights of commercial fishermen.

Chisik and Duck islands, at the mouth of Tuxedni Bay, are units of the Alaska Maritime National Wildlife Refuge, which was set aside to protect the sea-bird colonies.

Climbing

The possibilities for climbing in the park are virtually endless. The two volcanoes, Iliamna and Redoubt, receive the most attention, but literally hundreds of lesser peaks are alluring.

Kayaking the Lakes

Because the absence of trails can make hiking difficult, many visitors prefer to travel by boat or combine hiking and boating. Boats allow more freedom to explore a lake without moving base camp frequently. Lake Clark and Little Lake Clark, Kontrashibuna Lake, the two Tazimina Lakes, Crescent Lake, Twin Lakes, Turquoise Lake, Telaquana Lake, and the Two Lakes present interesting paddling. The choice of a lake should depend on the type of

Opposite: Trumpeter swan cygnets hatch after a thirty-five-day incubation period.

surrounding terrain and animal habitat desired. Not so very long ago, these lakes were huge tongues of ice lapping the terminal moraines that form their western shores. Boaters can see evidence of glacial scraping high on the mountainsides. Floatplane access generally limits the type of boats that can be launched to folding kayaks or rafts. Caution is advised: without warning, winds can whip waves to dangerous heights. Crossing the middle of Lake Clark should be avoided if possible.

Rafting the Wild and Scenic Rivers

Tlikakila, Mulchatna, Chilikadrotna: the names themselves conjure up exciting images, and so they should. These three rivers have earned the national designation of "wild and scenic." From Summit Lake in Lake Clark Pass, the Tlikakila drops past glaciers through a breath-taking valley lined with waterfalls. Beavers busy themselves in side creeks. Moose and bears wander the banks. In a raft, it is usually a relatively easy 3 1/2-day trip with some high standing waves and class III to IV (moderate to difficult) rapids. Varying water levels can change the river's character dramatically, and rafters should be prepared to take on water when they hit the haystacks (large waves in the rapids) on the second day out. Check with the rangers and fly over the river before floating.

The Chilikadrotna and Mulchatna drain from Twin Lakes and Turquoise Lake, respectively; they flow through tundra caribou land, waterfowl sanctuaries, and some sections of spruce forest. On the 60-mile, 4-day float of the Chilikadrotna to the Mulchatna, some class II (sometimes III) rapids and long, rocky sections require constant attention. Logjams and sweepers (trees lying across the river) are abundant, and scouting is advisable. Once on the Mulchatna, the 12-mile float to the pickup at Dummy Creek (outside the park) is wide open and easy. The upper Mulchatna is rocky and must be run at high water. The scenery throughout is superb.

With three such exceptional rivers in one park, other rivers are too often overlooked. Short trips down the Kijik (from Kijik Lake), the Tazimina, and the Tanalian rivers are tantalizing and challenging. A portage around the falls on the Tanalian and Tazimina rivers will be necessary under all river conditions. Obtain a copy of *Alaska Float Trips: Southwest Region* or *The Alaska River Guide* by Karen Jettmar, and talk with the rangers for more information.

Whether one is interested in rafting, kayaking, climbing, or hiking, Lake Clark National Park and Preserve yields treasures that exhilarate, satisfy, and demand a return visit.

Opposite: One of many waterfalls along Little Lake Clark by-passes a shallow cave.

MOUNT RAINIER
NATIONAL PARK

In Mount Rainier's low-elevation forest, evergreens grow to heights of 250 feet or more.

MOUNT RAINIER NATIONAL PARK
TAHOMA WOODS, STAR ROUTE
ASHFORD, WASHINGTON 98304
TEL: (360) 569-2211

HIGHLIGHTS: Mount Rainier • Glaciers • Willis Wall • Kautz Mudflow Deposit • Reflection Lake • Box Canyon • Wonderland Trail • Wildflower Meadows • Grove of the Patriarchs

ACCESS: By car, Nisqually Entrance is 70 miles southeast of Tacoma, 95 miles southeast of Seattle, and 103 miles west of Yakima. Take Washington 7 and 706 to Nisqually; White River Entrance accessible from Enumclaw via Washington 410; White River and Stevens Canyon entrances are accessible from Yakima via Washington 12 and then Washington 123 or (in summer) Washington 410.

HOURS: Daily, 24 hours. Depending on snow conditions, all entrances should be open by Memorial Day, except White River, which opens around June 15; use Nisqually entrance in winter.

FEES: At entrance, for car or motorcycle, and for person on bus or by foot, and for camping. Golden Eagle, Golden Access, and Golden Age passes honored.

PARKING: Ample parking, but crowded on holidays and summer weekends.

GAS: None available in park.

FOOD AND LODGING: Year-round at National Park Inn in Longmire; Paradise Inn and cafeteria open from late May to early October.

VISITOR CENTER: Paradise Visitor Center open daily, mid-May through mid-October, weekends and holidays for the remainder of the year.

PETS: Leashed pets allowed, but not on park trails or in buildings.

PICNICKING: At designated areas.

HIKING: Longmire and White River provide information and permits.

BACKPACKING: Backcountry permits required for overnight camping, year-round. Season normally extends from mid-July to mid-October; some trails open earlier or later, depending on elevation and snowfall.

CAMPGROUNDS: Visitors on backcountry trails must use established campsites; cross-country campers must camp .25 mile from any trail. Ample vehicle/tent campgrounds along paved roadways, with treated water, fire rings, and parking area. Fourteen-day use limitation in effect during summer, for both backcountry and vehicle campgrounds. Group sites available. Portable stoves necessary.

TOURS: Ranger-guided nature walks.

OTHER ACTIVITIES: Snow sliding, cross-country skiing, snowshoeing, fishing, mountain climbing, some boating.

FACILITIES FOR DISABLED: Access to all public use buildings; some rest rooms.

For additional information, see also Sites, Trails, and Trips on pages 266–276 and the maps on pages 248–249 and 274.

FROM A HUNDRED MILES AWAY, MOUNT RAINIER appears to float like an ethereal cloud in the distance. This massive, sleeping volcano, with its gleaming cap of ice, is the best-loved landmark in Washington State, visible from all directions on a clear day. Only by driving mile after mile toward the mountain can the traveler begin to comprehend its huge scale; at 14,411 feet, it is the fifth tallest peak in the contiguous 48 states.

No high mountains stand nearby; Mount Rainier soars from low foothills to its majestic height in dramatic isolation. From its shining summit, rivers of ice hang in suspended streams down its sides to the 5,000-foot level, where they meet subalpine meadows that are brilliant with wildflowers during the short summer.

The base of the mountain is mantled in dense forests of conifers, evergreen giants that tower to heights of 250 feet and canopy the opulent undergrowth of the shaded forest floor. Icy glacial streams, clear upland lakes, and an abundance of wildlife add to the striking beauty of this wilderness park.

Mount Rainier, 60 miles southeast of Seattle, Washington, is the highest in the chain of volcanoes that dominate the Cascade Range. The enormous bulk of the mountain occupies more than one-fourth of the park's 378 square miles. Eighty miles of paved road and more than 300 miles of trail make Mount Rainier National Park's sublime scenery accessible to all.

Mount Rainier is a treasured and highly visible Washington State landmark.

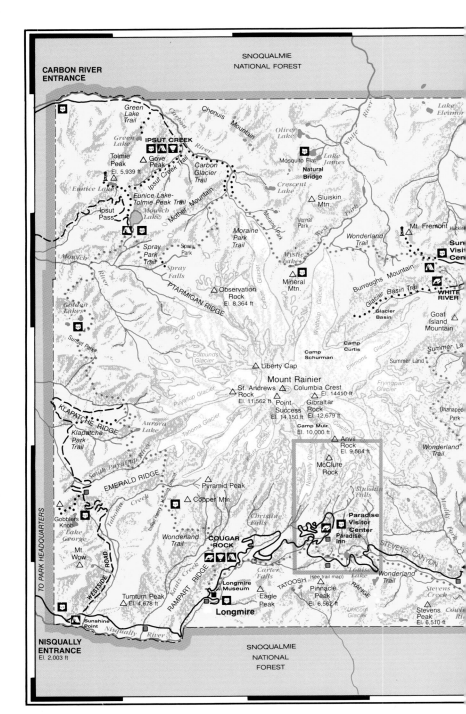

SNOQUALMIE
NATIONAL FOREST

**CARBON RIVER
ENTRANCE**

Green
Lake
Trail

Chenuis Mountain

*Lake
Eleanor*

White River

*Oliver
Lake*

Green
Lake

IPSUT CREEK

Tolmie
Peak
El. 5,939 ft

Gove
Peak

*Carbon
Glacier
Trail*

Ipsut Creek Trail

Eunice Lake

*Eunice Lake-
Tolmie Peak Trail*

Mother Mountain

*Mowich
Lake*

Ipsut
Pass

Mowich River

Spray
Park
Trail

*Spray
Park*

*Spray
Falls*

PTARMIGAN RIDGE

*Golden
Lakes*

Sunset Park

Mosquito Flat

*Lake
James*

**Natural
Bridge**

*Crescent
Lake*

Sluiskin
Mtn.

*Vernal
Park*

*Moraine
Park
Trail*

Moraine Park

*Mystic
Lake*

Mineral
Mtn.

Observation
Rock
El. 8,364 ft

Carbon Glacier

Winthrop Glacier

Mt. Fremont

Huckle

**Sun
Visi
Cen**

*Wonderland
Trail*

Burroughs Mountain

Glacier Basin Trail

**WHITE
RIVER**

*Glacier
Basin*

Goat
Island
Mountain

Summer La

KLAPATCHE RIDGE

*Aurora
Lake*

Klapatche
Park
Trail

South Puyallup River

EMERALD RIDGE

Puyallup Glacier

Tahoma Glacier

Liberty Cap

St. Andrews
Rock
El. 11,562 ft

Columbia Crest
El. 14,410 ft

Point
Success
El. 14,150 ft

Gibraltar
Rock
El. 12,679 ft

Mount Rainier

Camp
Schurman

Camp
Curtis

Emmons Glacier

Summer Land

*Fryingpan
Glacier*

*Ohanapec
Park*

Camp Muir
El. 10,000 ft

Kautz Glacier

Anvil
Rock
El. 9,584 ft

McClure
Rock

*Sluiskin
Falls*

*Wonderland
Trail*

Pyramid Peak

Copper Mtn.

Indian Henry's Hunting Ground

*Christine
Falls*

Tahoma Creek

TO PARK HEADQUARTERS

Gobblers
Knob

*Lake
George*

Mt.
Wow

WESTSIDE ROAD

*Wonderland
Trail*

**COUGAR
ROCK**

Kautz Creek

**Paradise
Visitor
Center**

**Paradise
Inn**

(see trail map)

Nisqually Glacier

STEVENS CANYON

*Louise
Lake*

*Wonderland
Trail*

Tumtum Peak
El. 4,678 ft

RAMPART RIDGE

**Longmire
Museum**

Longmire

*Carter
Falls*

Eagle
Peak

TATOOSH

Pinnacle
Peak
El. 6,562 ft

Cowlitz River

RANGE

*Unicorn
Glacier*

*Stevens
Creek*

Stevens
Peak
El. 6,510 ft

*Cowli
Ri*

Sunshine
Point

Nisqually River

**NISQUALLY
ENTRANCE**
El. 2,003 ft

SNOQUALMIE
NATIONAL
FOREST

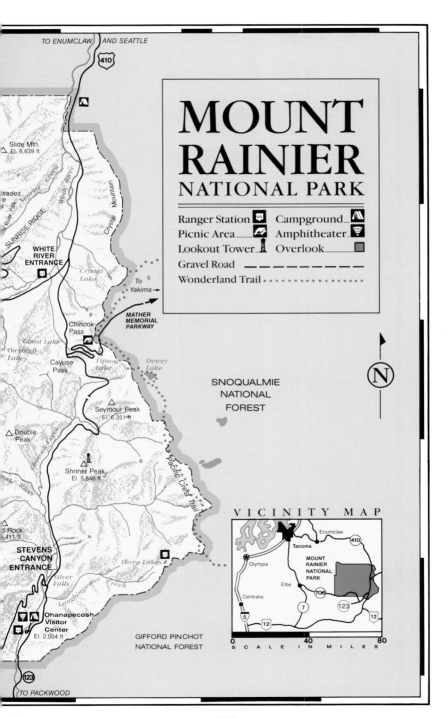

TO ENUMCLAW AND SEATTLE

410

Slide Mtn.
El. 6,639 ft

sades

White River

Silver Creek

SUNRISE RIDGE

Crystal Mountain

WHITE RIVER ENTRANCE

Crystal Lake

Crystal Creek

To Yakima

Chinook Pass

MATHER MEMORIAL PARKWAY

Ghost Lake

Ouylugh Lakes

Cayuse Pass

Tipsoo Lake

Dewey Lake

Seymour Peak
El. 6,351 ft

Double Peak

Chinook Creek

Shriner Peak
El. 5,846 ft

Pacific Crest Trail

d Rock
,411 ft

STEVENS CANYON ENTRANCE

Silver Falls

Three Lakes

Laughingwater Creek

Ohanapecosh Visitor Center
El. 2,004 ft

123

TO PACKWOOD

MOUNT RAINIER
NATIONAL PARK

Ranger Station **RS**   Campground ▲
Picnic Area ___ ⬠   Amphitheater ___ ☗
Lookout Tower ___ ⬙   Overlook ___ ■
Gravel Road ___ ___ ___ ___
Wonderland Trail · · · · · · · ·

SNOQUALMIE
NATIONAL
FOREST

N

GIFFORD PINCHOT
NATIONAL FOREST

VICINITY MAP

Enumclaw

Tacoma

410

Olympia

MOUNT RAINIER NATIONAL PARK

Elbe

706

Centralia

7

123

5

12

12

0   40   80
S C A L E   I N   M I L E S

The First Americans and "The Mountain"

When the Pacific Northwest became inhabited by Indian tribes nearly 12,000 years ago—at the end of the last ice age—various tribes moved about in the lowlands that surround the Cascades. They found it an idyllic region with rivers full of fish, lush forests alive with large and small game animals, and huge flocks of migrating birds.

The white settlers who began to arrive in the mid-1800s found western Washington populated by the Nisqually, Yakima, Puyallup, Klickitat, and Cowlitz Indians. There is no evidence that any tribes established permanent settlements in the area now enclosed by the park, but hunting parties followed game up the mountain's slopes as the previous winter's snows retreated, and groups of women camped in Mount Rainier's high meadows every summer, gathering herbs, picking berries, and digging roots to dry and store for winter use.

The Indian name for the snowy peak that towered above their villages was Takhoma or Tahoma, which means (in a superlative sense) "The Mountain." Legends told of an early time when the mountains to the west, now known as the Olympics, were really warriors. One of the warrior peaks took a wife named Tahoma, who came to live with him from her home across the Sound. Because the peaks there were still growing, the Olympic Peninsula eventually became too crowded to hold them all, and Tahoma decided to go back to her tribe, taking her small son with her. But when she crossed the water and stepped from her canoe, she was frozen in solitude as a punishment for leaving her husband. Her son became a peak called Little Tahoma, held high on her eastern shoulder. Tahoma grew taller and broader until she became a huge, snow-capped mountain and could look across the sound to keep an eye on her former husband.

Other legends told of the mountain god within Tahoma who could, when angered, send fire and molten rock flying out of the top of the mountain or pour sudden floods of water from melted ice and snow down its flanks to inundate villages.

Explorers and Climbers

In the late 1700s, Spanish and English explorers sailed along the Washington coast, but none of them mentioned seeing the great white mountain until 1792. In that year, Captain George Vancouver of the British Navy sailed into Puget Sound and recorded in his log

Longmire, once a homestead cabin, is now a historic structure.

251

MOUNT RAINIER

Top: First touring buses, 1908.
Right: Washingtonian elegance on Mount Rainier.
Above: President Taft was the first motorist to Paradise in 1911.

for May 7 the sighting of a "high, round mountain covered with snow." In the custom of the time, he named it for a friend, Rear Admiral Peter Rainier, who never came to America to see his namesake.

In the years that followed, English and American scouts and fur traders passed through the Puget Sound country in increasing numbers. By 1833, the British-owned Hudson's Bay Company had established the first settlement near Mount Rainier—an outpost called Fort Nisqually, not far from the present-day city of Tacoma. In August 1833, Dr. William Tolmie, a botanist stationed at the fort, organized an expedition to the mountain to collect plants and explore the countryside. He was probably the first white man to set foot on Mount Rainier's slopes.

A small but steady stream of immigrants made their way to western Washington in the 1850s, and many settled in its lush valleys, despite troubles with Indians who resented being displaced from their lands by the newcomers. One early settler, James Longmire, helped pioneer a route across the Cascades. He made his home—and later built a resort—at the mineral springs on the south side of the mountain, now called Longmire.

The towering presence of Mount Rainier was an almost irresistible lure to the settlers, and attempts to climb to the summit were made as early as 1852. A local newspaper told of four men who said they had reached the summit in that year, and an Indian guide recalled, some years after the fact, that two men had climbed to the top in 1854 and reported seeing steam vents at the summit.

The first well-documented climb was made in August, 1870 by Hazard Stevens and Philemon Van Trump. In an article in *Atlantic Monthly*, they wrote that their Indian guide, Sluiskin, tried to discourage them by telling of Takhoma's dangers. He warned of "precipices whence avalanches of snow and vast masses of rock were continually falling" and of furious winds at the summit—so strong that the men would be "torn from the mountain and whirled through the air by this fearful blast."

They persisted against his advice, leaving Sluiskin at the base camp, but vastly underestimated the time it would take for the final assault up the glaciers. By the time they reached the summit, night was falling and a storm was approaching. They had carried no blankets on their final ascent and would have died of exposure if they had not smelled sulfur fumes and upon investigation discovered that steam vents had melted caves in the ice. They crawled into one and spent the night amid hissing steam jets and acrid fumes, uncomfortable but safe. The next morning they scrambled down to meet their astonished guide, who had given them up for dead.

More and more climbers came to Mount Rainier to take up the

challenge. The first ascent by a woman—Fay Fuller—took place in 1890, and the next year a party included Susan Longmire, age 13. More than a dozen routes were pioneered up the treacherous glaciers, and in 1921 an entire 16-person wedding party celebrated a marriage ceremony at the summit. At the present time, about 8,000 people attempt to climb Mount Rainier each year.

Establishment of the Park

The first suggestions that Mount Rainier be protected as a national park were made in the early 1890s, and in 1894 a concerted effort was begun to preserve the area in the face of growing visitor use. Local newspapers led the campaign, including the National Geographic Society. These efforts succeeded, and the bill establishing Mount Rainier as the nation's fifth national park was signed by President William McKinley in 1899. Today, more than two million visitors come to Mount Rainier each year to climb, hike, fish, and to glory in the scenery of this magnificent national park.

GEOLOGY

Mount Rainier is a classic example of the battle between fire and ice: volcanic eruptions building a huge mountain, and glacial erosion grinding it away. These two geologic processes have often occurred at the same time during the almost million-year life span of Mount Rainier, but for clarity it is best to consider them separately.

The Volcano

Almost everyone in the Seattle-Tacoma area realizes that the giant snowcapped peak that looms over their cities is a volcano. Many, however, think that Rainier's volcanic fires are dead or dying and that future eruptions are only science fiction speculation. Most geologists disagree. Although there is no precise way to predict future volcanic activity, it seems unreasonable to assume that Mount Rainier, which has been intermittently active for hundreds of thousands of years and which last erupted only about 150 years ago, is now dead. Such a conclusion is analogous to deciding that a mature person in apparent good health, who has been asleep for several hours, is dead. Possibly so, probably not.

Geologist François Matthes once described Mount Rainier as resembling an "enormous tree stump with spreading base and broken top." This shape formed largely because of the character of the volcanic eruptions it has experienced over its long life span. A volcano built out of a combination of lava flows from relatively "quiet"

A view of Mount Rainier over the ruined summit of Mount St. Helens.

eruptions and of ash and fragmental layers from explosive eruptions is called a stratovolcano, or composite volcano. Mount Rainier is a good example of this type. Stratovolcanoes have steep, often concave-upward slopes. Unless modified by glaciation, as Mount Rainier has been, or summit collapse, they form graceful sharp-pointed cones.

During its long life, Mount Rainier has produced thousands of lava flows. Some of these were of enormous volume, filling 2,000-foot-deep canyons for distances of more than 12 miles. After exposure to glacial erosion, these massive flows now form spreading ridges at the base of Rainier's high cone—the roots of Matthes's giant tree stump.

Thousands of explosive eruptions have also added their deposits to the growing volcanic pile. Air-fall deposits of ash and pumice (fragments of light, frothy volcanic glass) form many layers surrounding Mount Rainier, particularly on the east (the generally downwind) side of the volcano. Ashflow and mudflow deposits are another product of Rainier's explosive eruptions.

An ashflow consists of hot but solid volcanic fragments suspended in hot, turbulent gases. Before the gases escape, this mixture can build into a glowing avalanche that sweeps down the flanks of a volcano at high speed, destroying everything in its path. A mudflow is a liquid slurry of volcanic debris and water that floods down a stream canyon on the flank of a volcano like a great torrent of wet concrete. The overall deposits from an explosive eruption are com-

Red heather grows in soil deposits in Stevens Ridge Breccia Formation, near Sunrise.

plex: giant landslides, blasted rock fragments, fine air-fall ash deposits, mudflows, and ashflows, all parts of a deadly shroud spread over the landscape surrounding the exploded volcanic stump.

About 75,000 years ago, some time before the onslaught of the most recent major ice age, Mount Rainier was even more imposing than it is now. Geologists believe that its peak was a symmetrical cone reaching between 15,000 and 16,000 feet above sea level. Glacial erosion has continued to rasp away the rocks even after the last ice age ended some 12,000 years ago, and about 5,700 years ago a major landslide also contributed to the destruction of the high summit. The release of a small amount of pumice marked the last significant eruption, sometime between 1820 and 1854.

Will Mount Rainier erupt again? Most probably. In our lifetime? Probably not. Dwight Crandell and Donal Mullineaux, the two U.S. Geological Survey scientists who correctly forecast that Mount St. Helens would erupt, have also studied Mount Rainier. They estimate that small-scale avalanches, floods, mudflows, and steam explosions can be expected at Mount Rainier at intervals of 10 to 100 years. Larger versions of these same hazards may occur once every 2,000 years; pumice eruptions and glowing avalanches, once every 2,500 to 5,000 years; and a major lava flow, once every 10,000 years.

These are fairly comforting statistics, but when the larger events occur they can affect vast areas of land at considerable distances from the summit of the mountain. The towns of Orting,

Buckley, and Enumclaw, which lie 25 miles northwest of Mount Rainier, are built on giant mudflow deposits that swept from the volcano down the valleys of the Puyallup River 500 years ago and White River 5,700 years ago—ancient history to a town planner, but only yesterday to a geologist.

The Glaciers

Mount Rainier is so high and cold and receives so much snowfall that at its summit the latest ice age is not over. In fact, the 26 major glaciers on its slopes form the largest mass of year-round ice anywhere in the United States except Alaska. Glaciers form where snowfall in the winter exceeds snowmelt in the summer. The lower boundary of this zone is often marked by a distinct snowline, which on Mount Rainier occurs about 7,000 feet above sea level. As snowpack accumulates, its weight compresses loose snow into dense ice. The ice in turn deforms under pressure and slowly flows down valleys in great "rivers of ice" called valley glaciers.

As the front of a glacier descends to warmer elevations, the increased melting it undergoes balances with the surplus of snow and ice formed at higher elevations. This point of balance between ice accumulation and ice melt is sensitive to slight long-term changes in climate, and especially to trends in average temperature or precipitation. Advancing glacial fronts are a sign of cooler average temperatures or more snowfall, while retreating glaciers signal an increasingly warm or dry climate.

Ice on the surface of a valley glacier flows most rapidly near the glacier's center, and its speed varies with the slope. Typical speeds for glaciers such as those on Mount Rainier are about 1 foot per day, although they may move up to 10 feet per day where the slopes are steeper. At higher speeds, the ice breaks up into great jumbled blocks called icefalls. Where speed increases rapidly, great cracks called crevasses open to form beautiful but dangerous chasms deep in the ice.

Meltwater often carves ice caves within and beneath the glaciers. For years, the Paradise Ice Caves provided a glittering pearly blue environment in which light and color changed with every step. This cavern, however, had melted out by the early 1990s.

The landscape features that are carved and heaped by the flowing ice are as magnificent as the glaciers themselves. The huge ridges of rock separating the glaciers that radiate down the slopes of Mount Rainier are called cleavers; they are thin remnants of the lava flows that once formed the high volcanic cone. If Rainier's glaciers melted away, the deep U-shaped valleys they have carved would be revealed. Without their ice these valleys would end in

Carbon Glacier is one of the few glaciers in the park that maintain a constant size.

high amphitheater-shaped basins called cirques, each probably with a cirque lake surrounded by great cliffs of the eroded lava flows. Moraines—ridges consisting of loose broken rocks bulldozed by the glaciers—mark the far edges of former glacial advances. Medial moraines—bands of rock debris riding on the active glaciers—form when tributary glaciers merge and grind away the lower edges of the bedrock cleavers between them.

The glaciers on Mount Rainier cover 38 square miles and contain about 1 cubic mile of ice. Emmons Glacier on the east flank, more than 4 miles long and 1 mile wide, is the most massive glacier in the United States south of Alaska. Carbon Glacier on the north flank is 6 miles long, and has carved a great cirque cliff known to rock climbers as Willis Wall.

The Nisqually, the best studied of Mount Rainier's glaciers, flows some 4 miles from the summit down the south flank to about the 4,700-foot elevation. Its front has shifted nearly 2 miles since it was first observed in 1840 at about the 3,600-foot elevation. After retreating for more than a century, the Nisqually Glacier reversed its trend in the early 1960s and advanced slowly until the mid–1980s. Hindsight now shows that after a century of warming, the earth's climate cooled slightly from the late 1940s until 1983. These trends are too gradual to be detected on a year-to-year basis because yearly weather is so variable. The use of glaciers as climate gauges to smooth out these annual variations is a good example of the serendipity of science; studying "rivers of ice" led to an unexpected conclusion about a trend in global climate.

Opposite: Winter at the Christine Falls Bridge, on Mount Rainier.

Climate

The Cascade Range, of which Mount Rainier is a part, constitutes one of the world's most striking climate boundaries. Winds sweep in from the Pacific Ocean, heavy with moisture and comparatively warm from the influence of the sea. When they meet the massive barrier of the Cascade Mountains—especially a mountain as formidable as Rainier—they rise and cool, and the condensing moisture falls as rain or snow.

Rainfall and snowfall are prodigious on the west side of the mountain, with Paradise at the 5,400-foot level averaging about 100 inches of precipitation a year. Most of this precipitation falls as snow, which accumulates 15 or 20 feet deep in normal years. In an exceptional year, the build-up may reach 30 feet of snow by March at Paradise. Meanwhile, the land to the east of the Cascades is a desert, with annual precipitation of 10 inches or less.

Rainier's summit rises above the lower-level clouds. Condensation in the upper air stream sometimes creates a cloud cap that can hide the peak for days with no relation to the lowland weather.

During the winter, when clouds and fog shroud Rainier much of the time, views of the mountain are hard to obtain; but in the spring the frequent snow flurries are interspersed with some warm, clear days. Snow remains in the high meadows well into summer, and snow may fall in any month; in general, though, July, August, and early September are fine and warm. In some years, clear Indian-summer weather can linger into late October.

Forest and Flowers

The heavy moisture that falls on Mount Rainier as snow or rain produces a lovely, luxuriant growth of trees, ferns, mosses, and flowers. The park encompasses four plant zones (belts controlled by the climate found at different elevations), and all are accessible by road or trail.

At the lowest elevations, up to about 3,500 feet, is the Humid-Transition Zone. Here, in dense forests, specimens of Douglas-fir, western redcedar, and mountain hemlock may grow over 250 feet high. Slender vine maples wind among these giants, above shrubs such as the spiny Devil's club, red huckleberry, Oregon grape, and salal. Ferns and mosses cover the damp, shady forest floor. The total effect is one of being submerged in a moist greenness.

Opposite: Vine maples enjoy the sunlight that penetrates taller evergreens.

Here and there beams of sunlight break through, touching fragrant needles on the forest floor and patches of delicate flowers such as trillium, beadruby, vanilla leaf, and bunchberry dogwood.

In the Canadian zone, 3,500 to 5,000 feet, the forest is less dense, and not as tall. The noble fir, western white pine, and western hemlock predominate. Shrubs are profuse, and many—including red and blue huckleberry, salal, salmonberry, and Pacific blackberry—bear fruit, to the great pleasure of bears and hikers.

In the Hudsonian zone, 5,000 to 6,500 feet, forests mix with meadow. The trees are mostly velvety Alaska cedar, subalpine fir, mountain hemlock, and whitebark pine. All typically grow in dense clusters on the fringe of meadows, becoming more sparse with increasing altitude.

The subalpine meadows themselves, when carpeted with drifts of white, pink, purple, and yellow blossoms, are a stunning sight. As the snows retreat up the hillsides, yellow glacier lilies and white avalanche lilies push through the last few inches of snow, followed by marsh marigolds, western anemones, and purple shooting stars.

As the summer progresses, dozens of other flowers tint the meadows—blue lupine, red and yellow monkeyflowers, whole hillsides of magenta painted cup, or paintbrush, and white Sitka valerian.

The Arctic-Alpine zone is from 6,500 feet to the summit, with the treeline varying from 6,500 to 7,500 feet. Few trees can survive in the hostile windswept environment just below the snowline, but scattered whitebark pine and an occasional subalpine fir grow in prostrate, contorted forms called *krummholz*—a descriptive German word meaning "elfin timber" or "crooked wood."

Clumps of alpine flowers cling to the sparse soil, growing in ground-hugging mats; these include patches of alpine phlox, white anemone, and the Tolmie saxifrage, a delicate cushion of flowers named for the first botanist to collect plants on Mount Rainier.

The thin soil gives way to rock, then to the permanent snowfields and glaciers. But at the very summit some touches of green can be found; a few mosses and lichens grow in the steam-heated ice caves within the crater.

Animals and Birds

At least 50 mammals call Mount Rainier National Park home. Because many are nocturnal as well as shy and secretive, visitors are likely to see far fewer than that.

Of the large mammals, probably the most intriguing are the mountain goats that live high in the Arctic-Alpine life zone, grazing on meadow grasses and climbing to precarious rocky perches on the steep slopes. These shaggy white "goats"—actually rock antelope—easily cross glaciers and snowfields, staying at as high an altitude as possible most of the year.

Black-tailed deer, a subspecies of the mule deer and the most frequently encountered large mammals in the park, spend the winter in the lowlands. They follow the melting snow into the highest country and in summer are found in all parts of the park up to timberline. Their fawns—usually twins—are born in June and are seen with the herd in the summer range, especially in quiet meadows in early evening.

The Roosevelt elk resembles a deer but is much larger. Mount Rainier's largest animal weighs up to 800 pounds at maturity. The several large herds in the park browse in high meadows in summer and move to lowlands when winter snows arrive. The only bear in the park, the black bear, may be black, brown, or cinnamon in color.

Small mammals such as the busy Townsend chipmunk, the Douglas squirrel, and the Cascade golden-mantled ground squirrel are everywhere. Sociable and always hungry, they are especially fond of campgrounds, but must not be fed. At the higher elevations near the snowline, the rabbit-like pika, or cony, collects grasses to store in its rocky home for the winter. Here, too, marmots sun themselves on rocks and signal to each other with shrill whistles.

Even the highest snowfields have touches of life. Tiny snow fleas, or springtails, hop wildly across the snow when disturbed, and thin black ice worms wiggle on the glacier ice, eating the red algae that sometimes stain the snowfields pink.

More than 140 species of birds have been identified at Mount Rainier, though many of those are migrants. The most visible resident birds are the bold, camp-robbing Oregon jay, or gray jay, and, at higher elevations, the noisy Clark's nutcracker. The nutcracker feeds on other hard seeds of the whitebark pine, tearing the cones apart with its strong beak to reach them.

The deep forests are home for woodpeckers, sapsuckers, and flickers, as well as for smaller birds such as creepers and juncos. Anticipating the winter, chickadees hide pine seeds and spider eggs in cracks in the pine bark.

Ravens, red-tailed hawks, and golden eagles are sometimes seen circling high over the open meadows, looking for mice and other small rodents. One of the best-adapted birds is the white-tailed ptarmigan, a grouse-like bird living at high elevations, whose dark summer feathers turn white for camouflage when winter snows begin.

Overleaf: Blue lupine and magenta paintbrush, among other flowers in a mountain meadow.

A Drive to Paradise

From the park's Nisqually Entrance, 19 miles of paved road climb from 2,000 feet in elevation to Jackson Visitor Center at 5,400 feet.

The first 6 miles, from the park entrance to Longmire, are along one of the most beautiful forest roads anywhere. The road, which climbs gently eastward along the north side of the rushing Nisqually River, could have been bulldozed and laid out almost straight. Instead, because of thoughtful planning, it winds among and around giant Douglas-firs, redcedars, and western hemlock, many of them thicker at the base than a car is wide. The trunks of these trees rise like temple columns into a thick canopy of branches that hides the sky.

Except for occasional glimpses, the river, less than a half-mile away to the south, is also hidden by the deep forest. Western sword ferns fringe the roadside with lighter green, and shade-loving flowers like trillium and vanilla leaf embroider the virgin forest.

Three miles inside the park is a slash of destroyed forest that was inundated by the *Kautz Creek mudflow*, a torrential mudflow up to 50 feet thick that swept down Kautz Creek in a 1947 flood. About 6 inches of rain fell in one day, triggering a flood of ice, boulders, sand, and mud from the Kautz Glacier. The flood apparently became temporarily dammed by debris in a box canyon high in the valley, but then broke through and surged downstream.

Mudflow deposits are common among the streams draining Cascade volcanoes. Severe rainstorms often trigger small mudflows, but the larger ones seem to be related to volcanic eruptions, whose heat melts volumes of snow and ice or whose tremors cause huge avalanches from the high volcanic cones. Nature slowly heals the scars, and forests grow again on the new layers of debris and mud.

Longmire, 6 miles from the park entrance, was once a homestead near the warm springs in the meadow. The museum maintains the historical flavor of early Longmire, and features exhibits that explain the geology and natural history of Mount Rainier.

Beyond Longmire, the road to Paradise climbs 2,600 feet in 13 miles of gentle grades and switchbacks. This was one of the first roads built in a national park, and President William Howard Taft came in 1911 to ride in the first car to make the trip. Because the road was still rough and muddy, teams of horses had been hidden along the way, and they emerged from the trees to pull the car over the worst spots, much to the amusement of the president.

The road passes *Christine Falls*, a short walk from the road for

Moisture-laden winds from the Pacific condense into a cloud over the summit.

the best view, and then crosses the *Nisqually Bridge*. The Nisqually Glacier reached to a point 300 yards downstream from here in 1840. By 1911, the glacial front had retreated to just above the present bridge location, and it is now out of sight around the bend about one mile above the bridge.

The road climbs out of Nisqually River and at *Ricksecker Point* offers a fine view of the summit of Mount Rainier and the Nisqually Glacier. The forest thins as the road climbs upward, and alpine meadows gradually replace it. The views of Rainier's high slopes, and the surrounding gardens of wildflowers, inspired James Longmire's wife to name this area "Paradise."

The *Henry M. Jackson Visitor Center* at Paradise offers interesting exhibits and programs, but in good weather the real show is outside. One can spend several hours or even days in Paradise, walking along the wildflower trails and hiking to Reflection Lakes and Camp Muir.

The road is kept open to Paradise throughout the winter, but it is not plowed beyond this point.

The Road to Sunrise

In summer, the Paradise Road is open for 23 miles eastward down Stevens Canyon and across Cowlitz Divide to the Ohanapecosh (Clearwater) River near the southeast corner of the park. Along the way are several sites worth seeing.

Reflection Lake, ponded up by an ancient mudflow, provides a mirror image of Rainier's majestic summit. It is difficult to tell top from bottom on photographs taken here on a still day. *Box Canyon*, 11 miles from Paradise, is a narrow Cowlitz River gorge more than 180 feet deep and only 15 to 30 feet wide.

From Box Canyon, the road continues to the Stevens Canyon Entrance of the park. Here, Washington 123 leads south and out of the park by way of the *Ohanapecosh Visitor Center*. At the Visitor Center, exhibits tell the story of northwest forests and their ecology.

Washington 123 also leads north toward Sunrise, skirting the eastern base of Mount Rainier for 33 miles. It climbs the valley of the Ohanapecosh River, crosses *Cayuse Pass* at 4,694 feet, drops into White River Valley as Washington 410, and then climbs again in zigzags up the ridge to Sunrise.

Sunrise Visitor Center, at 6,400 feet, has even better views of Mount Rainier than does Paradise, and the wildflower display in the surrounding area is almost as lavish. Emmons Glacier and White River Valley are visible from here. The Visitor Center contains exhibits explaining the geology and botany of the area, and a fine flower walk—the *Sourdough Ridge Trail*—leaves from here.

In the Sunrise area are layers of ash and pumice that fell following prehistoric eruptions of Mount Rainier, Mount St. Helens, and even Mount Mazama 7,700 years ago. The light gray lumps of pumice about the size of cherry pits that are found in the uppermost surface of the soil were produced by a small explosive eruption of Mount Rainier in the mid-nineteenth century.

After returning from Sunrise to the White River Entrance, visitors may follow the Mather Memorial Parkway (Washington 410) north down the White River Valley and out the northeast corner of the park.

The Summit Climb

The long climb to the summit of Mount Rainier, an arduous but thrilling adventure, can be accomplished by anyone in good physical condition who is determined to reach the top. All climbers must

Opposite: Snowy Little Tahoma Peak rises high above the eastern shoulder of Mount Rainier.

register with park rangers, and inexperienced climbers should participate in a one-day snow- and ice-climbing school provided by the guide service at Paradise. Good equipment and sufficient provisions are required both by the National Park Service and by common sense. Accidents on Mount Rainier have claimed more than 50 lives. Eleven died on Father's Day in 1981 as a result of an icefall.

The summit climb, beginning at Paradise (5,400-foot elevation), takes two days. The first goal is *Camp Muir*, 4.5 miles distant. After traversing the flowery meadows of Paradise, the trail leaves the thinning alpine soil to cross rough rocks of old lava flows. Beyond *Pebble Creek*, the route stays on steep snowfields. It is important to follow well-used tracks on the snow; the danger of concealed crevasses is real. A beautiful hike in clear weather, this trek can be hazardous if clouds close in and the trail becomes lost in fog.

Camp Muir is a rock-walled shelter surrounded by tent platforms, high in the bare rock and snowfields at 10,000 feet. It provides magnificent views of the Cascade Range to the south: snow-capped Mount Adams and Mount Hood and the stump of Mount St. Helens appear from left to right on the horizon.

If a hiker finds the climb to Camp Muir difficult, he or she should return to Paradise. The route ahead is much more strenuous.

The final ascent begins the next morning between 1 and 2 A.M., with the climbers using flashlights and roped together in groups of two or more. This part of the trail crosses deeply crevassed glaciers and steep rock cleavers. The flickering lights of climbing parties ahead and behind create a dreamlike vision of initiates marching with torches to some mysterious revelation. And so it is; dawn breaks when the climbers are about halfway to the summit, and the unfolding day, the stark beauty of white snow, black rock, and blue sky, and the discovery of the great stamina of the human body and spirit combine to produce a sense of profound satisfaction as the last steep snowfield flattens into the level snow-filled crater of the summit.

All who make the climb are winners. Each climber competes not with other climbers, but against the challenge of nature to reach its hidden shrines.

The summit crater, 1,300 feet in diameter, is filled nearly to its rim with ice and snow. This flat summit provides just enough room to land a light plane, and a daredevil accomplished the feat in 1951. (He also managed to glide his plane off again before park rangers could rescue and arrest him). Columbia Crest, on the west side of the crater rim, is the highest point on the mountain.

Steam vents occur at the edges of the crater between the rock rim and the ice; the fumaroles are handy for a little steam heat or to melt a frozen water bottle. The steam apparently originates below the crater. In escaping to the surface, it has melted out a network of steeply inclined ice caves and tunnels within the crater. Expert cavers with good lights and special equipment have explored this cave complex to depths of 350 feet below the flat snow and ice surface of the main crater.

Returning to Camp Muir by noon makes it possible to avoid the softening snow and small avalanches of loose rocks that the full day's sun would bring. After a rest there, the downhill walk to Paradise is easy. The 18-mile, two-day trip provides a true impression of the immense size of Mount Rainier; the difference between the upward climb and the descent instills great respect for the force of gravity.

The Wonderland Trail

The 93-mile Wonderland Trail, which encircles Mount Rainier, is as much of a challenge to the hiker as the summit trip is to the climber. With designated campsites placed 8 to 12 miles apart, the trail passes through every life zone in the park, winding through deep forests and flower-filled meadows, beside glacial streams, and across snow and ice. Magnificent views of Mount Rainier and its shining glaciers appear from every angle and in many moods; The Mountain becomes an intimate friend by the end of the trip.

The trail climbs and descends steeply as it crosses the ridges of old lava flows that radiate from the mountain. The Wonderland Trail gains and loses more altitude than does the summit climb—a total of about 20,000 feet.

Leaving Longmire in a clockwise direction, the trail rises and falls through forest and meadow along the entire west side of the mountain. It crosses Indian Henry's Hunting Ground, passes near the Tahoma Glacier, enters Klapatche Park, and continues on to Mowich Lake. The northern section of the trail is higher and colder, tracing along the Carbon Glacier to Mystic Lake at 5,800 feet and continuing past the Winthrop Glacier to Sunrise and White River.

The eastern section includes the highest point on the trail—6,700 feet—and passes glaciers, lakes, waterfalls, and the Box Canyon of the Cowlitz River, which was formed by glacier and stream action.

The whole circuit takes about 10 days of steady walking. It is preferable to allow two weeks. The trail touches the road at Longmire, Paradise, Sunrise, and a few other spots; supplies may be cached in advance at Longmire or White River to make backpacking easier.

Mount Rainier's Shorter Trails

With more than 300 miles of trail in the park, a trail can be found to suit any taste—one that features flowers, forests, glaciers, or waterfalls, whose route is easy or hard, and which is suited to almost any sort of weather. Only a representative few are described here.

Probably the most exciting and varied trails start from Paradise, including the summit climb described above. The *Wildflower Trails* are the most popular in the park. Paved trails radiate from the Visitor Center and Paradise Inn and lead through fields of yellow glacier lilies, blue lupine, red Indian paintbrush, gentian, and myriad other blooms that vary with the advancing season. Visitors can inquire at the Jackson Visitor Center to find which path has the best display at a particular time, but any choice will be dazzling.

The *Skyline Trail*, a 5-mile loop, involves an elevation gain of 1,400 feet and requires 4 hours to complete. It offers lovely displays of subalpine wildflowers, a good closeup look at Mount Rainier and the Nisqually Glacier, and, if the day is clear, a glimpse of mountains as far south as Mount Hood in Oregon. If one hikes clockwise, the trail climbs 2 miles to Panorama Point, then descends for 1 mile to the junction with the *Golden Gate Trail*. (To shorten the hike, one may take the Golden Gate Trail back to Paradise.) From the junction, a .75-mile hike on the Skyline Trail leads to the Stevens-Van Trump Memorial and the junction with the *Paradise Glacier Trail*. The 300-foot cascade of *Sluiskan Falls* is near the junction. From the junction, the Skyline Trail descends into Paradise Valley, climbs slightly to Myrtle Falls, and then returns to Paradise.

Several other trails from Paradise lead to excellent views of Nisqually Glacier. The shortest, only a 1.2-mile round trip to the edge of Nisqually Canyon from the Visitor Center parking area, provides a close look at this slow-moving river of ice.

A few short trails from Ohanapecosh make good low-altitude hikes when high-country weather is bad. The *Grove of the Patriarchs Trail* is a 1.5-mile round trip through a stand of gigantic Douglas-fir, western hemlock, and western redcedar estimated to be nearly 1,000 years old. Signs identify trees and plants along the loop trail through this lovely virgin forest. The trail leaves from the parking area just beyond the Ohanapecosh River Bridge.

The *Silver Falls Loop*, an easy 3-mile hike, starts at the Ohanapecosh Campground and follows the east bank of the river

Opposite: The Paradise River streams through grooves worn in volcanic rock.

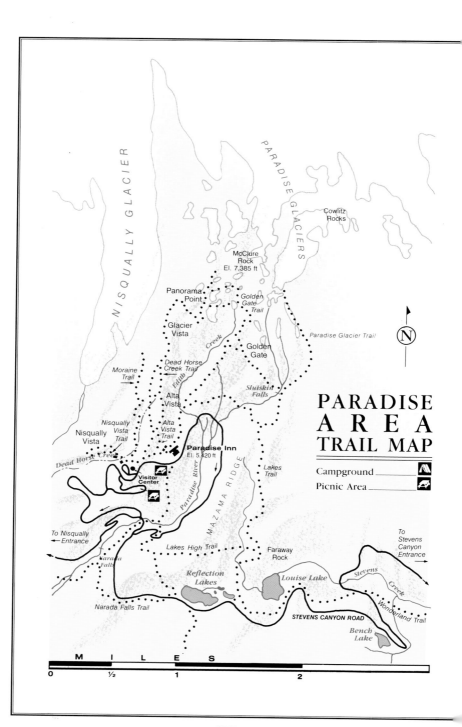

Cowlitz
Rocks

McClure
Rock
El. 7,385 ft

Panorama
Point

*Golden
Gate
Trail*

Paradise Glacier Trail

Glacier
Vista

Golden
Gate

*Dead Horse
Creek Trail*

Moraine
Trail

*Sluiskin
Falls*

Alta
Vista

Nisqually
Vista
Trail

*Alta
Vista
Trail*

Nisqually
Vista

Paradise Inn
El. 5,420 ft

Dead Horse Creek

Visitor
Center

PARADISE
A R E A
TRAIL MAP

Lakes
Trail

MAZAMA RIDGE

Paradise River

Campground ___
Picnic Area ___

To Nisqually
← Entrance

*Narada
Falls*

Lakes High Trail

Faraway
Rock

To
Stevens
Canyon
Entrance

Stevens

Reflection
Lakes

Louise Lake

Creek

Wonderland Trail

Narada Falls Trail

STEVENS CANYON ROAD

Bench
Lake

M I L E S

0   ½   1   2

TRAILS OF MOUNT RAINIER NATIONAL PARK

PARADISE AREA

LAKES TRAIL: Starts and ends at Jackson Visitor Center at Paradise; 5-mile loop; 4 hours; leads through subalpine meadows to Reflection Lakes; offers fine views of Stevens Ridge and the Tatoosh Range.

LAKES HIGH TRAIL: Starts and ends at Jackson Visitor Center; 4-mile loop; 3 hours; variation of the Lakes Trail; contains likely spots for viewing varied wildlife and abundant wildflowers.

SKYLINE TRAIL: Starts and ends at Jackson Visitor Center; 5-mile loop; 4 hours; highest trail at Paradise; leads above treeline to Glacier Vista and Panorama Point for views of Mount Adams, Mount St. Helens, and the Nisqually Glacier.

GOLDEN GATE TRAIL: Starts and ends at Paradise Inn; 4-mile loop; 3 hours; variation of the Skyline Trail; offers views of wildflowers in the Edith Creek basin.

ALTA VISTA TRAIL: Starts and ends at Jackson Visitor Center; 1.5-mile loop; 1 hour; leads through flower fields to prominent knoll overlooking Paradise River, Mount Adams, and Mount St. Helens.

NISQUALLY VISTA TRAIL: Starts and ends at Jackson Visitor Center; 1.2-mile loop; 1 hour; views of entire length of Nisqually Glacier.

MORAINE TRAIL: Starts at Jackson Visitor Center; ends at edge of Nisqually Glacier; 3 miles round trip; 2 hours; spur trail leading to rocky moraine at edge of Nisqually Glacier; wear sturdy boots and use caution while crossing loose rocks on moraine.

PARADISE GLACIER TRAIL: Starts at Paradise Visitor Center; ends at Paradise Glacier; 6 miles round trip; 5 hours; leads through area recently shaped by glacial ice.

NARADA FALLS TRAIL: Starts along Lakes Trail near Reflection Lake; ends at Narada Falls and Wonderland Trail; 1.4 miles round trip; 2 hours; follows Paradise River to falls.

DEAD HORSE CREEK TRAIL: Starts at Jackson Visitor Center; ends at Skyline Trail; 2 miles round trip; 1 hour; close view of Nisqually Glacier at Glacier Vista.

through deep forest and across Laughingwater Creek for a fine view of Silver Falls. The trail crosses a bridge at the falls, continues a little higher for a view from the top of the falls, and then returns down the west side of the valley.

At Longmire, the *Trail of the Shadows* is a .75-mile nature walk that starts across the highway from the hotel. The trail proceeds along the edge of a verdant meadow, passing the mineral springs discovered by James Longmire and an old cabin built by his son in 1888. Self-guiding signs identify interesting features along the trail.

The *Kautz Creek Trail* goes to Indian Henry's Hunting Ground, an 11-mile round trip; for an interesting short hike take the first part of this trail as it winds along the smooth top of the Kautz Creek mudflow. The devastation of the 1947 torrent is impressive, but a new forest is beginning to take form.

From the Sunrise Visitor Center, a trail to the *Mount Fremont Lookout* ascends 1,200 feet through meadowland and over rocky crags. Mount Rainier and the Cascades and the Olympics are visible on clear days. The trail follows Sourdough Ridge west to Frozen Lake, where it intersects with four other trails. The round-trip hike, a distance of 5.5 miles, takes three hours. Camping is not permitted at or near the lookout.

This is only a sample of Mount Rainier National Park's beautiful and enticing trails; other trips leave from Stevens Canyon, from the Carbon River–Mowich Lake area, and from the Westside Road.

Other Recreational Activities

The park is open to fishing according to Washington state seasons, but fish are not plentiful. Park waters are not stocked and depend on limited natural reproduction to replenish the fish population. The park encourages anglers to use barbless hooks and artificial lures and asks that uninjured fish be released.

Non-motorized boating is permitted on all lakes except Frozen, Reflection, Ghost, and Tipsoo. About 100 miles of park trails are open to the use of pack and saddle animals. Horse camps are situated at Ipsut Creek, Deer Creek, North Puyallup River, Mowich River, and Three Lakes.

Several winter activities are feasible in the Paradise area. Snow sliding on inner tubes and saucers is permitted on three constructed and supervised runs. From January to March, naturalists lead snowshoe walks to introduce visitors to snowshoeing and winter ecology. When snow is sufficient, park rangers mark three cross-country ski trails for visitors' use.

Opposite: The masses of glacial ice at the summit mimic the most recent ice age.

NORTH CASCADES
NATIONAL PARK

NORTH CASCADES NATIONAL PARK
2105 HIGHWAY 20
SEDRO WOOLEY, WASHINGTON 98284
TEL.: (206) 856-5700

HIGHLIGHTS: Picket Range • Cascade Pass • Stehekin River Valley • Skagit River • Challenger Glacier • Ross Lake and Lake Chelan National Recreation Areas

ACCESS: North Cascades Highway (Washington 20) from Burlington on the west and Twisp on the east, or Washington 542 from Bellingham.

HOURS: Daily, 24 hours, year-round. North Cascades Highway closed from November to April (varies).

FEES: For camping; none at entrance.

PARKING: At public-use facilities and pullouts.

GAS: At Marblemount.

FOOD AND LODGING: At Ross Lake resort, and in Stehekin at North Cascades Stehekin Lodge. Groceries in Marblemount and Newhalem.

VISITOR CENTERS: Golden West Visitor Center in Stekehin; North Cascades Visitor Center near Newhalem. Both offer audiovisual programs and exhibits.

GIFT SHOPS: At Stehekin Landing; book stores in Visitor Centers.

PETS: Permitted on leash in front country, Pacific Crest Trail, and in National Recreation Areas.

HIKING: On established trails and cross-country routes. Check on conditions.

BACKPACKING: Permit required for all overnight trips. Camp at designated sites. No camping on alpine or subalpine meadows. Fires only in designated grates; stoves recommended. Treat water unless from an approved source.

CAMPGROUNDS: Numerous sites along North Cascades Highway and more remote locations. Goodell Creek group sites must be reserved. Fourteen-day use limitation in summer. Horse camping in designated areas only.

TOURS: Ranger-led nature walks at Stehekin, Newhalem, and Colonial campgrounds. Commercial raft tours on Skagit and Stehekin rivers.

OTHER ACTIVITIES: Boat launching; state license required; Coast Guard certificate necessary if vessel uses mechanical propulsion. Fishing with state license. Mountain climbing; cross-country skiing at Stehekin; horseback riding.

FACILITIES FOR DISABLED: Many restrooms; Stehekin shuttle bus; North Cascades Visitor Center; Happy Creek Forest Walk and the Sterling Munro Trail in Ross Lake National Recreation Area.

For additional information, see also Sites, Trails, and Trips on pages 303–310 and the map on pages 282–283.

DESCRIPTIONS HAVE NEVER COME EASY IN the North Cascades. In 1859, topographer Henry Custer wrote: "Nowhere do the Mountain masses and Peaks present such strange, fantastic, dauntless and startling outlines as here." But the more Custer trekked the wild mountains, the less satisfactory his own words seemed to him. Ultimately, he wrote that the North Cascades Range "must be seen . . . it cannot be described." Other pioneers used such adjectives as *wondrous* and *spectacular*—nice choices, yet none of them seemed suitable. Adjectives that worked elsewhere failed here, as if our language had evolved in a world without comparable scenery.

At a loss for words, someone once reached back to a European heritage and gave the North Cascades their most popular epithet: the North American Alps. The range exhibits quintessential alpine features. Jagged peaks, hanging glaciers, mountain meadows, and sapphire lakes dot the upper elevations, while the deeply furrowed valleys below are filled with conifers and waterfalls. This is the North Cascades, tucked into the northwest corner of Washington State. The Cascade Range as a whole extends from British Columbia to northern California.

The park is divided into a North Unit and a South Unit. Between them stretches Ross Lake National Recreation Area, and to the south is Lake Chelan National Recreation Area. The four are administered as North Cascades National Park Service Complex.

Glaciers sculptured the ridges and peaks of the North Cascades Range.

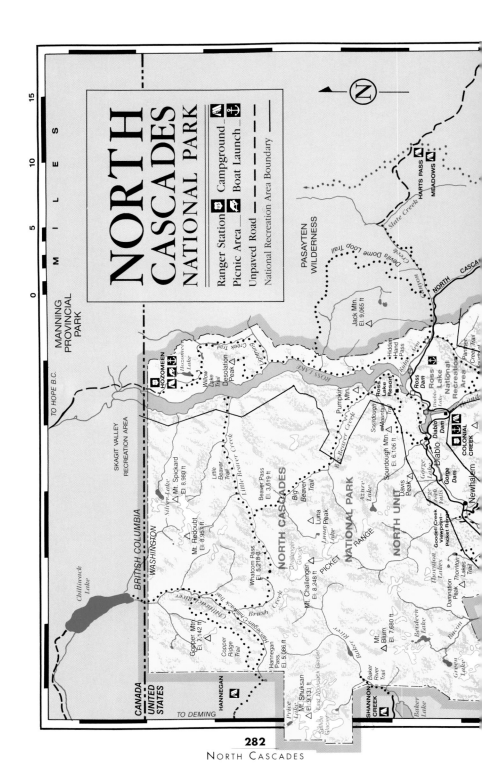

NORTH CASCADES NATIONAL PARK

Ranger Station 🏢
Picnic Area 🏕
Unpaved Road
National Recreation Area Boundary

Campground ⛺
Boat Launch ⚓

MILES
0   5   10   15

N

MANNING PROVINCIAL PARK

TO HOPE B.C.

SKAGIT VALLEY RECREATION AREA

CANADA
UNITED STATES

BRITISH COLUMBIA
WASHINGTON

Chilliwack Lake

Silver Lake
Mt. Spickard El. 8,980 ft
Mt. Redoubt El. 8,957 ft
Copper Mtn El. 7,142 ft
Copper Ridge Trail
Chilliwack River

Hozomeet Lake
HOZOMEEN
Willow Creek Trail
Lightning Creek Trail
Desolation Peak El. 3,619 ft

PASAYTEN WILDERNESS

Jack Mtn. El. 9,065 ft

Slate Creek
Devils Dome Loop Trail
HARTS PASS
MEADOWS
NORTH CASCA

ROSS LAKE

Pumpkin Mtn
Beaver Creek
Sourdough Mountain Trail
Ross Lake Resort
Hidden Hand Pass

Little Beaver Trail
Little Beaver Creek
Beaver Pass El. 3,619 ft
Big Beaver Trail
Luna Peak El. 8,248 ft
Luna Lake
Azure Lake

NORTH CASCADES RANGE

NATIONAL PARK

NORTH UNIT

Challenger Glacier
Mt. Challenger El. 8,248 ft
Whatcom Pass El. 5,218 ft
Brush Creek
Hannegan-Chilliwack Trail
Hannegan Pass El. 5,066 ft

Sourdough Mtn El. 6,106 ft
Davis Peak

Diablo Lake
Gorge Lake
Ross Dam
Diablo Dam
Gorge Dam
Gorge Creek Falls
Goodell Creek Viewpoint
Picket Ranger
Newhalem

Ross National Recreation Area
COLONIAL CREEK

HANNEGAN
TO DEMING

Mt. Shuksan El. 9,131 ft
Price
Little
East Nooksack Glacier
Sulide Glacier

Mt. Blum El. 7,680 ft
Baker River
Baker River Trail

Thornton Lakes
Thornton Lakes Trail
Damnation Peak
Thornton
Berdeen Lake
Bacon

SHANNON CREEK
Baker Lake
Green Lake

282
NORTH CASCADES

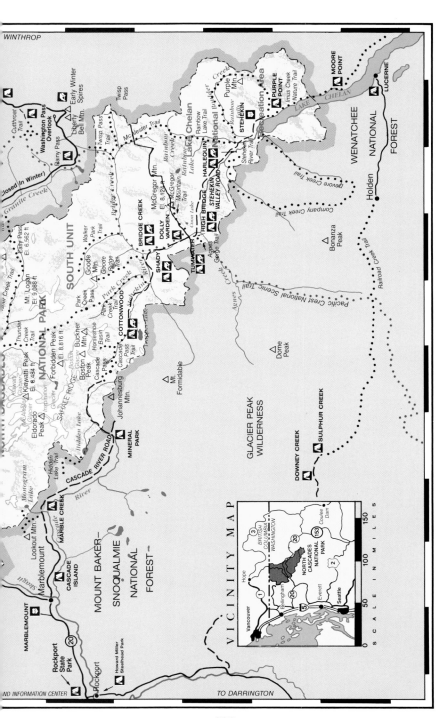

Winter hits hard in the North Cascades. There is little likelihood that many Native peoples had permanent villages there. Instead, it served as a summer home. Indians from at least ten tribes came to collect roots, pick berries, quarry stones for tools, hunt, fish, and trade. They often met in large valleys, such as the Stehekin and Skagit. There they may have traded bone needles for making fishnets and deer ulnas for work in basketry. They left behind clamshell middens and stone points, some dating back thousands of years. The Indians had been in the North Cascades for a long time and doubtless knew the mountains well.

Breaching the Unbreachable

In 1811, Alexander Ross, employed as an officer in John Jacob Astor's Pacific Fur Company, helped establish Fort Okanogan on the Columbia River—the first permanent white settlement in what is now Washington State. He then turned westward, determined to reach Puget Sound.

In 1814, Ross and three Indian guides traveled up the Methow River. Their exact route is unclear. They may have pioneered the course now followed by the North Cascades Highway, or they may have hiked via Bridge Creek, the Stehekin River, and finally over Cascade Pass. Either way, a battered Ross wrote in his journal that "a more difficult route to travel never fell to man's lot." Two of his guides departed, but Ross pushed on. When he was about 150 miles from Fort Okanogan and just shy of the Skagit River, Ross encountered a sudden storm that leveled a stand of huge trees before him. His last guide retreated, and he was alone. At last, cold, tired, and low on provisions, he turned around. The North Cascades remained unbreached by whites.

In 1853, Captain George B. McClellan, who would serve later as general-in-chief of the Union Army in the Civil War, was assigned to find "a suitable wagon route" over the North Cascades. He investigated the Lake Chelan area, listened to local Indians talk about trails up the Stehekin River, and wrote a commendable report, but he found no promising route. In his view, the North Cascades were "impenetrable."

Henry Custer, a young topographer with (according to one account) "a passion for climbing mountains and a talent for recording what he saw," had been assigned to demarcate the United States–Canadian border. In 1859, Custer was sent to survey what is now the northern extremity of North Cascades National Park.

Custer enlisted a party of two whites and nine Indians, and they

Ross Dam, which rises 540 feet high, is one of the world's tallest dams.

set off, "winding our way along steep slopes of the mountains . . . or breaking our way through dense tissues of bush vegetation always found in the bottom of these streams." They entered the Ensawkwatch Creek drainage in what is now the far northwest corner of the park. They crossed ridges into the Little Chilliwack Valley and climbed Copper Mountain, from which Custer first described Mount Baker and Mount Shuksan on the western horizon.

Following the Chilliwack River, Custer apparently turned up Easy Creek into terrain unfamiliar even to his Indian guides. They climbed to Whatcom Pass, and Custer beheld the Picket Range and Challenger Glacier to the south. "All the glaciers in the surrounding mountains, and there are many of them," Custer wrote of Challenger, "vanish before it into insignificance."

Custer and his party eventually floated the Skagit River to Ruby Creek—twice the distance he was assigned to cover—and they pulled ashore just upstream (luckily) of a large waterfall where towering Ross Dam stands today. Returning east, Custer crossed over Devils Dome mountain and explored far east of the present park boundary. At summer's end, Custer estimated that he had walked, floated, or climbed more than 300 miles, and had "made suitable to be mapped" more than 1,000 square miles.

In 1882, Lieutenant Henry Pierce searched for an "elusive army corridor" through the mountains. With a small party he battled his way along a "most imperfect" Indian trail up the Stehekin River, crossed Cascade Pass, found the Skagit River, and eventually reached a small settlement near the present site of Sedro Woolley. The North Cascades had at last been traversed by someone of European descent, but Pierce recommended that no road be built.

"Hard Luck and Rough Country"

No miner made a fortune in the North Cascades, although many tried. Tides of ore seekers flowed and ebbed in the mountains, including a large wave in 1880 and another in 1890. They found some gold dust and rubies, plus a little silver, copper, mercury, iron, chromium, lead, and molybdenum; but there were no big strikes.

For years, steamers plied the Skagit River, carrying men and supplies from Puget Sound to Bacon Creek. These miners filed hundreds of claims in Thunder and Cascade valleys and along Ruby and Canyon creeks. They found, in one writer's words, plenty of "hard luck and rough country" and hiked countless miles over trails "so rough that even blasphemous old prospectors were hard pressed to denounce them sufficiently."

Operations expanded in the late 1800s from riverbank panning to hard-rock drilling. Explosives and machinery were introduced. Well-financed corporations built mining camps and power plants, but ultimately went bankrupt. "Lady Luck" was gone. In fact, she had never been in the North Cascades. In 1898, the Klondike gold rush lured miners north to Alaska and the Yukon. They gathered their picks and bedrolls and left behind the land they had defiled.

A few pioneers remained in the North Cascades, making it their home. Steamships first carried settlers up Lake Chelan in 1889; by 1892 Stehekin boasted a "fancy hotel" and a one-room school. Across the mountains, the Davis family between 1901 and 1907 built cabins and a roadhouse near the present site of Diablo. They charged 50¢ a night for room and board, and $100 for a ton of hay.

The Dam Builders

By the turn of the century, Puget Sound's population was growing rapidly. Energy became a problem, and the North Cascades became a solution. In 1905, a Colorado company chose the upper Skagit River Valley as a site to develop for hydroelectric power. The mountainous terrain offered ideal conditions—a large volume of water, high canyon walls, and a solid rock floor. Costs skyrocketed, however, and one firm sold to another until Seattle Power and Light, a city-owned utility, acquired the project.

Construction began in 1919. Fleets of ferries delivered materials upriver while workers built roads, railways, and tunnels. The towns of Diablo and Newhalem rose overnight as construction crews worked nonstop. The last concrete for that phase of construction was poured in 1949. Thirty years of labor had produced three dams—Gorge, Diablo, and Ross—with a combined power output of 694,000 kilowatts. Disappearing in the process, however, were the canyons upstream of the dams, now drowned and, tragically, lost to human sight.

Climbers and Conservationists

Recreational mountain climbers first entered the North Cascades as early as 1869. These men and women found the alpine country

The Portland Mazamas in the North Cascades.

irresistible, as had the miners, but they loved the land not for what it could produce or become but simply for what it was. They climbed peaks, discovered canyons, and photographed vistas. They wrote eloquent accounts that focused public attention on the unique beauty of these mountains. In so doing, the mountaineers helped promote an attitude toward conservation in the Pacific Northwest that would eventually result in protection for the North Cascades.

The Seattle Mountaineers and the Portland Mazamas organized early climbs. They explored Snowfield and Colonial peaks and the southern Pickets in 1931 and 1932, and Eldorado Peak was climbed in 1933. In the mid-1930s the Mazamas concentrated their efforts south of Cascade Pass. Many major summits, including Dome, Bonanza, and Goode, were first climbed in 1936 after several unsuccessful attempts. However, the banner year for first ascents was 1938. A team of young climbers called the Ptarmigans pioneered the now-famous Ptarmigan Traverse. They hiked from the Miner's Ridge-Dome Peak area to Cascade Pass; along the way, they stood atop Formidable, Magic, Johannesburg, and Boston. By 1942, most major peaks in the North Cascades had been climbed.

Establishment of the Park

As early as 1892, people had suggested a North Cascades National Park. Five years later, President Grover Cleveland signed into existence the Washington Forest Reserve, which, by 1924, had been divided and redivided until the North Cascades province lay split among the Mount Baker, Wenatchee, and Okanogan national forests. The resulting level of protection was labeled "grossly deficient" by many organizations, including the Seattle Mountaineers. Public demand for greater preservation finally induced a joint study by the U.S. departments of the Interior (Park Service) and of Agriculture (Forest Service). In 1965 the special study team released its proposal:

> The portion of the North Cascades in the Study Area defies description. Here occurs the most breathtakingly beautiful and spectacular mountain scenery in the 48 contiguous States. From Glacier Peak northward, particularly the Eldorado Peaks complex, the Picket Range and Mount Shuksan, are what have been termed the "American Alps." Here is scenic grandeur that unquestionably belongs in our national gallery of natural beauty.

On October 2, 1968, President Lyndon Johnson signed a bill creating North Cascades National Park.

White quartz in Skagit gneiss near Diablo Lake Overlook

GEOLOGY

The rocks of the North Cascades region exhibit effects of almost every type of turbulence known to the earth's crust. Almost everything, it seems, has been deformed by fracturing, faulting, and folding. And most of the formations have been altered, mixed, or lost; intruded or extruded; thrust into, over, or under others; tipped on end or turned upside down. Indeed, deciphering the geologic history of the North Cascades is a formidable task.

A Recipe for a Cake

Let's attempt a simplified explanation of one theory. Imagine the North Cascades province as a cake in a rectangular pan. The pan's long axis runs north-south. The geologic recipe includes a large variety of ingredients—rocks of all three major types: igneous, metamorphic, and sedimentary. The assembling process, from beginning to end, takes 10 hours (600 minutes), with each minute representing 1 million years.

By the early 1990s, geologists had concluded that distinct assemblages of rocks, called terranes, had formed in different locations, some far away, and had been brought to the Cascades area attached to plates of oceanic rock. During the first three hours of our cake bake, the ancient rocks settle down and harden.

Volcanism, tectonics, and erosion jumble the layers. Shallow seas invade and deposit more thick beds of sediments. At this time, the cake is about two-thirds complete (the processes having occurred between 600 and 200 million years ago). But now the mixing begins. Several cycles of mountain building and erosion take place. Shallow seas invade again and again. More sedimentary layers are deposited; like those before them, they are jumbled, stood on end, and scraped off.

Meanwhile, a molten mass of magma crystallizes into granite, and slowly begins to rise from deep within the cake. It shoves aside and further jumbles the older rocks, rising like a dome above all else around it. With only about 30 minutes remaining (30 million years ago), the granite uplift subsides and another major process begins. The cake fractures lengthwise into giant blocks that rise and fall adjacent to one another. Concurrently, the entire mass arches upward in the center, with the north end of the cake lifting higher. Erosion thus accelerates in the north end of these new mountains, exposing deeper and more ancient rocks.

This mountain-building process continues off and on for at least 25 minutes, leaving only 5 minutes. Soon thereafter (3 or 4 million years ago), the Mount Baker and Glacier Peak volcanoes rise above the surrounding summits. They are solitary mountains of lava formed deep in the earth's crust, where the subduction of ocean-floor rock beneath North America causes the rock to heat, expand, and at last climb to the surface.

The ice age begins in the last 2 minutes. During this period, great continental glaciers flow and ebb at least four times over northern North America. Alpine glaciers fill the new mountains, reshaping every landform from summit to streambed. Then, with one second remaining, the great glaciers retreat (this was the Fraser glaciation of the late Pleistocene epoch, which lasted from 25,000 to 13,500 years ago).

The completed assembly of the cake ingredients brings us to today. We see steep, abrupt mountains, rough-hewn and youthful. Nonetheless, their rocks tell complicated stories of tectonics, volcanism, metamorphism, deposition, and erosion: an anthology of change.

In contrast to the time since formation of the most ancient rocks, the ice age is remarkably recent. Massive glaciers filled the North Cascades in the final seconds of our 10-hour geologic cake bake, and carved the mountains almost as an afterthought. Yet this icing on the cake is not really the finishing touch of the recipe at all; on its own imperceptibly slow timetable, geological activity continues assembling ingredients for a recipe that will never be completed.

Opposite: A short but strenuous climb leads to this view from Cascade Pass.

A Sea of Peaks

A day hiker in the North Cascades might walk past exposures of granite, gneiss, schist, breccia, pumice, and tuff, as well as the more obscure rock types (or traces thereof) that only a trained geologist could identify. So greatly altered are the North Cascades rocks that a geology professor once suggested the area be called "Metamorphism National Park."

The Picket Range consists almost entirely of granite and probably constitutes the most homogeneous zone of rock in the park. Gneiss and schist lie exposed at many mountain summits and along Washington 20 near Ruby Mountain. The Yellow Aster Complex—the oldest rock in the North Cascades—remains buried except in a few places outside the park in the western foothills.

Although the composition of the rocks tells a remarkable story, it is the bold profiles of the North Cascades that most strongly command one's attention. Viewed from any summit, the mountains are reminiscent of the surface of a choppy sea; peaks are visible on every horizon, where sharp summits and serrated ridges rise between the cutting edges of the ice.

Tucked into cirques and hanging over valleys, more than 300

A bird's-eye view of glaciers.

alpine glaciers add a rich, dynamic element to the North Cascades. Among the largest are Redoubt, Challenger, Boston, Neve, Klawatti, McAlester, Fremont, and Inspiration. All are the vestiges of the vast ice mass that sculptured these mountains. Water spills off their flanks, polishes the rocks, and disappears into the forest below. The smallest glaciers have no names and border on being classified as snowfields. All of them put together would still be of insignificant size by Alaska standards. But size is not important. A veteran hiker of Washington's mountains, Harvey Manning, writes:

> For grand glaciers that overpower mountains, there are Greenland and Antarctica. For glaciers that leave room for flowers and trees, and lakes and rivers—and people—there are the North Cascades.

Natural History

Ocean, Cloud, and Rain

An Indian legend describing the creation and climate of the Cascade Range comes close to the modern scientific explanation.

Long ago, the land was flat and little rain fell. A tribe in the east asked Ocean for help, and he obliged by sending his children, Cloud and Rain. All went well until the tribe became greedy and refused to let Cloud and Rain return home to the west. After pleading with the tribe to no avail, Ocean finally appealed to the Great Spirit, asking that the tribe be punished. Suddenly the earth trembled and a huge pit opened in the land. Rock rose out of the pit and piled up in immense jagged peaks—the North Cascades. Meanwhile, into the pit flowed Ocean, forming Puget Sound. Cloud and Rain returned home to Ocean, west of the new mountains, and the land to the east grew even more parched and dry than before. Cloud and Rain now visit the east rarely, only when they can breach the mountains.

The Indians obviously understood the rain-shadow effect. They realized that the mountains catch the rain and have a significant effect on the variation in precipitation from west to east. The prevailing westerlies blow almost continuously off the Pacific Ocean and over Washington State. Moisture-laden air reaches the Cascades, rises, cools, and while still on the western slopes drops its moisture as rain in the low elevations and as snow higher up. The west side of the North Cascades, near the crest and with exceptions, receives an average annual precipitation of nearly 110 inches. Fifty feet of snowfall in a winter is not unusual at higher

Overleaf: Pacific silver fir appears on western slopes at about 1,800 feet.

According to legend, wherever Oregon ash grows, poisonous snakes disappear.

elevations, and between 4 and 5 feet may fall in a day. Moving east, the air descends, warms, and develops considerable capacity for evaporation. It can become a desiccating wind, completely devoid of moisture. Stehekin averages 35 inches of precipitation a year, while the Pasayten Wilderness, just to the east of the park, receives only 12 inches annually.

This is the dominant weather pattern of the North Cascades: wet west, dry east. Elevation also has an important effect in this mountainous region, where summits abruptly rise 6,000 to 7,000 feet above valley floors. The angle of slope and the amount of exposure then become significant. In combination, these factors dictate the abundance, type, and distribution of every organism that lives in the North Cascades.

From Conifers to Stonecrops and Back

Finding a predictable pattern in the occurrence of North Cascades plant life seems at first impossible. The convoluted topography, ragged at every edge, baffles casual attempts to classify and organize. The steep mountains are bordered on one side by the ocean and on the other by a near desert. Such conditions create a rich and varied flora. However, upon close inspection a subtle order emerges in the distribution of vegetation in the North Cascades.

Plant distributions and associations are dominated by two factors. First, from east to west the precipitation increases by as much

Black-tailed deer move in a series of bounds called "stotting."

as ninefold. Second, from valley bottom to ridgetop many living conditions worsen; soil quality deteriorates, air temperatures drop, slopes become steeper, and the growing season shortens.

Different species of large, shade-tolerant conifers define the limits of the region's various climatic zones. Each is able to set seed in the subdued light beneath a closed forest canopy. Above the treeline in the high Alpine zone, however, wildflowers cluster together in self-made microclimates, hugging the earth in rosette and button shapes. Primitive plants also fare well in the park. Botanists have counted 116 species of lichens and 124 species of mosses, most of them on the mountains' west slope.

Excluding the coastal Sitka spruce forests, western hemlock and western redcedar are dominant in the western lowlands from sea level to about 1,800 feet. Pacific silver fir then replaces redcedar in a zone that reaches to about 4,500 feet. The Western Hemlock-Silver Fir zone gives way to the Mountain Hemlock-Silver Fir zone, which extends up to the Alpine zone, approximately 6,000 feet above sea level.

The understory throughout these zones is determined by the overall environment. Large shrubs characterize the open forests. Vine maple, red elderberry, Indian plum, salmonberry, thimbleberry, and the smaller goat's beard are the most noteworthy. Beneath the canopy of the closed forest grow red huckleberry at lower ele-

Overleaf: Water, organic matter, and minerals may one day become fertile soil.

Pine needles collect in the shallow depressions of a rock outcrop.

vations and mountain and Cascade huckleberry at higher elevations near subalpine meadows. Along the streams grow devil's club
(notorious for its thorns), prickly currant, various species of willow,
and, again, salmonberry and thimbleberry.

A conspicuous plant of the western forest ecosystem is the fern.
Ferns grow nearly everywhere, especially sword and deer ferns.
Lady ferns form dense communities in moist habitats. Widely distributed flowering plants in the forest include wintergreen, foam
flower, princess pine, strawberry bramble, twin flower, ground
dogwood, queen's cup lily, and twisted rosy stalk.

In the higher zones, breaks in the forest occur at sites of
avalanche tracks, deep snowpack, and topographic irregularities
such as rock outcrops. Avalanche tracks contain diverse vegetation
normally associated with open forests, and dominated by slide alder,
vine maple, and yellow cedar. Rock outcrops, on the other hand,
support only sparse plant life; spreading phlox, Davidson's pentstemon, and stonecrops survive here. Sites of deep snowpack have a
meadowlike aspect in the summer, characterized mostly by sedges.

Mountain hemlock, subalpine fir, and silver fir all have the
capacity to invade highland meadows. Once one of them succeeds,
the others follow. They eventually form tree clumps with low profiles and spreading bases. Gracing the meadows are blossoms of
paintbrush, partridge foot, western anemone, fan leaf cinquefoil,

Queen Anne's lace blossom about to break open its dewy veil.

mountain bistort, Sitka valerian, bracted lousewort, and broad leaf arnica. White, five-petaled spring beauties and carpets of glacier lilies appear soon after the snow melts. White and red heather and Cascade huckleberry grow on the ridgetops, while down in the seepage areas saxifrages, gentians, bog orchids, and marsh marigolds prevail.

The highest zone is the Alpine, distinguished by unstable soils that easily erode. Most of this zone consists of talus slopes, snow-fields, glaciers, and treeless ground strewn with rocks. Nonetheless, yellow heather grows here, as do Cascade willow and Cascade huckleberry. The hardiest of flowering plants embrace the ground like a skin on the alpine topography. Blossoms include moss campion, alpine pussytoes, silky phacelia, shrubby cinquefoil, spreading phlox, desert parsleys, locoweed, stonecrops, daisies, and several species of pinks and of mustards. In such adversity, these plants put forth beautiful blossoms; and on the rock surfaces where the flowers cannot grow, colorful lichens survive.

Downslope to the east, subalpine and western larch reigns above clumps of Engelmann spruce and subalpine fir. Twisted and gnarled whitebark pines grow here, too. Farther downslope, drought-resistant trees begin to appear, and the forest understory thins out appreciably. Douglas-fir dominates at elevations equivalent to where western hemlock and silver fir grow on the Cascades' west side. Lastly, when the dryness of the soil has denied survival even to the adaptable Douglas-fir and the slopes are blanketed by bunch grasses, the ponderosa pine survives in the lowest eastern foothills of the North Cascades.

Well-Oiled Plumage and Flower-Filled Cheeks

The North Cascades wildlife is as diverse and abundant as its plant life. While some species live down low or up high, others tolerate a range of environmental stresses and seem at home everywhere.

Probably the richest wildlife zone in the park is the subalpine meadow. Mule deer graze and browse along the forest fringe. Black bears feast in the autumn huckleberry patches. Hoary marmots sunbathe on the dirt porches of their burrows, while pikas scamper across talus slopes, their mouths stuffed with alpine flowers.

Mountain lions, bobcats, and mountain goats live in the North Cascades, but they are seldom seen. Grizzly bears still survive in small numbers in the greater North Cascades area, and wolves are slowly returning.

Most conspicuous in the forest are the Douglas squirrel (or chickaree) and the red squirrel. These frisk from limb to limb, harvesting seeds from cones, berating all who approach. Also present is the Townsend chipmunk, which busily feeds on the forest floor. Even busier are fourteen species of shrews, voles, and moles, which taken together inhabit every vegetation zone in the North Cascades.

More than 120 bird species are year-round residents of the North Cascades, while at least 60 others visit regularly or occasionally. Gray jays and Clark's nutcrackers swoop and chatter in the subalpine treetops. Rufous hummingbirds searching for nectar hover in front of red-shirted hikers and then dart away. White-tailed ptarmigan explode from the brush at a traveler's approach, while nesting horned larks remain quiet, still, and unnoticed. From the forest come the tappings of woodpeckers, sapsuckers, and flickers, plus the nasal calls of nuthatches and the distinctive two-note song of the black-capped chickadee. Deeper still into the forest are the songsmiths, the thrushes; and there, too, is the ubiquitous winter wren, flying and scampering through the forest understory.

Most curious of all is a dark gray bird with an upturned tail and pointed bill that inhabits the park's forest rivers and streams, nesting behind waterfalls or beneath high-water cutbanks. In a most un-birdlike fashion, it dives into the frigid water and walks along the bottom to feed on aquatic insects. Its well-oiled plumage keeps it warm and dry. Popping out of the water, it stands atop a midstream boulder and dips methodically up and down. This is the dipper, or water ouzel, a bird very much at home in the North Cascades.

Herpetologists have counted thirteen species of amphibians (salamanders, newts, toads, and frogs) and fourteen species of reptiles (turtles, lizards, and snakes) in the park. Most of these animals prefer damp lowland habitats, but some range surprisingly high—even up to subalpine lakes and creeks. Most amphibians require a moist environment throughout their life cycles and are therefore more common on the mountains' western slopes. Of special interest is the tailed frog. Although a true tail is absent, it has vestigial tail-wagging muscles, and the male has a copulatory organ resembling a tail. Reptiles fare better than amphibians on the dry eastern side of the North Cascades.

Sites, Trails, and Trips

Washington 20

Completed in 1972 and dedicated as "the most scenic mountain drive in Washington," Washington 20 runs east to west over the North Cascades. It follows the Ross Lake National Recreation Area corridor between the park's North and South units, skirting the south sides of Ross and Diablo lakes and the north shore of Gorge Lake. Below Gorge Dam, it traces the Skagit River to Interstate 5.

Washington 20 passes through one town in the park, Newhalem, and near another, Diablo. The drive is beautiful, replete with forests, mountains, and waterfalls. Probably the most picturesque site along the route is at Washington Pass (5,483 feet) in the Okanogan National Forest east of the park, where Liberty Bell Mountain and Early Winter Spires rise immediately to the south.

The highway affords access to numerous trails that lead into the park. They begin in the Ross Lake corridor and Okanogan National Forest. Heavy snows close the highway each winter, usually from mid-November to mid-April, although the towns and the park's North Cascades Visitor Center at Newhalem remain accessible. The towns provide access to winter recreational activities.

Roads

Nooksack Valley Road. This road provides access to Hannegan Campground, in Mount Baker-Snoqualmie National Forest, from which hikers can enter the far northwest corner of the park via Hannegan Pass. Washington 542 runs from Bellingham (90 miles north of Seattle on Interstate 5) east to Mount Baker. At the Mount Baker Lodge turnoff, U.S. Forest Service Road 402 continues east into the mountains. It soon divides, the right fork leading to a trail that climbs toward Price Lake and Nooksack Cirque, and the left fork wrapping around Nooksack Ridge and eventually arriving at Hannegan Campground.

Cascade River Road. This is a long, bumpy ride into breath-taking country. The road branches off the North Cascades Highway at Marblemount, travels southeast for about 23 miles, and enters the park's South Unit. From there, it continues upward several miles and finally ends between the imposing summits of Johannesburg Mountain (8,200 feet) to the west and Boston Peak (8,894 feet) to the east. (Trailers are not allowed for the last few miles.) This is the trail head for a rigorous climb to Doubtful Lake and Cascade Pass, thirty-three switchbacks up.

Stehekin Valley Road. This old mine-to-market road is accessible only by ferry (see below). It begins at the Stehekin boat landing, near the north end of Lake Chelan, and winds 20 miles up the Stehekin Valley to Cottonwood Campground, passing seven other campgrounds and eight trail heads. Park Service shuttle buses travel the road regularly, from end to end. In 1995, the Park Service was considering closing the upper 7 miles of the road. The valley offers a wide choice of day hikes, most of which originate at the town of Stehekin or near the campgrounds. The mist from Rainbow Falls (312 feet), has created a small but lush fern grotto.

Lakes

Lake Chelan. The largest lake in the park was formed by Pleistocene glaciers and impounded by a moraine at its southern end. Subsequently, a power dam raised the water level. At its deepest point, the lake now measures 1,500 feet from surface to bottom, making it one of the deepest in North America.

Only the northernmost 5 miles of the 55-mile-long lake are in the park. A ferryboat runs daily, March 15 to October 15, between the town of Chelan and Stehekin, a 5-hour round trip. Canoes, kayaks, and other small craft also travel the lake. This can be dangerous, however, because powerful north winds often kick up rough water. It is best to paddle near the shore and to keep an eye on the weather.

Ross Lake. The only vehicle access—a long drive through British Columbia—and boat launch on Ross Lake is at its north end, at Hozomeen. Canoeists and kayakers can launch their craft onto Diablo Lake at Colonial Creek Campground, portage around Ross Dam on a one-mile jeep trail, and enter Ross Lake. Along the lake's

Opposite: The Skagit River, downstream from Diablo Dam.

shore are seventeen boat-access and camping areas, and seven trail heads. The trails climb either west into the park's North Unit or east into the Pasayten Wilderness.

Trails

More than 350 miles of trail wind and climb up and down throughout North Cascades National Park Service Complex. The various trails follow rivers, creeks, and contours, but sometimes also meet the topography head-on. The ever-present switchbacks are steep and occasionally rocky. Yet the hiker's rewards are plentiful.

In the high country it is important to tread lightly. The soils and vegetation have been badly damaged at several passes, which were subsequently closed to camping.

Whereas lowland trails might remain open all year, alpine trails are usually not snow-free until late June or July, or even later. An ice ax is a good idea, as are wool clothing and sturdy raingear. On some trails, streams must be forded. And throughout the North Cascades, mercurial weather may bring rain, hail, or snow in an instant.

Several long trails traverse or loop the North and South units of the park. Most of these have campsites spaced every 3 to 4 miles. Permits are required for overnight trips. Day hikes are more numerous in the national recreation areas.

Chilliwack River-Copper Ridge Loop. This trail measures about 35 miles from Hannegan Campground, through the park, and back to the campground. A 4-mile climb to Hannegan Pass opens sweeping views of Nooksack Ridge, Copper Mountain, and Chilliwack Valley. Another mile onward, the trail enters the park and then divides. The right fork is the *Hannegan-Chilliwack River Trail,* the lower end of the loop. This portion of the trail passes through stands of western hemlock and Douglas-fir interspersed with avalanche chutes that offer glimpses of the valley walls. After several river crossings, the forest deepens into groves of huge western redcedars that shade the trail throughout the day. About 5 miles from the Canadian border, the Copper Ridge Trail begins a steep series of switchbacks up and to the west. Mount Baker and Mount Shuksan stand out in bold relief from atop Copper Ridge. The fire lookout (6,260 feet) near Egg Lake is the highest point on the trail. Summer wildflowers and russet autumn tones enrich the trail as it follows the precipice where Copper Ridge falls away to the Chilliwack Valley.

Brush Creek-Little Beaver Trail. The Brush Creek Trail crosses Whatcom Pass between the Chilliwack River Trail and the Big and Little Beaver trails. Colorful meadows and rivulets of water bright-

Dormant Mount Baker, which is of volcanic origin, showed signs of activity in 1975.

en Whatcom Pass. A side trail to the south unveils excellent views of Challenger Glacier, from much the same prospect as Henry Custer had in 1859. The Little Beaver Trail offers easy hiking, assuming the Park Service is on top of damage in slide and stream areas; it follows switchbacks down the final mile to Ross Lake.

Big Beaver Trail. This trail begins at Ross Dam and can be followed 46 miles to Hannegan Campground (via Brush Creek, the Chilliwack River, and Hannegan Pass). It swings along a hillside above the west shore of lower Ross Lake, joins the Big Beaver drainage, and turns northwestward. This drainage was saved when conservationists prevented the raising of Ross Dam. Shortly upstream are some huge beaver dams believed to be 150 years old. At an active beaver pond near 39-Mile Creek these mammals may be seen in the evening or early morning. River otters live here also, and great blue herons may be seen along the shore. The area contains possibly the largest stand of western redcedars anywhere. The trail works gently upriver. Views of Luna Cirque and the Picket Range open to the west as the forest thins on the higher ground. Switchbacks climb to the top of Beaver Pass, from which the trail drops 2 miles to Little Beaver Trail.

Thunder Creek-Park Creek Trail. This popular trail runs 26 miles from Colonial Creek Campground to the Stehekin Valley Road. The trail offers many rewarding views of mountain scenery, especially the portion along Fisher Creek. Looking to the south, hikers can see Boston Glacier tucked beneath Forbidden Peak, Boston Peak, and Buckner Mountain. The trail climbs and drops several

TRAILS OF NORTH CASCADES NATIONAL PARK

Approximately 360 miles of trails offer access to more than 600,000 acres of wilderness in the Cascades. The weather can change quickly. Rivers and streams rise and fall, and altitudes vary widely. All hikers, therefore, should consult trail guides and rangers for information on current conditions.

STEHEKIN VALLEY AREA

LAKESHORE TRAIL: Starts at Golden West Visitor Center; continues beyond Moore Point to Prince Creek; 7 miles one way to Moore Point; 3.5 hours; several excellent views of Lake Chelan; trail crosses 5 streams; private property along trail should be respected.

McGREGOR MOUNTAIN TRAIL: Starts at High Bridge with Coon Lake Trail; ends at McGregor summit; 8 miles one way; 12 hours round trip; steep ascent of 6,200 feet; last .5 mile involves hand-and-foot scrambling up talus and ledges; rewarding views; weather conditions and snow level must be checked at ranger station before summit climb is attempted.

OLD WAGON ROAD LOOP TRAIL: Starts and ends off Coon Lake Trail at lake; 3.5 miles; 2 hours round trip; follows signs toward Bridge Creek and Cascade Pass; then cuts off to Stehekin Valley Road and follows it back to High Bridge.

RAINBOW LOOP TRAIL: Starts and ends at Rainbow Creek trail head; 5 miles one way; 2-3 hours round trip; elevation change of 1,000 feet in first 2 miles; trail crosses bridge over Rainbow Creek at 2 miles and passes through ponderosa pine forest back to road; road leads to starting point.

STEHEKIN RIVER TRAIL: Starts at Harlequin Campground; ends at Weaver Point on Lake Chelan; 4 miles one way; 4 hours round trip; level, cool, and shaded trail with spring flowers, birds, and fishing holes; stream floods in spring.

AGNES GORGE TRAIL: Starts at High Bridge; ends at Agnes Gorge; 2 miles one way; 2-3 hours round trip; 300-foot ascent; begins in dense ponderosa forest, then opens with views of gorge; fine views of Junction Mountain; cool in summer.

IMUS CREEK NATURE TRAIL: Starts at Golden West Visitor Center; ends at Purple Point Campground; .25 mile; .5 to 1 hour; short hike across and along wet stream environment and into contrasting drier, open environment; trail quickly escapes hubbub of Stehekin community. Interpretive brochure.

UPPER STEHEKIN VALLEY AREA

CASCADE PASS TRAIL (EAST): Approaches Cascade Pass from Cottonwood Campground, 5.5 miles east of pass; 8 hours round trip; 2,600-foot ascent; 1-mile hike up Sahale Arm from pass offers panoramic views of Sahale Mountain, Doubtful Lake, and Stehekin Valley.

HORSESHOE BASIN TRAIL: Leads off Cascade Pass Trail, 2.5 miles from Cottonwood Campground; good stopping point is Black Warrior Mine, 3.7 miles from trail head one way; 6 hours round trip; more than 15 waterfalls from snowfields to meadow floor; Sahale and Davenport glaciers dominate scenery; 2,000-foot ascent.

The shores of Ross Lake offer seventeen boat-access camping areas.

PARK CREEK TRAIL: Starts about 2.5 miles west of Bridge Creek on Stehekin River Road; ends at Park Creek Pass; 7.2 miles one way; 4-5 hours round trip; steep, with many switchbacks for first 1.5 mile, then level until meadow; climb from meadow to pass is 3 steep miles; magnificent views, fragile alpine area.

GOODE RIDGE LOOKOUT TRAIL: Starts at trail head just across Bridge Creek bridge; ends at site of old fire lookout (6,680 feet) on Goode Ridge; 5 miles one way; 8 hours round trip; trail runs through dense forest for 3.5 miles, then opens onto spectacular views; 4,600-foot ascent overall.

WEST SIDE AREA

SOURDOUGH MOUNTAIN TRAIL: Starts at main parking area at town of Diablo, off Washington 20 behind inflated dome of an indoor swimming pool; ends at Sourdough Lookout cabin; 10 miles round trip; 7 hours; 5,000-foot ascent; steep trail with numerous switchbacks; excellent views of park—Diablo and Ross lakes, Boston Glacier, Jack Mountain, and north into Canada.

THORNTON LAKES TRAIL: Starts at parking area on Thornton Creek Road, 5 miles from Washington 20 and 11 miles from Marblemount; ends at Thornton Lakes; 9.5 miles round trip to lower lake; 6-8 hours; first 2 miles on abandoned logging road before real trail begins; trail leads through forest to 4,900-foot ridge, then down 400 feet to lowest and largest of the three lakes; great views.

THUNDER CREEK TRAIL: Starts at .1 mile south of North Cascades Highway, off paved Colonial Creek Campground Road; ends at Park Creek Pass; 19.1 miles; 9 to 12 hours in, 6-8 hours out; 6,300-foot ascent; leads through forested valley exhibiting variety of ecosystems and wildlife typical of uncut forest areas.

times between Junction Camp and Thunder Basin. The highest point is at Park Creek Pass, with an elevation of 6,063 feet. Snow can linger here until August, and it may be necessary to follow the rock cairns in order to stay on the trail. Continuing south, the trail descends to the Stehekin Valley Road.

Easy Pass-Fisher Creek Trail. This trail begins off the North Cascades Highway, at a parking area about 5 miles north of Rainy Pass. A short but arduous climb leads to Easy Pass, where stands of subalpine fir open into mountain meadows. Vistas unfold to the east, where the highway follows Granite Creek, and to the west, where the trail drops into the Fisher Creek drainage. It follows many switchbacks to a meadow rich with wildflowers and then enters the forest. Several miles downstream along Fisher Creek, the trail joins the Thunder Creek–Park Creek traverse.

Bridge Creek Trail. This is a short fragment of the famous *Pacific Crest National Scenic Trail,* which extends from Canada to Mexico. It begins near Rainy Pass on the North Cascades Highway, parallels the highway for about a mile, and then turns south and west to follow Bridge Creek downstream. The *Twisp Pass, McAlester, and Rainbow Lake trails* all join Bridge Creek and offer hiking options to the south and east. Farther downstream, the Walker Park Trail turns north and climbs 7 miles up Bridge Creek's North Fork to a broad basin beneath Mount Logan and Goode Mountain. The main branch of the Bridge Creek Trail continues for a few more miles through dense woods to the Stehekin Valley Road and Bridge Creek Campground.

Cascade Pass Trail. This is a demanding hike, short on mileage but long on work. It begins at Cottonwood Campground at the end of Stehekin Valley Road. Just above Basin Creek, a side trail leads to Horseshoe Basin, a formerly active mining area where prospectors tried their luck and failed. Today, wildflowers and more than a dozen waterfalls help to soften the century-old scars. Back on the main trail, a climb leads to Cascade Pass. From here, a side trail climbs to beautiful alpine vistas atop Sahale Ridge. Footing here must be chosen carefully; the entire Cascade Pass area is heavily visited and deserves gentler treatment than it has received in the past. Please stay on the trail. The last leg of the trail drops for 4 miles to the Cascade River Road. There are thirty-three sweeping switchbacks and, as on most trails in the North Cascades, countless ecological transitions from ridgetop to valley floor.

Opposite: Mount Shuksan, one of the North Cascade's "American Alps."

OLYMPIC
NATIONAL PARK

OLYMPIC NATIONAL PARK
600 EAST PARK AVENUE
PORT ANGELES, WASHINGTON 98362
TEL.: (360) 452-0330

HIGHLIGHTS: Mount Olympus • Lake Quinault • Lake Crescent • Blue Glacier • Hurricane Ridge • Hoh Rain Forest • Hall of Mosses • Enchanted Valley

ACCESS: From Portland, take I-5 to U.S. 101, which provides main access to the park. From Seattle, use the ferry system and the Hood Canal Bridge. Air service from Seattle.

HOURS: Year-round, 24 hours, daily.

FEES: At entrance, per vehicle, and for camping.

PARKING: Available at all visitor centers and trail heads.

GAS, FOOD: Gas at Fairholm Visitor Service Area and Kalaloch Lodge. Restaurants at Kalaloch Lodge, Lake Crescent Lodge, Log Cabin Resort, and Sol Duc Hot Springs Resort. Snack bar at Fairholm and Hurricane Ridge.

LODGING: Variety available in park; make reservations well in advance. For information, contact Olympic Park Visitor Center.

VISITOR CENTER: Olympic Park Visitor Center in Port Angeles (open all year), the Storm King Visitor Center at Lake Crescent, Hurricane Ridge, Kalaloch, and Hoh Rain Forest. Port Angeles has an audiovisual program; all centers have exhibits and numerous publications and maps for sale.

MUSEUM: Olympic Park Visitor Center in Port Angeles.

GIFT SHOP: At Sol Duc Hot Springs Resort, Lake Crescent Lodge, Kalaloch Lodge, Log Cabin Resort.

PETS: Permitted on leash in campgrounds and parking lots, prohibited on trails and in backcountry.

BACKPACKING: Permits required for all overnight trips, available at all ranger stations and some trail heads. Minimum-impact camping techniques recommended, as well as familiarity with the park's backcountry guidelines.

CAMPGROUNDS: Check with park headquarters about facilities available during the off-season. Summer season campgrounds may be crowded; all sites available on a first-come basis. Trailer hookups, showers, and laundry facilities available at privately owned lodges. Campers must use designated sites. Fourteen-day stay limit in summer. Fires prohibited in some areas; stoves recommended.

OTHER ACTIVITIES: Cross-country skiing, mountain climbing, horseback riding, swimming, water skiing, boating, and fishing per regulations.

FACILITIES FOR DISABLED: All visitor centers.

For additional information, see also Sites, Trails, and Trips on pages 337–350 and the map on pages 316–317.

The Olympic Mountains, as seen from the Seattle suburb of Magnolia.

SEASHORE, RAIN FOREST, AND MOUNTAIN, three distinct environments, embody Olympic National Park. The ocean forever pounds the shore, its thundering surf a counterpoint to the calm, cathedral-like forest nearby. Inland, glaciers cut the Olympics' summits, streams pour through alpine meadows, and rivers carry sediment to the sea. Marmots hibernate in the heart of the park, while starfish populate its coastal periphery.

Olympic National Park lies in the center of the Olympic Peninsula, where Washington State juts westward to challenge the Pacific Ocean. Thus isolated, the park supports a rich natural history and a colorful human heritage. And one soon discovers that Olympic is not only a geographical peninsula but an ecological island as well.

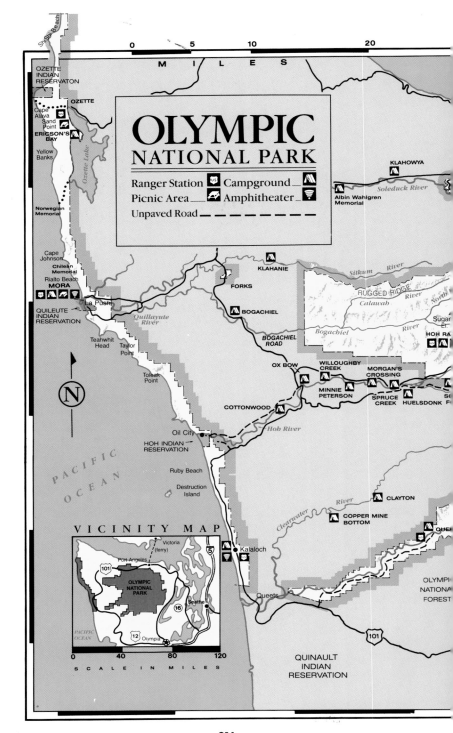

OLYMPIC
NATIONAL PARK

Ranger Station | Campground
Picnic Area | Amphitheater
Unpaved Road

OZETTE INDIAN RESERVATON

Cape Alava
Sand Point
Ozette Lake
ERICSON'S BAY
OZETTE

Yellow Banks

Norwegian Memorial

Cape Johnson
Chilean Memorial
Rialto Beach
MORA
La Push

QUILEUTE INDIAN RESERVATION

Teahwhit Head
Taylor Point
Toleak Point

N

Quillayute River

KLAHANIE

FORKS

BOGACHIEL

BOGACHIEL ROAD

OX BOW
WILLOUGHBY CREEK
MORGAN'S CROSSING
MINNIE PETERSON
COTTONWOOD
SPRUCE CREEK
HUELSDONK

KLAHOWYA

Soleduck River

Albin Wahlgren Memorial

Sitkum River

RUGGED RIDGE
Calawah River
Bogachiel River
North

Sugar El
HOH RA

Oil City
HOH INDIAN RESERVATION

PACIFIC OCEAN

Ruby Beach

Destruction Island

Hoh River

CLAYTON

COPPER MINE BOTTOM

Clearwater River

QUE

OLYMPI
NATIONA
FOREST

VICINITY MAP

Victoria (ferry)
Port Angeles
101
OLYMPIC NATIONAL PARK
5
16
12 Olympia
Seattle
PACIFIC OCEAN

0   40   80   120
S C A L E   I N   M I L E S

Kalaloch

Queets

101

QUINAULT INDIAN RESERVATION

0   5   10   20
M I L E S

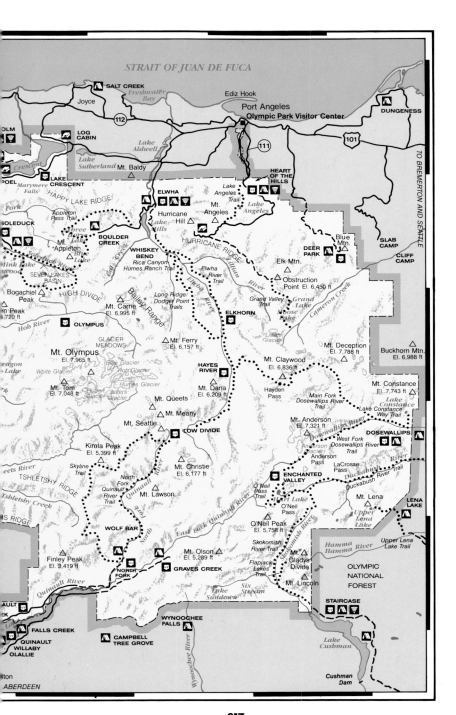

STRAIT OF JUAN DE FUCA

SALT CREEK
Joyce
Freshwater Bay
Ediz Hook
Port Angeles
Olympic Park Visitor Center
DUNGENESS

OLM
LOG CABIN
112
111
101
TO BREMERTON AND SEATTLE

Lake Aldwell
Lake Sutherland
Mt. Baldy
SPOEL
LAKE CRESCENT
Marymere Falls
HAPPY LAKE RIDGE
ELWHA
Lake Angeles Trail
HEART OF THE HILLS
Lake Angeles
SLAB CAMP

Fork
SOLEDUCK
Appleton Pass Trail
Three Lake
Hurricane Hill
Mt. Angeles
HURRICANE RIDGE
Blue Mtn.
DEER PARK
CLIFF CAMP

Mt. Appleton
Blue Lake
BOULDER CREEK
WHISKEY BEND
Rica Canyon
Humes Ranch Trail
Elwha River Trail
Elk Mtn.
Obstruction Point El. 6,450 ft

Mink Lake
SEVEN LAKES BASIN
HIGH DIVIDE
Cat Creek
Long Ridge Dodger Point Trails
Grand Valley Trail
Grand Lake
Moose Lake
Cameron Creek

Bogachiel Peak
Mt. Carrie El. 6,995 ft
Bailey Range
ELKHORN
Lillian Glacier
Mt. Deception El. 7,788 ft
Buckhorn Mtn. El. 6,988 ft

Hob River
OLYMPUS
GLACIER MEADOWS
Mt. Ferry El. 6,157 ft
Mt. Claywood El. 6,836 ft
Mt. Constance El. 7,743 ft

Mt. Olympus El. 7,965 ft
Blue Glacier
Hoh Glacier
HAYES RIVER
Hayden Pass
Lake Constance Way Trail

White Glacier
Hubert Glacier
Jeffers Glacier
Humes Glacier
Mt. Dana El. 6,209 ft
Main Fork Dosewallips River Trail
Lake Constance

Mt. Tom El. 7,048 ft
Mt. Queets
Mt. Anderson El. 7,321 ft
West Fork Dosewallips River Trail
DOSEWALLIPS

Mt. Meany
Anderson Glacier
Anderson Pass

Mt. Seattle
LOW DIVIDE
LaCrosse Pass
Duckabush River Trail
LENA LAKE

Kimta Peak El. 5,399 ft
Skyline Trail
North Fork Quinault River Trail
Mt. Christie El. 6,177 ft
ENCHANTED VALLEY
O'Neil Pass Trail
Hart Lake
Mt. Lena
Upper Lena Lake

TSHLETSHY RIDGE
Mt. Lawson
O'Neil Pass
Upper Lena Lake Trail

WOLF BAR
O'Neil Peak El. 5,758 ft
Skokomish River Trail

Finley Peak El. 3,419 ft
NORTH FORK
Mt. Olson El. 5,289 ft
GRAVES CREEK
Flapjack Lakes Trail
Mt. Gladys
Mt. Lincoln
OLYMPIC NATIONAL FOREST

Quinault River
Lake Sundown
Six Stream
STAIRCASE

AULT
FALLS CREEK
WYNOOCHEE FALLS
CAMPBELL TREE GROVE
Lake Cushman

QUINAULT WILLABY OLALLIE
Cushman Dam

ABERDEEN

Native Americans

Nature was generous to the early people of the Olympic Peninsula. Comfortably quartered in multifamily long houses built of wooden planks, they had to endure neither extremely cold winters nor very hot summers.

In the forest they gathered roots and berries and hunted deer and elk. They fished salmon, trout, and steelhead from the rivers. The women collected clams, mussels, limpets, and barnacles from tidal pools. The men felled cedar trees and carved canoes in which they hunted whales, eight men to a canoe, casting harpoons made of mussel shells and elk bone fastened to tethers of twisted cedar bark.

Nine tribes shared the lowlands of the Olympic Peninsula. They spoke one of three languages, all lived in long houses, ate the same foods, and followed similar religious practices. They traded wares and sometimes even intermarried. Nonetheless, the tribes occasionally warred with each other and enslaved captives. Only through trade could a slave be freed. The cost: two otter skins, or one canoe, or one gun, or fifteen to twenty baskets.

All differences dissolved at a "potlatch," the most distinctive event in Northwest Indian culture. It signified an important birth, marriage, or death. As many as a thousand guests from twenty tribes traveled hundreds of miles to pay their respects. The preparations could take many months. Characteristically, the host of a potlatch sought to establish his high rank by giving valuable possessions to his guests.

Early Explorers

In 1788, Captain John Meares of the British Royal Navy sailed down the coast of present-day Washington State. Where a broad peninsula reached northwest into the sea, he sighted a crown of coastal summits. A fair wind blew, while sunset bathed the peaks in cinnabar light. Captain Meares exclaimed in his ship's log: "If that be not the home where dwell the Gods, it is beautiful enough to be, and I therefore call it Mt. Olympus."

Though Meares did not know it, the mountain had been named by the Spanish navigator Juan Perez in 1774, and long before that by the local Indians. The name Olympus gained ascendancy, however, as British influence in the region was consolidated by successive waves of settlers.

Opposite: A hunting lodge in Enchanted Valley, built in 1931, is now a ranger station.

An unsuccessful attempt was made in the United States in 1849 to christen the peninsular mountains the Presidents Range, and to reject the name Mount Olympus in favor of Mount Van Buren. But in 1864 the *Seattle Weekly Gazette* spearheaded a campaign that finally produced an official name for the range, the Olympic Mountains. Mount Olympus, home of the gods, had received its court.

Isolated and distant, the mountains hardly constituted a travel route, let alone a destination. On late-nineteenth-century maps of the Pacific Northwest, the one blank spot was the Olympic Mountains. Superstition began to prevail. The Olympics were called "haunted" and "bewitched," and madmen were said to live in them.

In a report to the U.S. Department of the Interior in 1888, Eugene Semple, the territorial governor of Washington, repeatedly referred to the "riddle of the Olympics." This impressed Elisha P. Ferry, first governor of the state, who called for a major exploration of the mountains. The *Seattle Press* organized an expedition to be led by James Christie, a Scotsman who had journeyed "as far north as water will run." Facing great odds, the six-man Press Party departed Port Angeles in December 1889, southbound along the Elwha River, determined to traverse the mountains. Almost six months later they achieved their goal and emerged at Quinault Lake.

Lieutenant Joseph P. O'Neil of the U.S. Army led two expeditions into the mountains. The first, in 1885, explored the northeast corner of the peninsula. The second, in 1890, included three scientists from the Oregon Alpine Club. The party pushed through the southern Olympics, up the North Fork of the Skokomish River, and out the East Fork of the Quinault. Two resolutions emerged with them. The scientists strongly advocated more extensive research of the peninsula, while O'Neil sought to protect the unspoiled mountains. Both succeeded.

Establishment of the Park

In describing the mountains he had explored, O'Neil said that the Olympics were absolutely unfit for anyone except perhaps as a national park where elk and deer could be saved. In 1897, President Grover Cleveland issued a proclamation creating the Olympic Forest Reserve. President Theodore Roosevelt created the Mount Olympus National Monument in 1909. But national monuments could be reduced in size by presidential whim, and three such reductions between 1912 and 1929 left the monument with only half of its original acreage. Finally, in 1938, Congress gave approval for an 898,000-acre Olympic National Park, and President Franklin Roosevelt signed the bill into law. Most of the 50-mile-long coastal strip was added to the park in 1953.

Three members of Lt. O'Neil's 1890 expedition reportedly scaled one of the three peaks of Mount Olympus and left there a copper box containing a record of the climb. The box has never been found, however, and the exact route and peak ascended by the expedition is unclear.

Theodore Rixon and Arthur Dodwell spent 3 years surveying the Olympics for the U.S. Geological Survey. In August 1899, Jack McGlone, one of their packers, reached the top of the East Peak after a solo ascent.

In 1907, two teams of climbers aimed for the unattained summit of Mount Olympus. A team of east-coast climbers scaled the Middle Peak of Mount Olympus in July 1907. Then, unable to see nearby peaks through the clouds, they assumed they had reached the mountain's highest point and returned home. A second party, the Seattle Mountaineers, set off soon afterward. As they approached Mount Olympus, the weather cleared. Led by L. A. Nelson, the eleven-member party first climbed the East Peak and then proceeded to the Middle Peak, where they found the cairn built by the east-coast party. Looking westward, they at once realized that the unclimbed West Peak was higher. Euphoric, the Mountaineers scaled the true summit, 7,965 feet, on August 13, 1907.

By 1920, most major peaks of the Olympics had been climbed except for Mount Constance. In 1922, after at least five unsuccessful attempts, three Seattle Mountaineers "solved the approach puzzle" and stood on its top.

Mining and Logging

Early prospectors discovered small deposits of manganese and copper along the eastern valleys of the mountains, and by 1906 several claims had been staked. In 1908, the American Manganese Corporation built a mine in Dungeness Valley. Most subsequent activity took place around the North Fork of the Skokomish and west of Lake Crescent. All in all, though, the Olympics yielded very little valuable ore.

Logging, the backbone of the peninsula's economy, began in the 1860s and has hardly abated since. Early lumberjacks prided themselves on felling trees 200 feet high and 15 feet in diameter. An old photograph shows twenty-eight people standing on top of one Douglas-fir stump.

Today, the peninsula produces more than 200 million board feet of lumber per year, mostly from Olympic National Forest, which surrounds the park. As western redcedar is downed and higher-yield Douglas-fir is planted, the native forest loses its diversity. It will gradually deteriorate from a heterogeneous temperate rain forest into a monoculture tree farm. As a result, the quality of wildlife habitat will decline. Certain animals, such as spotted owls, will disappear; elk, deer, otter, fish, and other animals that migrate along rivers will encounter greater risks from human activity. Even though all logging today (though not in the past) is outside the park, its ecological repercussions are not.

Geology

Sediments Beneath the Sea

The oldest rocks in the core of the Olympic Mountains began to form on the floor of the Pacific Ocean 55 million years ago. North America had already broken away from a massive supercontinent and was probably drifting westward—as it continues to do today—at a rate of about 1 to 2 inches per year. Tremendous amounts of sediment washed off the continent and into the sea.

Just as water maintains its integrity on land while flowing beneath less dense air, separate slurries of sand, silt, clay, and water flowed beneath sea water along the ocean floor. The sediments collected into layers, some thick, others thin. Meanwhile, deep fissures opened in the ocean floor, exuding lava that spread out and interspersed with the layers of sediment. Broad volcanoes also formed, pouring out lava that mounted high enough in some places to breach the surface of the sea. As the layers of lava and sediment collected, they hardened. The increasing weight and pressure of the topmost beds cemented those below. The sand hardened into sandstone, the mud and clay into shale, and the lava into basalt.

Occasionally, thick slurries deposited rounded pebbles and cobbles onto the ocean floor. These hardened into conglomerate. Other slurries broke off and carried away angular fragments of partly consolidated mud, which solidified into shale-chip and slate-chip breccias. And during all this time limestone was being created as the shells of marine organisms—most of them from now-extinct families—rained down through the sea and collected at the bottom in the sediments.

Thus formed the rocks of the Olympics, preserving in their shape and detail the assaults, caresses, and inhabitants of the sea. Next came the mountain building.

Opposite: Brightly colored acid-producing lichens, algae, and fungi begin to cover a basalt outcrop.

A Collision Near the Shore

North America, one of many drifting plates on the earth's mantle, tended to float over the denser Pacific Ocean plate as it continued its northwesterly migration. About 25 million years ago, the two plates collided just east of the present-day shore of Washington State.

The Pacific plate plunged beneath the continent, carrying old rocks deep into the earth's mantle. But as this subduction began, the uppermost ocean-floor strata struck the continental edge. The top stratum of basalt slid atop the continent's margin. The sedimentary strata, however, did not fare as well. The layers peeled back and piled seaward against and beneath the basalt, many horizontal beds being turned to the vertical. As a result of the collision, and the relative "buoyancy" of the shale and sandstone, the once neatly layered ocean-bottom strata were pushed into a huge dome-like pile of jumbled rock—the Olympic Mountains. The basalt formation now rings the mountains' perimeter, opening like a horseshoe toward the west. Within the perimeter the sedimentary rocks lie folded, fractured, and faulted.

After the mountains had risen from the sea, they were shaped by a great force. From out of the north came the Pleistocene glaciers.

Ice on the Rocks

The ice age (Pleistocene epoch) began between one and two million years ago. It was characterized by alternating periods of glacial activity and quiescence, most lasting hundreds of thousands of years. At least four major continental ice sheets advanced and retreated over the whole breadth of northern North America.

The westernmost lobe of the last glacier left indelible marks on the Olympic Peninsula. It proceeded out of British Columbia, buried Vancouver Island, and piled up against the Olympics at a thickness of about 3,000 feet. Unable to breach the mountains, the glacier split. One lobe flowed east around the Olympics and carved Hood Canal and Puget Sound. The other flowed west of Lake Crescent. Huge glacial outwash rivers spilled south around the mountains. Within the Olympics themselves, the alpine glaciers grew and coalesced, leaving only the topmost peaks free of ice. Beginning about 12,000 years ago, for reasons not yet understood, the continental ice sheet began to withdraw and the high alpine glaciers started to shrink. Left behind was a solitary mass of mountains, carved by ice.

The Evidence

The Olympics are not a mountain range in the usual sense.

Instead, the mountains form a tight circular cluster. The jagged peaks, set above timbered slopes and labyrinthine valleys, at first seem chaotic, but one design dominates. From the innermost mountains thirteen rivers radiate like the spokes of a wheel. They are: the Bogachiel, Dosewallips, Duckabush, Dungeness, Elwha, Hamma Hamma, Hoh, Humptulips, Queets, Quinault, Skokomish, Soleduck, and Wynoochee.

This radial drainage from a circular mountain cluster confirms that the Olympic Mountains uplifted as one unit, independent of the coastal ranges to the south and north. Indeed, at 7,000 to 8,000 feet in elevation, the Olympics are generally higher and more rugged than their counterparts in California, Oregon, and British Columbia. These Olympics are unique mountains; their summits consist of rocks containing marine fossils and they are surrounded on three sides by water. It is entirely fitting, therefore, that local residents call their mountains a "gift from the sea."

Pleistocene glaciers scooped out the U-shaped valleys and the basins of Quinault Lake, Lake Cushman, and Lake Crescent. They shaped the peaks and ridges, and carried in and abandoned huge boulders—"erratics"—from Canada. Faint grooves, or striations, on smooth rocks offer further evidence that glaciers transporting rock debris once passed by.

Today, about sixty glaciers, seven of them on Mount Olympus, cut away at the Olympics. The Blue Glacier (just above Glacier Meadows on Mount Olympus) receives about 500 inches of snow a year and flows downslope at a rate of 5 inches per day. The Mount Carrie, Mount Anderson, and Mount Christie areas also have several glaciers each.

Far above timberline and soils, the naked mountaintop rock strata are bent and warped from the tectonic pressures that lifted the Olympics. Visible here are the slate- and shale-chip breccias, the jumbled conglomerates, and the half-hidden fossils, all in mixed beds of sedimentary and igneous rock. Also exposed here—and along many road cuts (including Hurricane Ridge)—are the pillow basalts. This globular form of basalt usually occurs when freshly expelled lava hardens beneath the sea.

Sea stacks, sea arches, and islets add lively detail and form to the Olympic coast. The surf, heavy with suspended sand, pounds the rocks with a great force. Under such pressure, landforms change rapidly. Many sections of the coast look quite different than they did in photographs taken in the early 1900s.

Overleaf: Rivers carry smoothly polished jasper and quartz pebbles down from the mountains to the sea.

Precipitation

To most residents of the Pacific Northwest, the Olympic Peninsula immediately suggests one thing: rain. It can fall hard, fast, and non-stop—or in a soft mist. Rivers can rise six feet in a day.

The three elements that produce the wet climate are the warm Japan Current, the prevailing westerly winds, and the Olympic Mountains. The seaward slopes of the Olympics receive more precipitation than any other place in the forty-eight contiguous states. Between 120 and 150 inches fall annually in the Hoh and Queets valleys. Mount Olympus itself catches the equivalent of 220 inches per year, three-fourths of that total falling between October and March. Northeast of the mountains, though, less than 18 inches fall in the town of Sequim. Farmers there have to water their summer crops.

The Olympics have notoriously capricious weather. Hikers on Hurricane Ridge might be sunning themselves among the mountain goats and marmots while visitors in the Hoh River Valley huddle in a downpour. Or vice versa. Valley temperatures are always moderate, seldom dipping below freezing in winter or rising above 80° F in summer.

Sea anemones use stinging cells, or nemacysts, on their tentacles to catch prey.

Seashore

Change and beauty are the two constants along the Olympic seashore. The dynamics of change apply to the competitive positioning of intertidal invertebrates or of gulls feeding at a river mouth, to the shape of a headland, and to the subtle curve of a beach.

Processes hidden elsewhere seem more tangible here. The pounding surf, diaphanous salt mist, and opaque tidal pools leave unmistakable impressions. Sand and salt etch the white wood of drift logs thrown up on the beach. Bear tracks circle a stranded sea urchin—picked clean by gulls—and lead into the forest. Sanderlings scamper along the surf's leading edge, moving up and down the beach in perfect unison, crossing the half-buried rib of a gray whale.

The seashore's richness is exemplified in the intertidal communities. A one-foot-square area can support 4,000 individual animals belonging to more than twenty species. Many intertidal animals produce thousands or millions of eggs at a time. Yet the survival rate to maturity might be only one in every quarter million—just enough to perpetuate the species. The ones that do not survive help to perpetuate other species, sustaining the food chain.

Intertidal organisms live in specific zones between the lowest low

Abundant numbers and species of starfish are found on northern Pacific shores.

Ruddy turnstones eat small crustaceans and mollusks.

tide and the highest high tide. Each is adapted to a particular type of substrate, amount of tidal exposure, and degree of surf disturbance. Pacific razor clams, butter clams, horse clams, and cockles bury themselves in mudflats and beaches. A razor clam can dig down 9 inches in less than a minute. In the tidal pools and eelgrass flats live multicolored sea anemones, giant and lined chitons, and several members of the echinodermata, including purple stars, brittle stars, sea urchins, and sea cucumbers. Other residents of these zones are purple shore crabs and the curious but bashful hermit crab.

Littoral rock surfaces provide a home for shield, white-cap, and keyhole limpets, gooseneck and acorn barnacles, spindle snails, wrinkled purple snails, periwinkles, and mussels. These animals take a beating. The "wave shock" along the Olympic coast measures higher than it does almost anywhere else in North America. Holding their ground, keyhole limpets grip the rock with a force equivalent to 70 pounds per square inch.

Many birds work the shore. Bald eagles perch in Sitka spruce and western hemlocks, watching for fish. Sandpipers probe the beach for small crustaceans—isopods and amphipods—while turnstones do what their name implies. Cormorants, grebes, scoters, and murres dive for fish far offshore. The black oystercatcher uses its long red bill to pry open mussels. Gulls and northwestern crows, however, have learned to crack tightly clamped clamshells by carrying them whole to a height of about 50 feet and dropping them onto a rock. If the clam were relaxed, the trick would proba-

Opposite: Seagull tracks on a sandy stretch of beach.

bly fail. But because the bivalve's muscles are tensed, the impact is intensified and the clam pops open. The bird then descends to eat, calling and calling as if smitten with its own ingenuity.

Rain Forest

When nature combines a mild coastal climate, heavy summer fog, and 12 feet of rain per year, it creates the temperate rain forest. This rare and wondrous environment is best developed in Olympic in the southwest-facing valleys of the Quinault, Queets, and Hoh rivers. Deep within the valleys, greenness infuses everything, even the air. Stately limbs of conifers and maple close out the sky. Sounds are quickly absorbed by the ubiquitous moss. It is a placid, untroubled place.

Sitka spruce distinguishes the rain forest. Western hemlock and western redcedar attend the spruce. Specimens of spruce and redcedar may measure 15 to 25 feet in diameter and 200 to 300 feet high. Because water is never in short supply, the giant conifers anchor in roots only 5 to 6 feet deep. As a result, the wind sometimes topples them, opening apertures in the forest canopy and allowing rare spokes of sunlight to spill through. The fallen giants become "nurse logs," supporting rows of seedlings that otherwise cannot readily germinate on the fern- and moss-covered forest floor. The log eventually rots away, leaving behind a colonnade of mature trees, each standing on stilted roots.

Bigleaf maples grow beards of moss from every limb, speckled with licorice ferns. More than ninety species of epiphytes (nonparasitic plants that grow on other plants) live in the rain forest. They are generally harmless to the host species and at times may even be beneficial. However, so many epiphytes can crowd a maple that its overweighted branches break off and crash to the forest floor.

The most noticeable feathered resident of the rain forest is the winter wren. A weak flier, it flits and chatters among maidenhair ferns, sword ferns, vine maples, and red alders on the forest floor. What it lacks in size and color, it compensates for in busy behavior.

The park contains the largest herd anywhere of Roosevelt elk. The elk browse on the seedlings of hemlock, but not on those of spruce, and thus add an interesting twist to the rain-forest ecology. Columbian black-tailed deer, a subspecies of the mule deer, are also forest browsers.

Upslope, grand fir replaces Sitka spruce at elevations between 800 and 1,000 feet. Higher still, western redcedar surrenders en masse at about 2,000 feet, while western hemlock continues to 3,500 feet in favorable conditions. Other species include Pacific silver fir, a shade-tolerant tree of the upper elevations that forms dense stands, and Douglas-fir, a comparatively thick-barked, fire-resistant species common in the eastern Olympics. On the eastern slopes, the evergreen rhododendron, a large broadleaf shrub, spreads its lovely pink blossoms across many miles in late spring.

Mountain

The most fascinating ecological story in the Olympic Mountains involves twenty-seven species of plants and animals: the "missing eleven" and the "endemic sixteen."

When ice and water surrounded the peninsula, organisms in the Olympics reacted in three ways: some migrated south, an option open chiefly to birds and a few large mammals; many perished; and others remained trapped in the mountains but adapted to the cold.

Black bear, black-tailed deer, and Roosevelt elk are representatives of the first group, ranging widely from high to low elevations. They were able to leave the Olympics, move south to more hospitable conditions, and then return after the ice receded. Although

As Olympic marmots feed, a sentinel watches for danger. Overleaf: Mountain lions may track a hiker for miles, but seldom attack unprovoked.

many mammals restricted to high elevations could not escape or adapt and consequently died out, many others probably never lived in the isolated Olympics. The "missing eleven," in any case, are mammals that survived throughout the Cascades and the Rocky Mountains, but not in the Olympics. They are the grizzly bear, wolverine, red fox, lynx, porcupine, golden-mantled ground squirrel, pika, water vole, northern bog lemming, mountain sheep, and mountain goat. The red fox was introduced but remains rare.

Long-eared owl.

Such is not the case, however, with the mountain goat, which was introduced in the 1920s and is now by no means rare. From an original population of eleven, 1,200 goats were flourishing by the 1980s. Their grazing, wallowing, and trampling significantly altered vegetation patterns. Live capture and sterilization had some success in limiting numbers, but the National Park Service continues to study other options.

Among the Olympic plants and animals that clung to life above the ice, eight wildflowers, five mammals, and one fish evolved into new species or subspecies. They are Cotton's milk vetch, Piper's bellflower, Flett's fleabane, Thompson's wandering fleabane, Henderson's rock-spirea, Webster's senecio, Olympic mountain synthyris, Flett's violet, Olympic snow mole, shorttail weasel, Olympic marmot, Olympic chipmunk, Olympic Mazama pocket gopher, and the Olympic mudminnow.

The surviving plants were probably "pre-adapted" to life above the ice. Not surprisingly, they grow today in the high rock crevices and talus slopes of the Alpine zone.

Olympic marmots live in colonies usually consisting of one adult male, two adult females, several two year olds, a few yearlings, and a litter of newborn young. While the colony feeds together in the alpine meadows, a solitary sentinel sits on the rocks above. At the first sight of a coyote, mountain lion, hawk, or eagle, the sentinel whistles and all the marmots run for their burrows. The system works most of the time, failing just often enough to maintain the population balance.

Roads and Trail Heads

U.S. 101 loops around the Olympic Peninsula and encircles all but the southern end of the park. It enters the park twice: along the Pacific coast between Kalaloch and Ruby Beach, and to the north along Lake Crescent.

Roads to the coast follow the Hoh and Quillayute rivers, and a spur from Washington 112 leads to Ozette Lake. Elsewhere, twenty roads radiate inland off U.S. 101, follow drainages, and end at trail heads. Some of these are wide, paved roads that enter the park; others are narrow logging roads that end before reaching the park's boundary.

For visitors who want to experience the diversity of the park but have little time, Hurricane Ridge, Ruby Beach, and the Hoh Rain Forest offer easy access and outstanding sights.

The following descriptions begin with Quinault Lake, at the park's southwest corner, and proceed clockwise around the peninsula.

Quinault River Roads. Two roads enter the park at Quinault Lake, about 40 miles north of Aberdeen. The *North Fork Road* offers occasional glimpses of the lake through mixed stands of Sitka spruce and western hemlock. It ends at the North Fork Ranger Station, 18.4 miles from U.S. 101. The *Quinault River Road* winds 17.7 miles up the valley and ends at the head of the *East Fork Quinault River Trail.* It originates on the Quinault Indian Reservation, passes several small farms, enters the rain forest, crosses the river at 13 miles, and passes the Graves Creek Ranger Station at 18.6 miles. Elk are common in this area.

Queets River Road. Twenty miles up U.S. 101 from Quinault, this road offers excellent views of the rain forest. It traces the south side of the river and affords several good views of the snow-capped Olympic peaks. It passes the ranger station at 14 miles and the campground a mile thereafter. The road ends just beyond the campground where the 15.5-mile *Queets River Trail* begins.

Kalaloch–Ruby Beach Highway. Two miles north of Queets Village, U.S. 101 enters the park and follows the coast for about 14 miles. Seven short but unusual beach trails lead from the highway to the ocean. Sunsets and storms color the beaches and accentuate the forms of sea stacks, arches, and offshore inlets.

Hoh River Roads. At Ruby Beach, U.S. 101 turns inland and fol-

lows the Hoh River. This is the entrance to the heart of the rain forest, where western hemlock, western redcedar, Douglas-fir, and bigleaf and vine maples grow to their greatest size. The *South Fork River Road*, which progressively narrows after crossing the South Fork of the Hoh River, ends short of the park boundary, but provides access to the 4.5-mile *South Fork Trail*. The well-paved *Upper Hoh River Road* probes deep into the rain forest and ends at the Hoh Visitor Center, 19 miles from U.S. 101. Roosevelt elk forage in this valley in late fall and winter. Harlequin ducks breed along the river in summer.

Oil City Road. Between the upper and lower Hoh River Road turnoffs, the unpaved Oil City Road branches westward and follows the Hoh River for 9 miles, almost to its mouth. From here, hikers can enter the park and begin a beach trek north to La Push.

Bogachiel River Road. Midway between the Hoh River and the town of Forks, U.S. 101 crosses the Bogachiel River. Here a logging road turns inland and winds 4.5 miles through clear-cut land to the head of the *Bogachiel River Trail*, 2 miles short of the park boundary. The trail provides access to Seven Lakes Basin.

Lower Quillayute River–La Push Road. Two miles north of Forks, the Lower Quillayute River Road turns west off U.S. 101 and, after passing trail heads, arrives 14 miles later at the Quileute Indian fishing village of La Push. At 8 miles, motorists can bear right and drive 5 miles to Rialto Beach, on the north side of the mouth of the Quillayute River, opposite La Push.

La Push is a corruption of the French *la bouche*, which means "the mouth" and refers to the opening of the Quillayute River. Quileutes still fish from canoes fashioned from cedar logs, but today they use chain saws and square off the sterns to support outboard motors.

Calawah–Sitkum Rivers Road. Also two miles north of Forks, a graded road turns inland and begins a steady 13-mile climb up to Rugged Ridge. This extremely rugged road ends at the head of the *Indian Pass Trail*. From there, at the park boundary, a 6-mile up-and-down hike on the poorly marked trail leads to the Bogachiel River.

Ozette Lake Road. This 33-mile drive begins at Sappho, 50 miles

Opposite: In the rare and lush Hoh Rain Forest, everything seems suffused with the color green.

west of Port Angeles. It follows the Burnt Mountain Road north to Washington 112, turns northwest toward Neah Bay, and then picks up the Ozette Lake Road just past Sekiu. At the end of the road is the Ozette Lake Ranger Station. A boardwalk trail leads to the beach and to the Ozette Village archeological site, which is closed to the public. Here, 300 to 500 years ago, a mudflow buried a village, preserving its cedarplank lodges and other artifacts. Artifacts from Ozette Village are on display at the Makah Cultural Research Center in Neah Bay, at the western end of Washington 112.

Upper Soleduck River–Hot Springs Road. U.S. 101 follows the broad Soleduck Valley toward Lake Crescent. At the park boundary, 1.5 miles west of Fairholm, the Upper Soleduck River–Hot Springs Road turns south and traces the river for 14 miles. At Salmon Cascades (7.5 miles) salmon fight their way upstream each fall, leaping to reach higher pools along the way. The road continues through a beautiful forest and passes Sol Duc Hot Springs Resort to reach a trail head at 14.2 miles. Trails from here and from the resort lead to Seven Lakes Basin, Glacier Meadows, Boulder Creek, and down the North Fork of the Bogachiel River.

Along Lake Crescent. U.S. 101 winds for 10 miles along the south shore of Lake Crescent, the largest lake in the park. The 600-foot-deep lake owes its creation to glacial carving during the Pleistocene epoch and to an ancient landslide that dammed the eastward drainage between it and Lake Sutherland. At both ends of Lake Crescent, roads branch off along its north shore.

Lower Elwha River–Boulder Creek Road. Midway between Lake Crescent and Port Angeles, the Elwha River Road turns south off U.S. 101 and follows the river into the park. This is a rich wildlife area, with Roosevelt elk down at lower elevations and mountain goats at higher ones. It is also home to the Pacific madrone, or madrona tree, easily recognized by its smooth reddish-brown bark.

The road divides at 4.1 miles, just beyond the Elwha Ranger Station. Elwha River Road ends in Boulder Creek Canyon. From here, trails lead to the Soleduck River, to Lake Crescent, and to Glacier Meadows on the north slope of Mount Olympus. The 5-mile-long *Whiskey Bend Road,* which is dirt, branches to the left and provides access to the head of the *Elwha River Trail.*

Heart of the Hills Road to Hurricane Ridge. Hurricane Ridge has become famous for its breath-taking vistas, alpine scenery, and plentiful wildlife. The road begins at First and Race streets in Port

Angeles. One mile up the road is a park Visitor Center and museum. The road climbs steadily up the east end and south flank of Klahhane Ridge. At 17.8 miles, it joins *Alpine Drive* atop Hurricane Ridge. To the east is the scenic but rough (no trailers) 8-mile-long road to Obstruction Peak. To the west is Hurricane Ridge Lodge. Numerous trails lead into the park from along Alpine Drive.

From December to April, the road to Hurricane Ridge is plowed open on weekends. Heavy winds sometimes pile snow 20 feet deep. The lodge rents skis and snowshoes. Come summertime, wildflowers appear along the fringes of retreating snow patches. The first lilies usually emerge in mid-June; the russet tones of autumn peak in early October. Black-tailed deer and Olympic marmots are commonly seen on adjacent slopes, while mountain goats watch from rocky ledges above.

Deer Park Road. The Deer Park Road turns south off U.S. 101 at Mount Pleasant, 5 miles east of Port Angeles. It begins as a blacktop, enters the park at 10.9 miles, and ends as a narrow, winding dirt road (no R.V.s!) atop the Blue Mountain Overlook. Like Hurricane Ridge, this overlook provides spectacular views of the Strait of Juan de Fuca, Vancouver Island, the San Juan Islands, the Cascade Mountains, and the central Olympics. Trails from here lead to Obstruction Peak, Low Divide (in the center of the park), Dosewallips, and Slab Camp.

Slab Camp Road. Two miles west of Sequim, a paved road turns south off U.S. 101 and climbs 14 miles to Slab Camp. Trails are not maintained between here and the park boundary, about 4 walking miles away.

Tyler Peak–River Road. The 20-mile-long River Road follows the Dungeness River after branching off U.S. 101. It climbs through Forest Service land to the Tyler Peak area. From the trail head, a 20-mile hike south reaches Dosewallips Ranger Station.

Dosewallips River Road. This road turns west off U.S. 101 at Brinnon, on Hood Canal. Dosewallips Falls and cliffs of pillow basalt can be seen in the canyon near the end of the road. From the Dosewallips Ranger Station (15.5 miles), trails lead to almost all corners of the park.

Duckabush River Road. Originating in the town of Duckabush,

Overleaf: The Elwha River area is home to a rich array of wildlife.

just south of Brinnon, this road extends 7 miles up the Duckabush River. The park boundary is a 5-mile hike from there, and beyond it lies the Mount Anderson/Enchanted Valley area.

Hamma Hamma River Road. This road begins 15 miles north of Hoodsport and extends 8.5 miles up the Hamma Hamma River to *Lena Lakes Trail.* Hiking opportunities are limited, but beautiful.

Lake Cushman–North Fork Skokomish River Road. From Hoodsport, this road runs for 16 miles to the Staircase Ranger Station, just beyond Lake Cushman and a mile within the park. Trails lead north and west to the Enchanted Valley and the Graves Creek areas.

Camp Harps and Wynoochee Falls Roads. These roads approach the southern and least accessible quarter of Olympic National Park. Seekers of solitude might want to keep these areas in mind. The roads turn off U.S. 101, branch several times, and are 45 and 21 miles long, respectively. Both join trails that begin on Forest Service land, enter the park, and lead to the Graves Creek, Enchanted Valley, and Staircase areas.

This rain forest occurs only in the valleys of the Quinault, Queets, and Hoh rivers.

Trails

Olympic National Park has more than 600 miles of hiking trails. They are short, long, easy, difficult, solitary, and interconnecting, and they provide a tremendous range of scenic diversity and physical challenge. It would be possible to walk all summer in the Olympics and never retrace a footstep.

Rain is a regular, though intermittent, companion. Sunny skies can cloud over quickly and may not clear for days or weeks. Routes should be chosen carefully because snow can linger into August on alpine trails. Wilderness beach hikes and low-elevation forest trails remain open year-round. The beaches have no designated trails and thus invite open hiking.

Hoh River–La Push (South Wilderness Beach Hike). Beginning at the end of the Oil City Road (where there is neither oil nor a city), this 15.2-mile-long route follows beaches interspersed with forest trails that swing inland behind Hoh Head, Falls Creek, Taylor Point, and Teahwhit Head. The hike blends two of Olympic National Park's most arresting qualities: the pounding surf and the quiet forest. Each accents the other.

Logjams provide bridges over creeks, and two tattered shelters offer a respite from the rain. With so many beautiful distractions, walking can be slow. A good time allowance is twelve to twenty hours. At Teahwhit Head, the *Third Beach Trail* turns inland and joins the La Push Road. This last 1-mile leg through the forest makes an ideal halfday hike. More ambitious day hikers can walk from Third Beach to Toleak Point, an 11-mile round trip.

Rialto Beach–Ozette Lake (North Wilderness Beach Hike). This 18.5-mile stretch is as beautiful as the South Wilderness Beach Hike, but it requires more resourcefulness to traverse. Cape Johnson and Yellow Banks have no access trails through the forest. Instead, they must be crossed along their seaward sides, a feat that can safely be accomplished at low tide or at a falling medium tide. Hikers should check the tide table and proceed with caution; in fact, it is wise to carry an extra tide table in case the first is lost.

The retreating sea unveils many tidal pools on the rocky shore. At night, skunks and raccoons prowl the area for invertebrate meals, taking whatever they can get. Black bears also walk the beaches and forest, day and night.

This coast has claimed many sailors' lives. The Norwegian and Chilean memorials commemorate the dead of shipwrecks in 1903 and 1920. The Norwegians, whose helmsman mistook a simple

cabin light for the Tatoosh Island beacon, lie in a common grave beneath the memorial, shrouded together in the canvas sail of their ship. The Chileans were buried in coffins built from their ship's wreckage.

Hikers can reach the Ozette Lake Ranger Station via 3-mile trails from Sand Point or from Cape Alava, the westernmost point of the contiguous United States. The loop from Ozette Lake Ranger Station to Cape Alava to Sand Point makes a nice 9.5-mile day hike.

Hoh River Trail. The most popular rain-forest hike begins at the Hoh Ranger Station. A visitor who follows the trail into the silent forest for only a few minutes, beyond human voices and traffic noise, will quickly realize that here is a world unlike any other.

For 11 miles, the trail traces the river bottom beneath a cathedral-like canopy of Sitka spruce, western hemlock, western redcedar, bigleaf maple, vine maple, black cottonwood, and red alder. Shrubs and ferns blanket the forest floor. Birds sing from hidden perches, and the tracks of coyote, cougar, bobcat, and bear cross the trail.

At about 12.5 miles, the trail turns south along Glacier Creek. It crosses a bridge 150 feet above the river, which roars through a deep and narrow gorge, and then moves up the hillside to Elk Lake at 15.1 miles. Glacier Meadows is 2.2 miles ahead. To find both a glacier and a meadow, however, requires an additional half-mile hike to where the trail ends on the Blue Glacier moraine. This is the quickest route to Mount Olympus. Only experienced mountaineers should proceed higher.

For day hikers, the *Hall of Mosses* and *Spruce nature trails* make short forays (.85 and 1.3 miles, respectively) into the rain forest from the Hoh Visitor Center. Both have self-guiding signs that interpret the environment.

Seven Lakes Basin Trails. This water-jeweled, high cirque basin has several trails that meander along its alpine and subalpine contours. A handsome mix of mountain hemlock, subalpine fir, and open meadow surrounds the lakes, of which there are more than seven. In fact, one has been named Number Eight.

To the south rises Mount Olympus, visible in tantalizing glimpses from trails along the basin. Near Bogachiel Peak, a trail descends 6.5 miles past Hoh Lake and joins the *Hoh River Trail.* This junction is 7.1 miles down-valley from Glacier Meadows and 9.2 miles up-valley from the Hoh Ranger Station.

Opposite: The shallow root systems of red alders enable winds to topple them.

TRAILS OF OLYMPIC NATIONAL PARK

LAKE CRESCENT SUBDISTRICT

Seven Lakes Basin Loop Trail: Starts at Soleduck Seven Lakes Basin Trail Head 14.2 miles up paved Sol Duc Hot Springs Road; ends at Soleduck trail head; 18 miles one way; 2-3 days round trip; ascends gradually for 1 mile, then climbs 1,500 feet in 3 miles to Deer Lake; hazardous in off-season; excellent views in High Divide subalpine zone; best trail in park for wildlife, but very crowded.

ELWHA SUBDISTRICT

ELWHA RIVER TRAIL: Starts at Whiskey Bend trail head at end of unpaved Whiskey Bend Road (near southern end of Lake Mills); ends at Low Divide; 28.4 miles one way; 4-6 days round trip; grade generally gradual; only major elevation changes are near Lillian River, 4 miles in, and over last 2.6 miles during trail's steady ascent to Low Divide; Douglas-fir and western hemlock forests; good fishing at Mary Falls; three old homesteads are of historical interest.

RICA CANYON–HUMES RANCH TRAIL: Starts at Rica Canyon Trail junction with Elwha River Trail, 1 mile from Whiskey Bend; ends at Michaels Homestead, junction with Elwha River Trail, 1.8 miles from Whiskey Bend; 3 miles one way; 4–5 days round trip; follows Elwha River and offers view of Goblins Gates, where river water funnels into Rica Canyon; deer and elk are numerous.

LONG RIDGE/DODGER POINT TRAILS: Starts at junction with Humes Ranch Trail, .2 mile below Michaels Cabin at 1.8-mile point on Elwha River Trail; ends at Elwha River Ford at Remanns Cabin, 13-mile point on Elwha River Trail; 16.4 miles one way; 2–3 days round trip; commanding views of Mount Olympus and the Bailey Range after fording Elwha River at Remanns.

APPLETON PASS TRAIL: Starts at Boulder Creek trail head, .75 mile above Lake Mills on Olympic Hot Springs Road; ends at 4.9-mile point on Soleduck River Trail; 13.4 miles one way; 2–3 days round trip; steady climb with switchbacks for approximately 3 miles as trail gets above tree line; Olympic Hot Springs (natural area of 7 small hot spring pools) is at 2.4 miles; views of Mount Olympus, Soleduck River, and Boulder Creek at Appleton Pass.

HURRICANE SUBDISTRICT

LAKE ANGELES TRAIL: Starts at Heart of the Hills trail head; passes Lake Angeles and ends at Klahhane Ridge; 6.5 miles one way; 1–2 days round trip; 2,400-foot ascent over 3.5 miles; excellent view of interior Olympics from ridge; trail can be hazardous because of slide conditions and loose talus.

GRAND VALLEY TRAIL: Starts at Obstruction Point trail head at end of Obstruction Point Road, 8 miles from Hurricane Ridge parking area; ends at Grand Pass; 6 miles one way; 1–2 days round trip; entire trail is above treeline in subalpine environment; spectacular views all along route; very popular trail with heavy use.

ROYAL BASIN TRAIL: Starts at Dungeness trail head; ends at Royal Lake ranger station; 6.2 miles one way; 1-2 days round trip; part U.S. Forest Service trail; avalanche danger high in off-season; profusion of wildflowers in season.

MAIN FORK DOSEWALLIPS RIVER TRAIL: Starts at Dosewallips trail head; ends at Hayden Pass; 15.4 miles one way; 3–4 days round trip; several cross-country routes accessible off this trail; excellent views of interior Olympics from Hayden Pass.

WEST FORK DOSEWALLIPS RIVER TRAIL: Starts at Dosewallips trail head; ends at Anderson Pass and junction with Anderson Glacier side trail; 10 miles one way; 2–3 days round trip; gradually ascends through forests of Douglas-fir, hemlock, and cedar; one steep grade at 3 miles; last 3 miles climb by switchbacks; elk, deer, and bears are occasionally seen.

LAKE CONSTANCE WAY TRAIL: Starts at Lake Constance trail head; ends at Lake Constance; 2 miles one way; 6–8 hours round trip; reservations must be made at Staircase ranger station for campsite at lake; trail elevation change is 3,400 feet in 2 miles; limited fishing for eastern brook trout at lake.

DUCKABUSH RIVER TRAIL: Starts at Duckabush trail head; ends at O'Neil Pass; 23 miles one way; 5–7 days round trip; U.S. Forest Service maintains trail for first 6.2 miles; hazardous crossing of upper Duckabush River; good fishing; subalpine views for last 5 miles.

LACROSSE PASS TRAIL: Starts at 15.7-mile point on Duckabush River Trail; ends at 9.3-mile point on Dosewallips River Trail; 6.4 miles one way; 6–8 hours, ascends 5,000 feet; excellent panoramas from upper portions of trail.

UPPER LENA LAKE TRAIL: Starts at Lena Lake trail head; ends at Upper Lena Lake; 7 miles one way; 1–2 days round trip; fishing in both lakes; creek crossing 1 mile below Upper Lena Lake difficult after rainfall.

SKOKOMISH RIVER TRAIL: Starts at Staircase trail head; ends at junction with Duckabush River Trail; 19.4 miles one way; 4–5 days round trip; gradual ascent over first 3.8 miles; trail passes through Douglas-fir forest, ascends to Nine Stream, and begins steep climb into subalpine environment of First Divide at Skokomish headwaters; trout fishing in summer; snow remains in Home Sweet Home Basin area (17.2 miles) until late in season.

FLAPJACK LAKES TRAIL: Starts at junction with Skokomish River Trail, 3.9 miles from Staircase; ends at Mount Gladys Divide; 5.6 miles one way; 1–2 days round trip; lakes are side by side at tree line; reservations required for campground.

NORTH FORK QUINAULT RIVER TRAIL: Starts at North Fork trail head; ends at Low Divide, Lakes Mary and Margaret; 17.5 miles one way; 4–5 days round trip; gradual climb; campsites few; footlog crossing of creek at 13-mile point; swimming possible at high lakes.

SKYLINE TRAIL: Starts at Three Lakes; ends at Low Divide; 20.3 miles one way, plus 6.5 miles from North Fork Road; 5–8 days round trip; almost entirely above treeline, trail encompasses subalpine meadows, lakes, and rocky ridges; snow patches may remain throughout summer; trail can be treacherous in areas; conditions should be checked in advance; fine views; wildlife abundant.

Soleduck Trail Head. The Soleduck Trail Head and Sol Duc Hot Springs Resort (and, to a lesser extent, Boulder Creek) afford the quickest access to Seven Lakes Basin. From the Soleduck Trail Head, Deer Lake is a pleasant 2.9-mile hike. Of equal distance is the hike to Mink Lake from the hot-springs resort.

Elwha River–North Fork Quinault River Trail. It took the *Seattle Press* party six months to pioneer this route in 1889 and 1890. Today, hikers normally complete the 45.9-mile trail in 4 to 6 days. As the trail crosses the park, it invites careful study of the plant ecology. From both north and south, the trail climbs slowly through transitions in dominant and understory forest species. Where the trail crests at Low Divide (3,600 feet), the montane and subalpine forests meet. Western hemlock, western redcedar, western white pine, and Douglas-fir reach their upper limits and yield to mountain hemlock, yellow cedar, and subalpine fir. The forest thins out and opens into meadows visited by Roosevelt elk, black-tailed deer, black bears, and marmots. Several short trails radiate from Low Divide and make excellent half-day and full-day hikes.

Variations on this route might include the 23-mile trail from Hayes River Ranger Station (10.4 miles north of Low Divide) east to Dosewallips via Hayden Pass.

Climbing Mount Olympus

Mount Olympus, the highest peak in the Olympic Mountains at 7,965 feet, is a prime target for experienced climbers. Climbers in good physical condition will need one or two days to complete the round trip from Glacier Meadows. Those in average condition will need three or four days. Climbing is possible from as early in the year as April, when snow is firm enough to walk on, until late fall. As a glacial mountain, Olympus is dangerous because of its hidden crevasses and slick ice. The sudden onset of bad weather—a sunny day can turn stormy in a few hours—can trap climbers. Necessary equipment includes ice ax, rope, crampons, slings for crevasse rescue, warm and waterproof clothing, map, compass, and a hard hat. From the end of the *Hoh River Trail* at Glacier Meadows, a moderately steep route with variations leads to the top. Climbers often use a pass at the east end of Five Fingers Ridge to avoid a large bergschrund, or crevasse. Above the ridge, a gentle basin separates the West (highest) and Middle peaks. The round trip from Glacier Meadows totals 8 miles and includes a gain in elevation of 3,500 feet.

Opposite: A salal leaf quickly decomposes in Olympic's wet climate.

WRANGELL–
ST. ELIAS
NATIONAL PARK
AND PRESERVE

An iceberg breaks off Hubbard Glacier and drops into Disenchantment Bay.

WRANGELL–ST. ELIAS
NATIONAL PARK AND PRESERVE
P.O. BOX 29
GLENNALLEN, ALASKA 99588
TEL.: (907) 822-5235

HIGHLIGHTS: Bagley Ice Field • Wrangell Mountains • Chugach Mountains • Dall Sheep Herds • Copper River • Chitina Valley • Kennecott Mine • St. Elias Mountains • Malaspina and Bering Glaciers

ACCESS: Glenn Highway from Anchorage to Glennallen: Richardson Highway from Valdez. Chitina–McCarthy Road from Chitina (off Richardson Highway). Nabesna Road from Slana. Air taxi to Glennallen or to points within park.

Season: Best time is from May 15 to September 15.

FEES: None.

GAS, FOOD, LODGING: Gas and groceries in Slana and Chitina. Lodging at Kennicott Lodge in Kennicott, McCarthy Lodge in McCarthy, Sportsman's Paradise Lodge on Nabesna Road, or at many roadhouses on the periphery road network.

VISITOR CENTER: At mile 105.5 on Old Richardson Highway. Formal briefings and trip-planning assistance. Ranger stations maintained at Yakutat, Slana, and Chitina.

GIFT SHOPS: At lodges and roadhouses.

PETS: Permitted on leash, except in backcountry, on trails, or in public buildings.

HIKING: Permitted; treat water. No maintained trails.

BACKPACKING: Unrestricted, no permit necessary. Treat all water. Voluntary registration system suggested.

CAMPGROUNDS: No designated campgrounds. Campers requested to uphold highest standards of minimum-impact camping. Showers at lodges.

TOURS: Concessionaire-guided tours; no National Park Service tours.

OTHER ACTIVITIES: Horseback riding, cross-country skiing, jet boat charters, boating, rafting trips, fishing with Alaska State license, mountain climbing. Check with park headquarters for further information.

FACILITIES FOR DISABLED: Visitor Center accessible.

For additional information, see also Sites, Trails, and Trips on pages 377–379 and the map on pages 356–357.

Masses of snow and ice cover Mount Drum.

WHEN AN ANCHORAGE-BOUND JET TURNS gently along the Gulf of Alaska, the scene unfolding below invariably stirs even the most seasoned travelers. The pilot reaches for the public address microphone. Passengers clutching cameras scurry to the nearest windows. A bewildering array of summits and U-shaped valleys rise from an oceanfront of glistening bays and beaches. Massive ice fields bend to the horizon, and families of clinging glaciers suggest the raw power still shaping the land. Braided rivers wind through an apron of lowland forest that runs for mile after uninhabited mile. All these scenes blend in Wrangell–St. Elias National Park and Preserve.

The nation's largest parkland, six times the size of Yellowstone, bigger than Massachusetts, Connecticut, and Rhode Island combined, embraces an earthscape unmatched on our continent. The 13.2-million-acre park abuts the Canadian border and Kluane National Park in the Yukon Territory. Kluane and Wrangell–St. Elias became in 1980 the first International World Heritage Site designated under the UNESCO program. In Wrangell-St. Elias alone, six major river systems cut down from the icy fastness. The

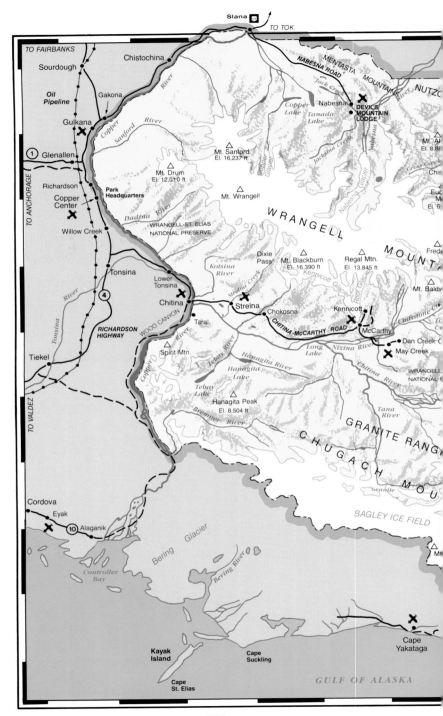

Slana

TO TOK

TO FAIRBANKS

Sourdough

Chistochina

MENTASTA MOUNTAINS

NABESNA ROAD

Oil Pipeline

Gakona

Copper River

Jack Creek

Nabesna

NUTZO

Copper Lake

Tanada Lake

DEVILS MOUNTAIN LODGE

Gulkana

Copper River

Sanford River

Jackshna Creek

Mt. Al El. 8.88

(1) Glenallen

Mt. Sanford El. 16,237 ft

Chis

TO ANCHORAGE

Richardson

Copper Center

Park Headquarters

Mt. Drum El. 12,010 ft

Mt. Wrangell

Eud M El. 6

Dadina River

WRANGELL-ST. ELIAS NATIONAL PRESERVE

WRANGELL

MOUNTA

Fred

Willow Creek

Kotsina River

Dixie Pass

Mt. Blackburn El. 16,390 ft

Regal Mtn. El. 13,845 ft

Tonsina

Lower Tonsina

Strelna Creek

Kennicott Glacier

Mt. Baldy

Chitistone C

(4)

Chitina

Strelna

Chokosna

Kennicott

Root Glacier

Tonsina River

RICHARDSON HIGHWAY

WOOD CANYON

Taral

CHITINA-McCARTHY ROAD

McCarthy

Dan Creek C

Chitistone C

Tiekel

Copper River

Spirit Mtn.

Tebay River

Hanagita River

Long Lake

Nizina River

May Creek

WRANGELL NATIONAL

TO VALDEZ

Hanagita Lake

Tebay Lake

Chitina River

Tana River

Hanagita Peak El. 8,504 ft

Bremner River

CHUGACH

GRANITE RANG

MOU

granite

BAGLEY ICE FIELD

Cordova

Eyak

(10) Alaganik

Bering Glacier

Controller Bay

Bering River

M

Kayak Island

Cape Suckling

Cape Yakataga

Cape St. Elias

GULF OF ALASKA

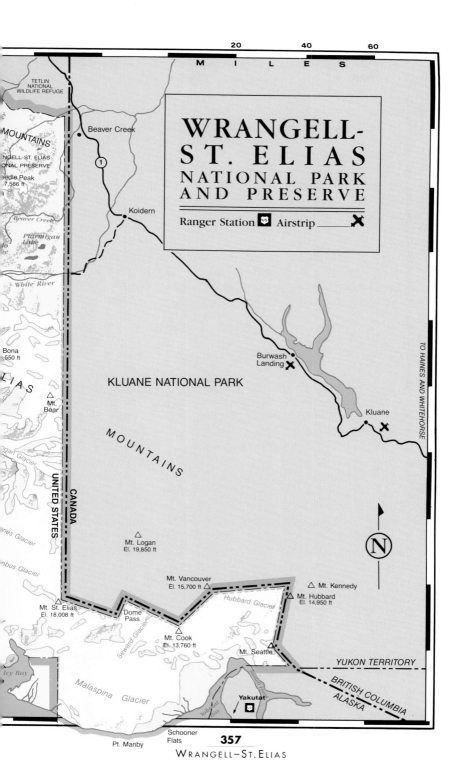

WRANGELL-ST. ELIAS
NATIONAL PARK AND PRESERVE

Ranger Station 🇺🇸 Airstrip ✈

MILES 20 40 60

TETLIN
NATIONAL
WILDLIFE REFUGE

MOUNTAINS

NGELL-ST. ELIAS
ONAL PRESERVE

edle Peak
7,586 ft

Beaver Creek

Beaver Creek

Ptarmigan
Lake

White River

Koidern

1

Bona
550 ft

Mt.
Bear

KLUANE NATIONAL PARK

Burwash
Landing ✈

Kluane ✈

LIAS

ogan Glacier

M O U N T A I N S

ries Glacier

UNITED STATES / CANADA

Mt. Logan
El. 19,850 ft

nbus Glacier

Mt. Vancouver
El. 15,700 ft

△ Mt. Kennedy

Mt. Hubbard
El. 14,950 ft

Hubbard Glacier

Mt. St. Elias
El. 18,008 ft

Dome
Pass

Seward Glacier

△ Mt. Cook
El. 13,760 ft

Mt. Seattle

YUKON TERRITORY

Icy Bay

Malaspina Glacier

Yakutat

BRITISH COLUMBIA / ALASKA

Pt. Manby

Schooner
Flats

TO HAINES AND WHITEHORSE

N

Copper River bounds the park on the west. Coastal glaciers and the Gulf of Alaska draw its southern boundary. There is a northern boundary, too, 170 miles distant from tidewater as the eagle soars, beyond the mountains and the greatest assemblage of glaciers on the continent, and bordering a rolling upland rimmed by foothills.

The broad span of climate, from maritime to dry interior, produces diversity in plant and animal populations. But the overpowering dimensions of the land almost eclipse the park's many natural, cultural, and historic features. Bands of magnificent Dall sheep can be dwarfed by hundred-mile vistas or by a single glacier five times as long as Manhattan Island. Evidence of humankind is scarce, and designation of the area as a park remains, in part, symbolic; wildlife is protected less by the stroke of a pen in Washington, D.C., than by the raw landscape, unfordable rivers, and unpeopled miles of muskeg and glacial rubble. Wrangell–St. Elias is a parkland to be approached in measured increments, studied as well as enjoyed. A lifetime of experience awaits the visitor.

HISTORY

Land of the "Ice People"

The first inhabitants of the Wrangell–St. Elias region were descendants of Asian hunters who crossed the Bering Strait from Siberia between 8,000 and 10,000 years ago. Four identifiable groups are prominent. Along the coast, Tlingit people became established at Yakutat Bay, while the Eyak Tribe made its homeland farther west in the Copper River delta. Two groups of Athapaskan origin dominated the interior regions: Tutchone Indians settled along the White River near the present Canada–United States border; and the Ahtna, or "Ice People," settled along the Copper River and in the Chitina and Nabesna valleys. Linguistically, Ahtna and Tutchone are distantly related to Indian cultures of California and the Southwest. Archeological evidence suggests that 500 Ahtna people may have inhabited Taral, an old village site near the confluence of the Chitina and Copper rivers. Sea-shell fragments discovered at Gulkana and dating to A.D. 1300 tell of trade with coastal people.

A distinctive mark of early Ahtna culture was the use of worked copper. Chitistone Canyon (*chiti* in the Ahtna language translates to "copper") was known to be a source of high-grade copper, and the people near Taral became proficient at using heat to work the crude metal. Copper spear points and blades found their way through trade to other tribes. Ahtna people relied heavily on fish for food, and a fine cutting tool could enhance survival in a region where starvation was not unknown. It has been estimated that more than 500 salmon per day could be processed by a family using sharpened copper blades.

Important groupings of Athapaskan prehistoric and historical archeological sites are found within both park and preserve. These sites include numerous villages, camps, and hunting and fishing

An old wooden bridge from the Copper River and Northwestern Railway.

locations, along with remains of other cultures, including the Tlingit and Eyak Indians and the Chugach Eskimo. A few of the well-known historical sites are found at Taral, Cross Creek, and Batzulnetas. Though largely unexplored, all of the major watersheds of the park and preserve are believed to be rich in archeological value, providing excellent opportunities for scientific research. More than ninety sites have been evaluated for possible listing in the National Register of Historic Places and are protected by federal and state laws.

European Exploration

European entry into the region came relatively early. Vitus Bering, a Dane in the employ of the Russian czar, explored the Gulf of Alaska in the summer of 1741 aboard the sailing ship *St. Peter*. Cape St. Elias on Kayak Island was named by the Danish navigator in honor of the saint whose feast day it was. On July 16, Bering saw for the first time the towering peak that Tlingits call *Yahtsetesha* and that would later be named Mount St. Elias. On July 20, sixteen of Bering's crew, along with the redoubtable Prussian naturalist Georg Wilhelm Steller, put ashore on Kayak Island—the first Europeans to touch Alaskan soil. Among Steller's many observations, he noted metallic implements, possibly of copper, at a hastily evacuated Native campsite.

The area's oceanfront was witness to famous navigators from different lands during the decades that followed. Captain James Cook, commanding the ships *Resolution* and *Discovery*, sighted Yakutat Bay in May 1778. He named Cape Suckling and Controller Bay, and claimed the surrounding regions in the name of Great Britain.

In 1790, a Spanish touch was added when Captain Salvador Fidalgo in command of the ship *Filipino* named Valdez Bay and claimed the surrounding area for Spain. Captain Alejandro Malaspina, an Italian in the employ of Spain, sailed into Icy Bay in 1791 in search of the Northwest Passage. His crew piled rocks into a pyramid and placed within it a Spanish coin and a bottle containing a proclamation claiming possession of the port "in the name of His Catholic Majesty." Coin and bottle have never been found.

Though Vitus Bering did not live to see Russia again, word of Alaska's vast fur resources soon brought the beginnings of Russian America to the Wrangell–St. Elias region. In 1795, Aleksandr Baranov established a Russian convict colony on the southeast shore of Yakutat Bay. Planned as an agricultural and shipbuilding colony, it was christened "Gloria of Russia." Ten years later, the town was destroyed and forty inhabitants were

The Kennecott Station, circa 1920.

killed by a raiding party of Tlingits.

Over the next thirty-five years, fur traders met with little success and much hardship along the Copper River. Short-lived trading posts were established at Taral, near Chitina, and at Gulkana for dealing with the *mednovtze*, Russian slang for Ahtna people. The well-documented fate of one notorious trading party lives on in Ahtna lore.

Rufus Serberenikoff, a Russian-Aleut, and eleven assistants spent the winter of 1847 trading for furs at Batzulnetas, a village at the confluence of the Slana and Copper rivers. Native food caches were routinely taken by party members during the winter, and the Ahtna men were driven from the area. In the spring, Serberenikoff and all of his men were killed by the Ahtna in retaliation for stealing and brutalizing Ahtna women, including the young daughter of a chief. Ahtna people traveled more than 100 miles to Nuchek, the region's main Russian outpost on Hinchinbrook Island, to return the trading party's belongings intact, including Serberenikoff's journal, and to explain the event to Russian leaders.

Although vague remnants of Russian culture persist today in communities of the Wrangell–St. Elias region, the characteristic independence of the Ahtna people kept them from developing close ties with the Russians. Direct Russian influence ended in 1867 with the purchase of Russian America for $7 million by the United States.

Lieutenant Allen's Odyssey

In contrast to the overbearing and brutal presence of Russian traders, the first significant American contact began on a humble note. Henry Allen, a young army lieutenant, and two enlisted men set out in 1885 to explore the Copper River and Chitina Valley and to go beyond if conditions allowed. At the confluence of the Copper and Chitina rivers, Allen observed dire poverty and hunger among the Ahtna. Food caches were low and it was still too early for "first fish" (salmon) of late May.

Yet Ahtna stories remember the Americans for their own extreme hunger and poor condition. Allen's party had traveled light, hoping to live off the land, but the land did not easily provide. The lieutenant's official journal contains gruesome details of the party's meager diet of rabbits and rotting moose meat. Their half-starved and bedraggled condition impressed Chief Nicolai, a powerful Ahtna leader, when Allen's party dragged into his camp on the Nizina River. Nicolai and his people were further impressed (and disarmed) when the famished Americans asked to eat with their hosts. Among the Ahtna, sharing food is a traditional sign of friendly intentions.

Good relations with Chief Nicolai assured a successful venture. The chief assigned guides to Allen's party, and they introduced him to chiefs farther upriver. They in turn supplied guides for the next leg of the journey. Allen explored part of the Chitina Valley and verified that Nicolai was a source of the copper being traded throughout the region. Allen crossed the Mentasta Mountains and traversed the Tanana Valley, ultimately reaching the Koyukuk River on the Arctic Circle. Dr. Alfred Brooks of the U.S. Geological Survey wrote in 1906: "No man through his own exploration has added more to a geographic knowledge of Alaska than Lieutenant Allen."

A Copper Bonanza

The historic gold strike of 1896 in Canada's Klondike region, and the lure of unstruck riches along the Tanana and Yukon rivers in Alaska, brought miners to the Wrangell-St. Elias area, first in a trickle and then in a flood. An "all Alaska" route from the port of Valdez to the gold fields appeared feasible. This was an alternative to the arduous Chilkoot Trail and White Pass route near Skagway—and would avoid Canadian customs fees and other requirements. The trail would top out over Thompson Pass and follow the Copper River northward to the gold fields. U.S. Army Captain W. R. Abercrombie surveyed the route.

In 1898, 4,000 prospectors landed at Valdez. While the greater number slogged northward through the Copper River Valley, a few were lured by dreams of local pay dirt. Oscar Rohn, a geologist with the U.S. Geological Survey, had described structures he called Chitistone Limestone and Nikolai Greenstone in the upper Chitina Valley. His analysis of volcanic contact zones occurring in the area compared favorably with Lake Superior Greenstone, which would produce some of the richest copper ore in the United States. In 1900, prospectors Clarence Warner and Jack Smith discovered the green cliffs of malachite above the Kennicott Glacier. Legend holds that they spotted the cliffs while seeking a grassy pasture for their horses. Their Bonanza Mine eventually became the central resource for the most significant mineral development in Alaska's history.

The pathway to successful operation of what would soon be known as the Kennecott Mine proved to be strewn with the snares and setbacks of which colorful history is made. (What began as a clerk's error was later standardized by the company as a distinctive spelling, *Kennecott*.) Financier Meyer Guggenheim, owner of the American Smelting and Refining Company, and the banking family of J. P. Morgan formed the Alaska Syndicate, which promptly acquired 3,000 acres of the Bonanza and adjacent claims for $2,987,500. Assays showing the ore to be 70 percent copper with an additional 14 ounces of silver per ton proved persuasive. A copper shortage on the world market added further incentive.

But the Kennecott Mine lay 200 miles from tidewater in the middle of a howling wilderness. The syndicate's grand scheme called for investing $20 million to complete a railroad from Cordova on the Gulf. This railroad proved to be one of the outstanding engineering feats of its day. An undeveloped coal field near tidewater at Katalla, east of the Copper River, was to be the smelter location as well as the source of fuel for the railroad. However, President Theodore Roosevelt, acting in 1906 to protect public resources, withdrew from development all Alaskan coal fields not already legally claimed.

In need of a fuel source, the syndicate began to acquire interests in coal leases from an organization which, some argued, had obtained its holdings illegally. Charges were also made that the Secretary of the Interior, Richard Ballinger, was implicated through his former roles as legal counsel to the claim holders and as commissioner of the General Land Office when the leases were evaluated. President William Howard Taft was challenged on the issue by Gifford Pinchot, chief of the U.S. Forest Service, who was a noted conservationist and a friend of ex-President Roosevelt.

Overleaf: Kennecott Mine is a reminder of the copper boom that came long before the Alaskan oil discovery.

Taft fired Pinchot amid a maelstrom of publicity. A congressional investigation exonerated Ballinger, but a subsequent inquiry proved that the coal leases were invalid in any case. Because of the Ballinger-Pinchot affair and for other reasons, Roosevelt left the Republican Party, ran against Taft for president on a third-party ticket in 1912, and inadvertently allowed the Democratic nominee, Woodrow Wilson, to win the election. The pursuit of wealth in the mountain environs of Wrangell-St. Elias had changed American political history.

The completed Copper River and Northwestern Railway linked the Kennecott Mine with the port of Cordova on March 29, 1911. One month later, the steamer *Northwestern* carried into Seattle the first load of 1,200 tons of high-grade copper ore, worth $250,000. By 1915, annual operating profits had jumped to $8 million. And World War I caused an even stronger upsurge in copper demand. On a glacier-scoured hillside hard by the lateral moraine of the Kennicott glacier, an immense mining complex sprang to life, including tramways, a power plant, bunkhouses, a hospital, a recreation hall, and many buildings for processing copper ore. About 2.5 miles down-glacier, the colorful community of McCarthy blossomed, offering such amenities as a dance hall, a roadhouse, two newspapers, a small schoolhouse, a pool hall, and a Chinese restaurant.

But eventually the high-grade reserves were nearly exhausted. The company developed an ammonia-leaching process to recover copper from tailings, but the downward trend continued. The Kennecott Mine closed in 1938. In its 27 years of operation it produced more than 1 billion pounds of copper and 9.7 million ounces of silver worth about $300 million. The Kennecott Mine stands as the single most significant industrial development in Alaska between the gold rush of the 1890s and the first major oil discovery in 1957. Today, the brick-red buildings of the old mine are listed on the National Register of Historic Places. The privately owned property, largely unmaintained, is slowly giving way to weather and snowpack and the shifting ground of glacier country.

Establishment of the Park

Shortly before shutdown of the Kennecott Mine, an official from the U.S. Department of the Interior visited the area. Ernest Gruening, then director for Territories and Island Possessions (and later governor and U.S. senator from Alaska) was so struck by the remarkable scenery of Wrangell–St. Elias that he recommended a national park be established there.

In 1978, after being studied for park status for almost eight years, Wrangel–St. Elias was proclaimed a national monument by

President Jimmy Carter. In 1980, Congress passed the Alaska National Interest Lands Conservation Act, which redesignated the area as a national park and preserve. Sport hunting and trapping are allowed in the preserve, which otherwise is managed as a national park. Many acres within the park are privately owned.

GEOLOGY

Alaska's Ring of Fire

Our continent's curve around the Gulf of Alaska coincides with the edge of the North Pacific's tectonic plate. This rocky segment of the earth's crust, which may reach 60 miles in depth below the ocean floor, grinds slowly north and west along the continental edge. The resulting interface—of which the Wrangell–St. Elias region is part—is known as the Ring of Fire, one of the most active seismic zones in the hemisphere. In September 1899, Yakutat was wracked by two severe earthquakes that measured 8.3 and 8.6 on the Richter scale. According to plate-tectonic theory, the North Pacific plate's ongoing collision with the continent has also contributed the force to uplift the landscape along the Gulf of Alaska and form the world's highest coastal mountain ranges.

In the Chugach and St. Elias regions, uplifting of marine sedimentation occurred during Mesozoic or early Tertiary times. Erosional forces then carved into the Tertiary sediments and exposed numerous plant and animal fossils. The sediments also contain some ancient glacial deposits and organic material that would one day produce naturally occurring oil seeps in the area. From uplifted zones, foothills along the oceanfront received sediments that formed localized beds of coal, such as those at the Bering River coal fields near Katalla.

During more recent Tertiary times, 70 to 100 million years ago, mountains of Wrangell–St. Elias were pushed so high that glaciers and ice fields became the dominant shaping force of the landscape. The ice mass expanded and shrank at least three times, softening lowland contours, rerouting waterways, and erasing many forms of ancient biota. Although less significant geologically, the Little Ice Age occurred in Wrangell–St. Elias as recently as 3,500 to 200 years ago. Some coastal areas were obliterated during this period. Icy Bay and Yakutat Bay were subjected to a glacial outwash that denuded and reshaped the landscape. Terminal moraines of this period continue to dam large lakes at the bases of ice fronts along the coast.

Overleaf: A geothermal mud volcano on Ahtna Native Regional Corporation lands.

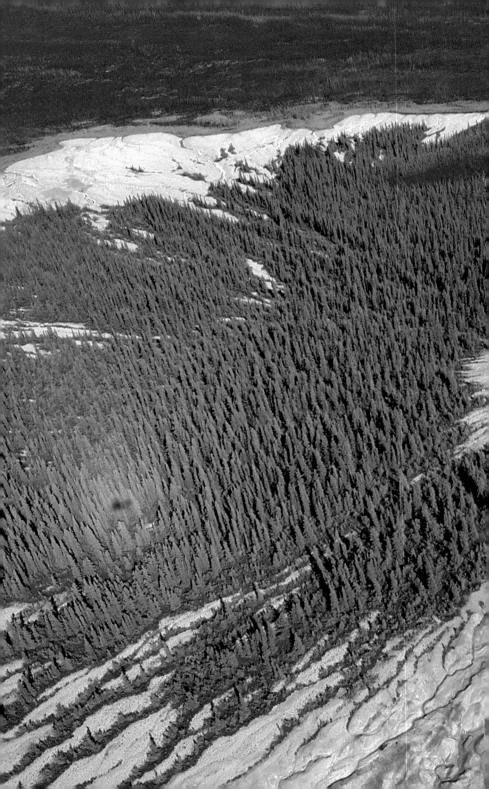

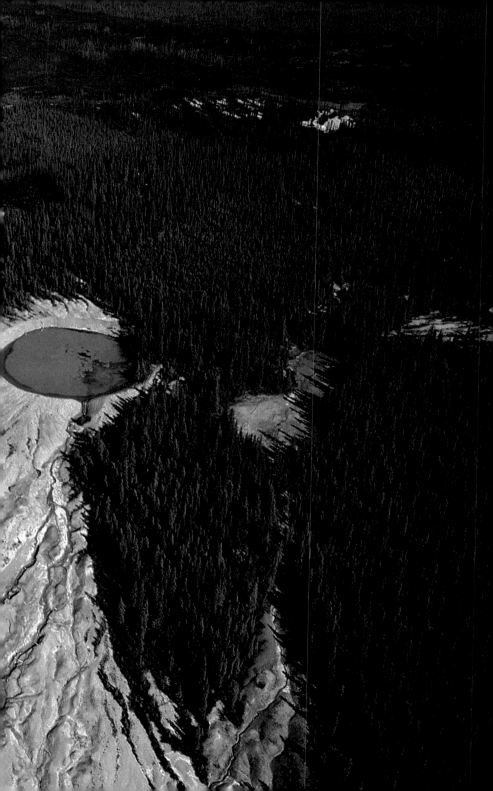

The Seashore Mountains

Today, three major mountain ranges lie within the boundaries of the park and preserve. The Chugach Mountains form the east-to-west barrier along the coast. In a trench atop this range, the massive Bagley Ice Field, 80 miles long, serves as the source of the Malaspina and Bering glaciers—the two largest in North America. Their terminal piedmont lobes extend down to tidewater. Altogether, ice fields cover about 4 million acres of the coastal mountains.

Joining the eastern Chugach to form the second prong of a mountainous wishbone, or slingshot, are the Wrangell Mountains, which display along their western frontage with the Copper River the well-known Alaskan skyline of Mount Drum (12,010 feet), Mount Wrangell (14,163 feet), and Mount Sanford (16,237 feet), all familiar to highway visitors. Major eruptions in this area occurred as recently as 1,500 years ago. Puffs of ash and vapor still rise occasionally from Mount Wrangell, and mud holes and mineral springs bubble along the flanks of Mount Drum. Mount Wrangell was named for Baron Ferdinand Wrangell, Russian governor of Alaska. Wrangell, one of Alaska's first non-Native conservationists, mapped and attempted to rotate sea-otter hunting grounds.

The handle of the slingshot is formed by the St. Elias Mountains, which cross into Canada's Yukon Territory and become the heartland of Kluane National Park. The St. Elias Mountains are the highest coastal mountains in the world. Mount St. Elias (18,008 feet), which helps define the Alaska–Canada boundary, and Mount Logan (19,850 feet) are the fourth and second highest peaks in North America.

Two smaller ranges, the Mentasta and Nutzotin mountains, surround a rolling upland. The Nutzotin range separates tributaries of the Tanana River in Alaska from those of the White River, which flows into Canada. These separated waters rejoin many miles later in the Yukon River in Alaska's central interior.

Some of the oldest rocks of the region are the Precambrian metamorphosed schists in the Wrangell and St. Elias mountains. These are largely covered by Permian marine sediments deposited 250 million years ago. They contain fossil assemblages, limestone, and greenstone.

The Nikolai Greenstone, a source of wealth in the twentieth century, had its origin about 200 million years ago during a series of undersea basaltic lava flows. Settling out of this material were small percentages of copper sulfides, later covered by layers of shale and dolomitic limestone. The process of uplift caused folds, fractures, and faults, and it gave the formation a northeasterly slant of 23 to 30 degrees. These formations were invaded by molten

Hubbard Glacier extends to tidewater.

porphyry about 75 million years ago, causing heated ground water to begin dislodging metallic copper from greenstone. This trickle of concentrate slowly worked into fissures in the dolomitic limestone, which proved to be an excellent host rock. Eventually exposed by erosion of the dolomite, the greenish outcrops awaited discovery by a pair of wandering prospectors with horses in need of pasture.

The area's greatest geological appeal to visitors is its diversity. Nizina and Chitistone canyons, for example, are comparable in size to the canyons of Yosemite and Zion national parks. They contain many unusual geological features, including excellent examples of eskers, moraines, and columnar jointing (or postpiling). Many features in Nizina and Chitistone canyons are not found in Yosemite or Zion. For example, Yosemite reveals only the effects of glacial activity, but Chitistone contains glaciers that continue to scour,

hang, and form. It has also been estimated that Nizina and Chitistone canyons display a record of about 25 percent of the earth's geologic time since the Precambrian. As a modest diversion, upper Chitistone Canyon includes a roaring 300-foot waterfall.

NATURAL HISTORY

Climate

The lands of Wrangell–St. Elias fall into three of the state's four climatic zones: Maritime, Transitional, and Continental. Only the Arctic zone is absent. Coastal regions near Yakutat receive up to 130 inches of precipitation annually, with winter low temperatures around 0° F, and summer highs in the 70s. Winter storms along the coast are severe. Annual snowfall at higher elevations averages more than 600 inches. The park's great mountain mass intercepts the moist maritime weather from the Gulf of Alaska and forms a barrier between coastal and interior climates.

The modest elevations of the Copper River basin fall into a Transitional zone between coast and interior. About 50 inches of snow occur here annually, along with 10 to 12 inches of rainfall. Advancing inland, toward the Mentasta and Nutzotin mountains, precipitation decreases and seasonal temperatures grow more extreme. In the weather shadow of these secondary mountains and foothills, rainfall drops to 8 inches annually while winter temperatures can fall to -70° F. Summer highs may reach 80° F. The northeastern perimeter of Wrangell–St. Elias overlaps an area along the White River Valley that consistently produces the lowest winter temperatures in arctic and subarctic latitudes. A reading of -85° F has been recorded at the small village of Snag on the White River just across the Canadian border.

The high-elevation mass of ice and snow in the Wrangell–St. Elias region forms a natural refrigeration system that shapes weather patterns as far south as Chicago and the central plains.

Riverways

The Copper River, the region's major waterway, forms the western boundary of the park and preserve. Major tributaries from within the park and preserve include the Sanford, Kotsina, Chitina, and Bremner rivers. All of the larger watercourses are fed with glacial meltwater and transport substantial amounts of "rock flour," or glacial silt, during summer. Waters laden with such powdered rock

Opposite: Trumpeter swan adults may be as large as 6 feet in length.

rarely support resident fish populations. Yet these waters form an important transitional and migratory habitat for coho, sockeye, and king salmon bound for spawning and wintering areas in lakes and clearwater tributaries. Wrangell–St. Elias's major clearwater streams are the Tebay and Hanagita rivers and Beaver Creek.

Some waterways—such as the Kennicott River—lie below ice-dammed lakes, sometimes called "booming lakes." These lakes can suddenly rupture their retaining ice wall and release an outburst flood to the river below. Such situations are extremely hazardous. The Kennicott River crossing at McCarthy is regularly affected by outburst floods from Hidden Creek Lake, a waterway along Kennicott Glacier's western edge.

The Thin Mantle of Life

Below lofty fields of perpetual snow, diverse vegetational communities form the true life zones of the park and preserve. Delicate alpine tundra is found at elevations between 3,000 and 5,000 feet. Dry tundra, consisting of low-growing species such as mountain avens, is found extensively on steep slopes and ridges. Grasses, sedges, and shrubs of the lower-elevation moist tundra form an important habitat for grazing caribou and provide winter forage for Dall sheep. Amid the low shrubs of dwarf birch, blueberry, and Labrador tea, thousands of migratory birds find nesting habitat in the tundra each spring.

River bottoms, punctuated with countless lakes and bogs, harbor white spruce that may reach 100 feet in height. A virgin stand of white spruce along the Chitina River has been designated as a representative "natural area" by the Society of American Foresters. Such stands of spruce are commonly interspersed with aspen, birch, and balsam poplar. In contrast, coastal forests consist mainly of western hemlock and Sitka spruce, often with an extensive understory of alder. Soils undergirded with permafrost have given rise to a slow-growth, or "stunted," forest of black spruce, an occasional tamarack, and paper birch. This type of plant sometimes occurs along the Nabesna Valley.

No plants known to be threatened or endangered inhabit the park and preserve. One possible candidate species, the false spring beauty (*Montia bostockii*), is found in the Chitistone Pass–Skolai Creek area. Numerous relict plant species, surrounded by Malaspina and other glaciers, have been found in the vicinity of Oily Lake and the Samovar Hills. Well over half the plants along

Opposite: The Amanita muscaria. The family of this dangerous mushroom causes almost all fatal mushroom poisonings.

the coastal lowlands are in some phase of re-establishment following general scouring of the landscape by glacial action. Pioneer species include dwarf willow, horsetail, and fireweed. A climax forest is a rare occurrence in a glacially active terrain.

Sheep and Other Wildlife

Alaska's majestic white sheep, named for the explorer and naturalist William Healey Dall, occur only in the northwest portions of North America. The finest of their kind—in both stature and number—are found in the high meadows and along ridgetops of Wrangell–St. Elias. Dall sheep form compact herd clusters, or bands, in alpine and subalpine zones of rugged uplands. Generally, their habitats coincide with ancient mountain refugia that were not invaded by ice during the most recent glacial period. They have adapted to life in one of the harshest environments on the continent.

Although mature rams sometimes explore new habitats that have recently emerged from glaciation, sheep customarily remain loyal to fixed home ranges. Distances between winter and summer habitats are short, usually less than 15 miles. Winter storms may drive scattered bands into long single-file migrations to sheltering basins or protective crags. In spring, the bands slowly follow the retreating snowline to the higher pastures of their summer range. Lambs are born in mid-May after a gestation period of 175 days. A newborn lamb weighs 6 to 10 pounds.

Major Dall sheep populations of Wrangell–St. Elias are found north of the Chitina River. About 12,000 to 16,000 sheep live in the park and preserve. Approximately 80 percent of these sheep reside on lands within the preserve and therefore are available for sport hunting. The remaining 20 percent are within the park, which is closed to sport hunting but open to subsistence hunting by local residents. The Dall sheep's summer habitat is remote and difficult of access, however, and the sheep do not play an important role in subsistence hunting. The use of aircraft for subsistence hunting is prohibited. The preserve supplies between 20 and 25 percent of all Dall sheep killed by sport hunters in Alaska.

Small herds of barren-ground caribou range within preserve lands along the north and northeast boundary and cross into Canada. Calving occurs on the gravel bars of the White and Chisana rivers, in the vicinity of Beaver Creek near the old mining camp of Bonanza and along the flanks of Mount Drum and Mount Sanford. Mountain goats range in the Chugach Mountains and Icy Bay area, occasionally overlapping with Dall sheep north of the Chitina River. Moose, the area's most widespread lowland ungulate, may be found anywhere at elevations below 6,000 feet, but they are most common along brushy areas near bogs where browse is abundant. They also frequent the forests of the Malaspina forelands.

Grizzly bears also range throughout the park and preserve at elevations below 6,000 feet. The Copper River attracts bears in the spring, and they also concentrate along fish streams in coastal areas. The "glacier bear," a gunmetal-blue color phase of the black bear, is found along the Malaspina forelands and is much sought by sport hunters. A variety of furbearers, including lynx, wolf, wolverine, marten, beaver, and muskrat, share habitats with the bear.

Introduced bison are found in the park and preserve in two small bands, one in the upper Chitina River Valley and the other near the Copper River between the Dadina and Kotsina rivers.

Bald eagles and golden eagles nest along waterways of the park and preserve. Many aeries occur along the Chitina River. Alaska's three species of ptarmigan are found in tundra and willow thickets throughout the area, along with such game birds as spruce and ruffed grouse. Trumpeter swans are found at several interior lakes along foothills and lowlands. The Malaspina forelands and Copper River flats are important migratory flyways.

Sea lions congregate along the Sitkagi Bluffs adjacent to Malaspina Glacier. Harbor seals are numerous in Icy Bay. Several species of whales can be seen offshore. White beluga whales swim near Grand Wash slough along the northwest coast of Yakutat Bay.

SITES, TRAILS, AND TRIPS

Three existing access routes naturally divide the park and preserve into north, central, and coastal regions, or districts. Along the coast, boats and aircraft may land anywhere safety allows along the broad oceanfront of the Malaspina forelands. The beach is noted for an often spectacular surf. One area known as Schooner Flats is recognizable by the broken masts of a turn-of-the-century wooden-hulled whaling ship that protrude from the burying sands. The forest lands bordering the ocean at Yakutat Bay are part of the preserve, where sport hunting is allowed in the fall. The town of Yakutat is the main point of access. It may be reached only by commercial or charter air service. The National Park Service maintains a district ranger station at Yakutat.

At the park and preserve's midsection, the Chitina–McCarthy Road provides surface access into the heartland of the Chitina Valley. The gravel road follows the historic route of the Copper River and Northwestern Railway, extending 61 miles to the Kennicott River crossing, 1 mile west of McCarthy. Broad vistas to the south and southeast offer a glimpse of the Chugach Mountains, some of the park's most remote and least known terrain, where nameless peaks and valleys fold away to the horizon. Balsam poplar and spruce muskeg parallel the road, which rises 500 feet above the Chitina River. From Strelna, the road offers access to Kuskalana Glacier via a 7-hour (18-mile) hike. The old mining settlement of Copper Town can be reached via Strelna Creek and Dixie Pass, with possible views of Dall sheep along the way. Motorists must leave their cars on the west side of the Kennicott River. To reach McCarthy, they have had to pull themselves across the river on a cable tram. (A footbridge was scheduled for completion in 1996.) Access to the old Kennecott Mine is via a 2.5-mile trail along the original railway grade. The Kennecott buildings, privately owned, constitute an in-holding within the preserve. Park Service contact points are at Chitina and at Wrangell–St. Elias headquarters at Copper Center near Glennallen. Drivers should inquire about conditions on the Chitina–McCarthy Road.

Motorists on Alaska 1 will skirt the base of Mount Sanford.

Road access into the northern district is from Slana along a state secondary route extending 43 miles to the abandoned and privately owned mining community of Nabesna. This route offers access to the popular Tanada Lakes area and the scenic high country above Jacksina Creek. The lower Jacksina Creek is a wild torrent of Class IV (very difficult) whitewater. Flights via charter aircraft to Sheep Lake or Grizzly Lake also offer a jumpoff point for access to alpine meadows favored by Dall sheep. The Nabesna Road offers vistas of Copper Glacier and Mount Sanford. A Park Service ranger station is situated at Slana.

The broad, silt-laden Copper River cuts through the rugged Chugach Mountains to the Gulf of Alaska. Beginning a raft or kayak trip on the Kennicott River near McCarthy in the heart of the park, a visitor can reach the Copper River after traveling on two more of its tributaries, the Nizina and the Chitina. The serpentine gorge of the Nizina River contains fast water and interesting forms on the canyon walls. In places, the Chitina is so widely braided that the opposite bank is beyond view, but then it narrows as it joins the Copper and flows through the slate gorges of Wood Canyon. Snow-capped mountains, several major glaciers, forests, and tumbling waterfalls are visible from the Copper River Valley. The river includes some class III (moderately difficult) rapids. Rafters and kayakers share the lower reaches of the Copper River with icebergs, and the calving of glaciers adds drama and some risk to the scenery. This trip, which takes 10 to 14 days, is an expedition, not a tour, and should be approached with that fact in mind.

Access to Chitistone Canyon is limited to three four-passenger aircraft at Skolai Pass. The hiking routes between the pass and the canyon require highly developed skills in crossing rivers and cross-country travel. Toby Creek and the Chitistone River can become impassable barriers overnight. In many places the historic trail through the canyon has become overgrown. In others, washed-out sections on steep scree slopes are traversed comfortably only by the sheep and goats that frequent the area.

Opportunities for wilderness backpacking, fishing, car camping, river running, mountain climbing, cross-country skiing, and other forms of winter and summer recreation are virtually limitless in Wrangell–St. Elias. Prospective visitors must bear in mind that this truly vast and remote part of Alaska contains no maintained trails or developed river crossings. Many of the safeguards and facilities usually found in National Park Service areas are not available here. Careful planning is the key to a safe and rewarding visit.

Overleaf: Slanting arctic light and sudden rainstorms produce many rainbows.

ANIMALS & PLANTS

OF THE PACIFIC NORTHWEST
AND ALASKA

This appendix provides a sample of animals and plants commonly found in the national parks of the Pacific Northwest and Alaska. The two-letter abbreviations indicate the parks in which these animals and plants are most often seen.

CL	Crater Lake	KA	Katmai	MR	Mount Rainier
DN	Denali	KF	Kenai Fjords	NC	North Cascades
GA	Gates of the Arctic	KV	Kobuk Valley	OP	Olympic
GB	Glacier Bay	LC	Lake Clark	WS	Wrangell-St. Elias

MAMMALS

ARCTIC GROUND SQUIRREL

DN, GA, KA, KF, KV, LC, WS

The arctic ground squirrel is usually grayish in color, with mottled fur and a short tail. Measuring about 14–18 in. and weighing about 1.5 lbs., it lives in colonies with elaborate burrow systems. The ground squirrel is mainly active from about 4 A.M.–9 P.M. during the long summer days, and hibernates from late September to April or May. It is sometimes called "Parka Squirrel" because Eskimos often use its fur for parka linings. The arctic ground squirrel is frequently seen on the banks of rivers and lakes; its diet consists mainly of the roots, stems, and leaves of grasses.

BEAVER

DN, GA, KA, KF, KV, LC, MR, NC, OP, WS

The beaver is North America's largest rodent; it generally is up to 4 ft. long, including a 1-ft., flat, scaly tail, and weighs 45–60 lbs., but can weigh up to 100. Mainly nocturnal, it can sometimes be seen during midafternoon. The beaver lives in lodges; on major rivers, it lives in dens along the bank. The beaver's diet is mainly the bark of trees, although in summer it feeds on water vegetation.

BLACK BEAR

CL, DN, GA, GB, KF, KV, LC, MR, NC, WS

The black bear may be a brownish or cinnamon color, but it can be distinguished from the grizzly and brown bear by its straight-profiled face (unlike the dished face of the others), its humpless shoulders, and by its comparatively smaller size (3 ft. at the shoulder, 4.5–6.25 ft. long, 203–595 lbs., although generally smaller in Alaska). The black bear feeds on grasses, buds, leaves, berries, nuts, bark, insects, rodents, carrion, and fish, particularly salmon; it forages near campsites. This is a powerful and potentially dangerous animal; although primarily nocturnal, it may be seen during the day.

BLACK-TAILED DEER

CL, GB, MR, NC, OP

Both the black-tailed deer and the mule deer are considered a subspecies of one deer species called the mule deer; although the two do not usually interbreed, they do intermingle. They are similar, with 5–6 in.-long ears, and differ from the white-tailed deer in that their antlers fork into equal branches, while the white-tailed deer's antlers grow from a single heavy beam. The black-tailed deer stands about 3.5 ft. at the shoulders and weighs between 100 and 400 lbs. It lives in hilly or mountainous regions where it feeds on herbaceous plants.

CARIBOU

DN, GA, KA, KV, LC, WS

The gregarious and migratory caribou is the only member of the deer family whose females grow antlers (although the female's antlers are smaller and less ornate than the male's). It is the North American representative of the Old World reindeer. Weighing as much as 600 lbs. (although most often considerably less than that), caribou will be found on the tundra in the summer and farther south during winter. Their diet consists of lichens, sedges, grasses, and willow.

DALL SHEEP
DN, GA, KV, LC, WS

In Alaska, the Dall sheep is usually white; in its Canadian range, it may sometimes be gray to nearly black. Related to North America's bighorn sheep, the Dall sheep has massive, tightly curled horns that can measure nearly 3 ft., considerably longer than those of the bighorn. Dall sheep, which may weigh up to 200 lbs., graze on various grasses and also eat sedges, willow, fireweed, and avens.

GRIZZLY BEAR
DN, GA, GB, KA, KF, KV, LC, WS

The grizzly is aggressive and extremely strong. (It is the

same animal as the Alaskan brown bear, which is found along coastal streams.) Berries, nuts, tubers, and insects form its major diet. The grizzly prefers the more open areas of the mountainous regions it inhabits.

LYNX DN, GA, GB, KA, KF, KV, LC, NC, WS

The lynx, one of the seven members of America's cat family, lives almost entirely in the coniferous forest zones of Alaska, Canada, and the most northern Rocky Mountains; in fact, its habitat can almost always be defined by where its main prey, snowshoe hare, abounds. Seldom does this 20-lb. cat with brown-gray fur venture beyond its square-mile territory, but it will migrate long distances if its prey has been depleted.

MOOSE DN, GA, GB, KA, KF, KV, LC, NC, WS

The largest member of the deer family, the moose is at once majestic and unpredictable. The male weighs up to 1,400 lbs. and stands up to 7.5 ft. at the shoulder. Its antler spread is 4–5 ft., but the record is 81 in.

Moose, identified by an overhanging snout and pendulous "bell" on the throat, live in spruce forests, swamps, and aspen and willow thickets, where they feed on willow, aquatic vegetation, and, at streams, the leaves of water lilies.

WOLF DN, GA, GB, KA, KF, KV, LC, WS

Recent studies have given more respect to the timber, or gray, wolf, which was once considered only a vicious predator; now its complex social behavior fascinates man. Its large doglike body measures 40–75 in., with a 13–19-in. tail, and weighs up to 130 lbs. Although usually grayish-brown, its fur can range from white to black. Its prey includes moose, deer, elk, caribou, sheep, and goats

WOLVERINE DN, GA, GB, KA, KF, KV, LC, NC, WS

The wolverine is one of the most powerful mammals for its size, about 3.5 ft. with a 10-in. tail. It feeds mostly on mice, lemmings, ground squirrels, and carrion. Usually dark brown with broad yellow stripes, the wolverine is found in forests or tundra.

BIRDS

AMERICAN ROBIN

DN, GA, GB, KA, KF, KV, LC, MR, NC, OP, WS

Best known of all North American birds, once called "robin," the American robin is gray-brown, with puffed-out, red or orange breast, white throat, and blackish head and tail. It measures 9–11 in. In Alaska, the robin feeds primarily on ground insects, not worms. In cold areas, the nest is built of twigs and mud and lined with fine material in low, densely leafed or needled trees and bushes; in hot areas, the nest is high in maple or sycamore trees.

ARCTIC LOON

GA, GB, KA, KF, KV, LC, OP, WS

The light gray head and neck of the arctic loon contrasts with its dark gray back in summer; it is two-toned like other loons in winter. This small loon measures 23–29 in. It migrates only during the day. The arctic loon is generally silent, except during the breeding season. The loon feeds mostly on fish.

BALD EAGLE

CL, DN, GB, KA, KF, LC, NC, OP, WS

The adult bald eagle, over 5 years old, has a snow-white head, neck, and tail; the rest of the body is brownish-black. The immature eagle is brown except for some white wing linings and whitish blotches on underparts; a white head and tail come gradually with each molt. The U.S. national bird, it measures 30–43 in. from head to tail, with a wingspan of 78–96 in. Primarily a scavenger, it also eats fish, carrion, and catches waterfowl. Hunting, poaching, and insecticides have diminished their numbers, but they can occasionally be seen nesting in tall trees.

COMMON MURRE

GB, KA, KF, LC, OP

Nesting on open ledges or cliff tops, this large, black-and-white sea bird measures about 17 in. In winter, its cheeks, throat, and neck are white with a thin black line that curves down behind the eye; in summer, the head is all black. When walking on land the common murre walks upright, like a penguin. Its diet consists largely of fish.

COMMON RAVEN

CL, DN, GA, GB, KA, KF, KV, LC, MR, NC, OP, WS

Considered to have an intelligence matching a dog's, applying reason to new situations, the raven is the largest of the Corvidae; it is 21.5–27 in. from bill to tail. It is black, with a thick bill and wedge-shaped tail. The raven nests in a large collection of sticks, bones, and soft material on a cliff face or in a tree, and feeds on almost anything.

GRAY-CROWNED ROSY FINCH

CL, DN, GB, KA, KF, KV, LC, MR, NC, WS

The ancestors of the rosy finch migrated from Asia;

the gray-crowned has stayed in Alaska and the extreme northwestern U.S. Its gray nape and crown give it its name, but its back and belly are dark brown, and its shoulder and rump are pink. A black forehead tops its gray face. During breeding, both the male and female develop a pair of pouches in the bottom of their mouths in which to carry food to their young.

GRAY JAY

CL, DN, GA, GB, KA, KF, KV, LC, MR, NC, OP, WS

Formerly called the "Canada jay," and sometimes called the "Camp Robber" or "Whiskey Jay," this bird of the northern forests is well known to campers. Measuring 10−13 in., it is dark gray above and light gray below, with a narrow, light band across the back. A blackish nape contrasts with an almost white face. Gray jays will consume almost anything they can find.

LEAST SANDPIPER

DN, GB, KA, KF, KV, LC, OP, WS

A common, tolerant sandpiper, this bird is smaller than the western sandpiper found along the Atlantic and Pacific coasts of the U.S. Measuring 5−6.5 in., with a short, thin, dark bill, yellowish legs, light brown breast, and striped brown underparts, this sandpiper frequents marshes and bogs. In flight this bird twists and turns, alternately showing its white belly and dark back.

PINTAIL

DN, GA, GB, KA, KF, KV, LC, NC, OP, WS

The pintail is a long-necked, slender duck with a brown head, white neck and underparts, and a grayish back and sides. Its tail is long, black, and pointed. The male is 25−29 in.; the female is slightly smaller. The pintail usually lives near marshes, small lakes, or ponds. While it usually eats seeds, it will on occasion feed on small aquatic animals.

SPRUCE GROUSE

CL, GA, GB, KV, MR, NC, OP

The spring display of this territorial male is most colorful; the large sound-amplifying pouches on its neck inflate and deflate with loud "hoots" as it courts. The male is a dusky or bluish gray overall with orange-yellow combs over its eyes; the female is a mottled brown with a dark tail. A large grouse, it measures 15.5−21 in., and nests near tree stumps or rocks.

SURF SCOTER

DN, GB, KA, KF, KV, LC, OP

The most common scoter of the Pacific coast spends most of the year on its Arctic breeding ground. It is 17−21 in. in length, has black-and-white patches on its forehead and nape, and a large bill with a bright white-black, orange-red pattern. The scoter feeds by diving and swimming underwater.

WHITE-CROWNED SPARROW

DN, GA, GB, KA, KF, KV, LC, NC, OP, WS

The white-crowned sparrow has a crown with alternating 5 white and 4 black stripes; a white stripe over the eye, and a black stripe through the eye; face and nape are grayish, and breast is pearl-gray. It is 6−7 in. long. Its grass nests are on or near the ground, and it feeds on seeds, insects, and small fruit.

AMPHIBIANS AND REPTILES

BOREAL TOAD
CL, GB, NC

The boreal, of the western toad family, ranges from southern Alaska to the Rockies to Baja California. It is gray to green overall, but has dark patches on its belly and a light stripe that bisects its back. The toad measures 2.5–5 in. The boreal toad is most active at twilight, but it can sometimes be seen moving during the day, especially in the higher elevations.

CASCADES FROG
CL, OP

The Cascades frog is usually an olive to brown color. Its back and legs are spotted with black, and it measures 1.75–2.25 in. Its face is masked in black and its underside is yellow. This frog can most frequently be seen taking a sunbath on a rock or near water.

COMMON GARTER SNAKE
GB, NC, OP

This is one of the snakes seen most often in North America, but its colors and identification marks vary from one region to another. It can best be recognized by three stripes, one on the back and one on each side; the side stripes occupy the second and third rows of scales above the belly. The area between stripes often has a double row of black spots and red blotches. The common garter snake can range between 1.5 and 4 ft. in length and generally lives near the water or in moist vegetation where it feeds on frogs, salamanders, earthworms, mice, and occasionally small fish.

GOPHER SNAKE
OP

The pine snake, bullsnake, and gopher snake are all of the same species. They are generally 4–8 ft. in length with a stout body, small head, and scales with ridges. Powerful constrictors, they are known to climb trees in search of birds or eggs. When afraid, these snakes hide under fallen trees or boulders.

LONG-TOED SALAMANDER
CL, MR, NC, OP

This variety of the long-toed salamander is black with a series of yellow to orange markings on its back. It is generally 4–6.5 in. long and is often found under logs near pools or ponds. The long-toed salamander inhabits moist northern forests and alpine meadows.

NORTHWESTERN GARTER SNAKE
MR, OP

Seen most often in moist meadows and open grassy areas, the northwestern garter is 15–26 in. in length, brown to greenish-blue or black and may have a red or yellow stripe down the middle of its back. Worms, salamanders, and frogs constitute its diet.

NORTHWESTERN SALAMANDER
CL, OP

This salamander is seldom seen except during breeding seasons. It is gray-brown to chocolate-brown with a light brown belly, and is 5.5–8.5 in. long. Large swellings behind each eye are formed by the salamander's parotoid glands. The northwestern salamander is found in damp areas in thick woods or open fields.

PACIFIC GIANT SALAMANDER
MR, NC, OP

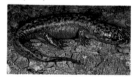

While most salamanders are silent, this one emits a low yelp when caught. It measures 7–11.75 in. The salamander is smooth-skinned and is brown or purplish in color, mottled with black. Its underbelly is a light brown to a yellowish-white. It feeds on large insects, garter snakes, and mice. This salamander thrives in moist woods, especially near rivers. The land-dwelling adults breed during the spring. They are generally found under stones or logs.

ROUGH-SKINNED NEWT
CL, NC, OP

On cool, wet days, this newt may be seen walking about on land, hunting for invertebrates. It lives in ponds and slow-moving streams. Measuring 5–8.5 in., it is light brown to black on top, with a sharply contrasting yellow to orange belly.

RUBBER BOA
MR, NC, OP

This constrictor measures 14–33 in. and curls up in a ball when picked up. Its short, broad snout and short, blunt tail makes it look two-headed. This boa may be reddish-brown, tan to chocolate colored, or olive-green. The rubber boa feeds on lizards, birds, and even small mammals and lives in moist coniferous forests.

TAILED FROG
CL, MR, NC, OP

This frog has vestigial tail-wagging muscles, although it does not have a true tail. Very small, 1–2 in. long, it has no voice. Generally olive or gray to almost black, the tailed frog has a spotted back. The tadpoles eat invertebrates, as well as algae. These frogs live in clean and fast-moving streams and brooks.

WOOD FROG
DN, GA, KV, LC, WS

This is the only North American frog that is seen above the Arctic Circle. Pink or light or dark brown, the wood frog has a dark mask that extends to behind its eardrum. Its belly is white and it has a light streak on the upper jaw. In some cases, there is a light line that runs down its back.

FLOWERS, SHRUBS, AND TREES

BLACK SPRUCE
DN, GA, KA, KV, LC, WS

The cold and short growing season of the north stunts the development of the black spruce; trees more than a century old may measure only 10 ft., while in other climates its heights may reach 30–40 ft. Generally found on bottomlands in the far north, its .25–.5 in. needles are 4-sided, pale blue-green and its cones (which hang down, unlike the erect cones of the fir) are purple-brown.

DOUGLAS-FIR
CL, MR, NC, OP

This tree is found primarily in the loamy soils on mountain slopes, in pure or nearly pure stands. It grows 80–200 ft. tall and the trunk measures up to 10 ft. in diameter. The evergreen needles are about .75–1.25 in. and quite flexible; cones measure 2–3.5 in. long and are light brown and egg-shaped. The foliage is eaten by grouse, deer, and elk; the seeds are eaten by birds and mammals.

ENGELMANN SPRUCE
CL, MR, NC

The Engelmann spruce ranges from Mexico to western Canada where it grows 80–100 ft. tall with a diameter of 1.5–2.5 ft. Its 4-sided, blue-green needles are 1 in. long and have a disagreeable skunklike odor when crushed; its light brown cones hang down. The wood of the Engelmann spruce is often used to make violins and piano sounding boards.

FIREWEED
DN, GA, GB, KA, KF, KV, LC, MR, NC, WS

Also called blooming Sally, this member of the evening primrose family grows in thick and colorful patches. Pink spires of flowers bloom above its tall, straight, leafy stem. Aggressive, it spreads in moist ground from tenacious underground stems.

GOATSBEARD
GB, KF, LC, NC, OP, WS

An explosion of small, delicate white flowers spreads from the top of tall, 3–7-ft. leafy stems. The 5-petal flowers are less than ⅛ in. wide. The name of the plant, *Aruncus sylvester*, derives from the Greek *aryngos* ("goat's beard"), and describes its long bunch of white flowers.

INDIAN PAINTBRUSH
DN, GB, KA, KF, LC, MR, NC, WS

The flower resembles a crimson or scarlet paintbrush, thus the name Indian paintbrush. Usually found in clumps of several stems in meadow areas, it grows to 1–3 ft. and flowers from May to September. Indian paintbrush parasitizes other plants through connecting roots.

LABRADOR TEA
DN, GA, GB, KA, KV, LC, MR, NC, WS

Sometimes called trapper's tea, this member of the heath shrub family blooms from June–August in roundish groups of white flowers about .5 in. wide. This shrub thrives in moist soil in the mountains.

MOSS CAMPION
DN, GB, KA, KF, KV, LC, MR, NC, WS

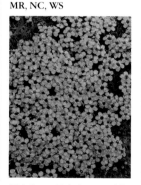

This beautiful alpine wildflower has adopted a low form as protection from frigid winds and resembles the purple saxifrage. Its pink

flowers bloom on short stems that are barely above thick mosslike mats. This plant is sometimes simply called "moss pink."

SITKA SPRUCE
GB, KA, KF, LC, MR, NC, OP, WS

The Sitka spruce is the main timber tree of Alaska, producing high-grade lumber and wood pulp for newsprint. It is the world's largest spruce, up to 160 ft. tall, with a tall, straight trunk, 3–5 ft. in diameter, that rises from a buttressed base, and a broad, conical crown of horizontal branches.

VINE MAPLE
MR, NC, OP

The vine maple is a handsome ornamental shrub or small tree, up to 25 ft. tall, with a short trunk. Several branches turn and twist from the base, which is often vinelike and leaning or sprawling. The vine maple's leaves are 2.5–4.5 in. long and are wide and rounded with 7–11 long-pointed lobes that are usually bright green but can turn orange and red in autumn.

WESTERN REDCEDAR
MR, NC, OP

This is the durable softwood of the Northwest Coastal Indians' totem poles. Particularly resistant to rot, it is the chief wood for shingles, fence posts, siding, boatbuilding, and outdoor-patio construction. It grows to 175 ft. and can measure up to 8 ft. in diameter. Its thin bark is reddish-brown and its .5-in. cones grow in upright clusters. The largest western redcedar measures 21 ft. in diameter, ranking second in size to the giant sequoia among native trees.

PHOTO CREDITS

Page 12: ©Pat O'Hara
15: ©David Muench
19: Peter Britt, Southern Oregon Historical Society
21, both: Oregon Historical Society
23: ©Pat O'Hara
24: ©Kevin Schafer/Tom Stack & Assoc.
26-27: ©Ed Cooper
28: ©Jeff Gnass
31: ©Tom Stack/Tom Stack & Assoc.
32-33: ©Jeff Gnass; inset: ©Joe Arnold, Jr.
35: ©Ed Cooper
37: ©J. A. Kraulis/First Light
44: ©Tom J. Ulrich
47: ©Tom Bean
51: Denali National Park
52, 53: Courtesy of Robert W. Stevens
55: ©John Johnson
56-57: ©Manuel Rodriguez
61: ©Rick McIntyre/Tom Stack & Assoc.
63: ©E.P.I. Nancy Adams/Tom Stack & Assoc.
65: ©Ed Cooper
67: ©Tom J. Ulrich
72-73, 76-77: ©Manuel Rodriguez
78, 81: ©Tom Bean
85: R. Marshall Collection, Alaska Historical Library
87, 88: ©Steven C. Kaufman
89: ©Boyd Norton
90: ©Dale Johnson/Tom Stack & Assoc.
92-93, 95: ©Robert Belous/National Park Service Photo
98-99: ©Boyd Norton
100: ©Tom Bean
103: ©Ruth and Louis Kirk
107: ©Arts & Illustrations Collection, Alaska Historical Library
109: Skinner Foundation Collection, Alaska Historical Library
110, 113, 116-117, 119: ©Tom Bean
124-125: ©Kim Heacox
127: ©John Johnson/DRK

Photo
129: ©Lewis Kemper
130: ©Tom Bean
133, 136: ©George Stroud
139, 140-141: Robert F. Griggs, ©National Geographic Society
145, 146, 148, 151: ©George Stroud
154: ©R. Ostermick/National Park Service Photo
156: ©Jeff Foott/Tom Stack & Assoc.
158: ©Tom Bean
160: ©Steven C. Kaufman
162-163: ©Stephen J. Krasemann/DRK Photo
164: ©Boyd Norton
167: ©Tom J. Ulrich
171: ©Centennial Collection, Alaska Historical Library
173: Skinner Foundation Collection, Alaska Historical Library
175: ©Karen Donelson/Tom Stack & Assoc.
177, 178, right: ©Boyd Norton
178, left: ©Manuel Rodriguez
179: ©Kent and Donna Dannen
180: ©Tom Stack/Tom Stack & Assoc.
181: ©Joe Arnold, Jr.
184: © Fred Hirschmann
187: ©Stephen J. Krasemann/DRK Photo
191: ©Boyd Norton
194: © Fred Hirschmann
196-197: ©Stephen J. Krasemann/DRK Photo
199: ©John Warden
201: ©Tom Bean
202: ©Alan G. Nelson/Tom Stack & Assoc.
205: ©Stephen J. Krasemann/DRK Photo
207: ©Kent and Donna Dannen
208, 211: ©Fred Hirschmann
215: Courtesy of Robert W. Stevens
216, 219: from the collection of Agnes Cusma

221, 222-223: ©Fred Hirschmann
225: ©Steven C. Kaufman
227, 228, 229: ©Fred Hirschmann
230: ©Spencer Swanger/Tom Stack & Assoc.
231: Wayne Lankinen/DRK Photo
234-235, 238-239: ©Fred Hirschmann
240: ©Steven C. Kaufman
243: ©Fred Hirschmann
244: ©Charles A. Mauzy
247: ©Ed Cooper
251: ©Bill West
252, all: Mount Rainier National Park Service
255: ©Neil R. Keller
256: ©Bill West
258: ©Keith Gunnar/West Stock
259: ©Ken Trimpe
260: ©David Muench
264-265: ©Charles A. Mauzy
267: ©Pat O'Hara
268: ©Kent Bowen
272: ©David Muench
277: ©Manuel Rodriguez
278: ©Lee Mann/West Stock
281: ©Ruth and Louis Kirk
285, 287: Washington State Historical Society
289: ©Michael Serecsko/Michael Serecsko
291: ©Pat O'Hara
292: ©Ken Trimpe
294-295: ©Ed Cooper
296: ©Ray Atkeson
297, 298-299, 300, 301: ©T. Schworer/Michael Serecsko
305: ©Ken Trimpe
307: ©Ed Cooper
309: ©Jon L. Shemerdiak / Michael Serecsko
311: ©David Muench
312: ©Jeff Gnass
315: ©Ken Trimpe
319: ©Ed Cooper
323, 326-327: ©Pat O'Hara
328: ©Ruth and Louis Kirk
329: ©Bill West
330: ©Pat O'Hara

331: ©Wayne Lankinen/DRK
Photo
333, 334-335, 336, 338:
©Tom and Pat Leeson
342-343: ©Galen
Rowell/High & Wild
Photo
344: ©Tom and Pat Leeson
346: ©Pat O'Hara
351: ©Stephen Trimble
352: ©Tom Bean/DRK Photo
355: ©Boyd Norton
359: ©Joe Arnold, Jr.
361: ©Skinner Foundation

Collection, Alaska
Historical Library
364-365: ©Tom Bean/DRK
Photo
368-369: ©Stephen J.
Krasemann/DRK Photo
371: ©Tom Bean
372: ©Stephen J.
Krasemann/DRK Photo
375: ©Ed Cooper
378: ©Boyd Norton
380-381: ©Stephen J.
Krasemann/DRK Photo

Appendix of Animals and Plants Photo Credits

384, col. 1, top: ©John W.
Warden, **bottom:** ©Larry
Thorngren/Tom Stack &
Assoc.; **col. 2:** ©Roy
Murphy: **col. 3, top:**
©Neil R. Keller, **bottom:**
©Jeff Gnass
385, col. 1, both: ©Mark
Newman/Tom Stack &
Assoc.; **col. 2, top:**
©Nadine Orabona/Tom
Stack & Assoc., **bottom:**
©G. C. Kelley/Tom Stack
& Assoc.; **col. 3, top:**
©Gary Milburn/Tom Stack
& Assoc., **bottom:** ©Tom
Stack, Tom Stack & Assoc.
386, col. 1, top: ©Stephen
Trimble, **bottom:** ©Alan
Nelson/Tom Stack &
Assoc.; **col. 2, top:** ©Tom
Stack/Tom Stack & Assoc.,
bottom: ©Kevin Schafer
/Tom Stack & Assoc.; **col.
3, top:** ©G. C. Kelley/Tom
Stack & Assoc., **bottom:**

©Alan Nelson/Tom Stack
& Assoc.
387, col. 1, top: ©Kim
Heacox, **bottom:** ©Siebe
Rekker/Tom Stack &
Assoc.; **col. 2, top:** ©John
Shaw/Tom Stack & Assoc.,
bottom: ©Alan Nelson
/Tom Stack & Assoc.; **col.
3, top:** ©Alan Nelson/Tom
Stack & Assoc., **bottom:**
©Anthony Mercieca/Tom
Stack & Assoc.
388, col. 1, top: ©John
Cancalosi/Tom Stack &
Assoc., **bottom:** ©David
M. Dennis/Tom Stack &
Assoc.; **col. 2, top:** ©John
Cancalosi/Tom Stack &
Assoc., **bottom:** ©John
Gerlach/Tom Stack &
Assoc.; **col. 3, top:**
©David M. Dennis, **bot
tom:** ©Milton Rand/Tom
Stack & Assoc.
389, col. 1, both: ©David M.

Dennis/Tom Stack &
Assoc.: **col. 2, top:** ©Jim
Yuskavitch/Tom Stack &
Assoc., **bottom:** ©David
M. Dennis/Tom Stack &
Assoc.; **col. 3, top:**
©Dennis M. Dennis/Tom
Stack & Assoc.,
©R. C. Simpson/Tom Stack
& Assoc.
390, col. 1, top: ©Jack
Wilburn, **bottom:** ©Jim
Yuskavitch/Tom Stack &
Assoc.; **col. 2, top:**
©Bullaty-Lomeo, **bottom:**
©Steven Anderson /
Michael Serecsko; **col. 3,
top:** ©Ed Cooper, **bot
tom:** ©Roy Murphy
391, col. 1, top: ©Rick
McIntyre, **bottom:** ©Fred
Hirschmann; **col. 2, top:**
©Tom Bean, **bottom:** ©Ed
Cooper; **col. 3:** ©Jeff
Gnass.

INDEX

Numbers in italics indicate illustrations.